ey Global Finance

Wiley Globa

Global Finance

Wiley Global Finance is a market-leading provider of over 400 annual books, mobile applications, elearning products, workflow training tools, newsletters and websites for both professionals and consumers in institutional finance, trading, corporate accounting, exam preparation, investing, and performance management.

Wiley Global Fir

obal Finance

Wiley Global Fina

www.wileyglobalfinance.com ⊛**WILEY** Global Finance
WHERE DATA FINDS DIRECTION

Accounting & Auditing Research and Databases

Accounting & Auditing Research and Databases

Practitioner's Desk Reference

Thomas R. Weirich
Natalie Tatiana Churyk
Thomas C. Pearson

John Wiley & Sons, Inc.

Published by John Wiley & Sons, Inc., Hoboken, New Jersey.
Published simultaneously in Canada.

Includes portions of modified and updated text from Wiley's *Accounting & Auditing Research: Tools & Strategies*, Seventh Edition, by Thomas Weirich, Thomas Pearson, and Natalie Churyk.

For general information on our other products and services or for technical support, please contact our Customer Care Department within the United States at (800) 762-2974, outside the United States at (317) 572-3993 or fax (317) 572-4002.

Wiley also publishes its books in a variety of electronic formats. Some content that appears in print may not be available in electronic books. For more information about Wiley products, visit our web site at www.wiley.com.

Library of Congress Cataloging-in-Publication Data:

Weirich, Thomas R.
  Accounting and auditing research & databases: practitioner's desk reference/Thomas R. Weirich, Natalie T. Churyk, and Thomas C. Pearson.
    p. cm.
  Includes index.
  ISBN 978-1-118-33442-3 (cloth); ISBN 978-1-118-41687-7 (ebk.); ISBN 978-1-118-42007-2 (ebk.); ISBN 978-1-118-43398-0 (ebk.)
  1. Accounting—Research. 2. Auditing—Research. 3. Accounting—Data processing.
  4. Auditing—Data processing. I. Churyk, Natalie T.   II. Pearson, Thomas C.   III. Title.
  HF5630.W388 2012
  657.072–dc23   2012017194
Printed in the United States of America
10 9 8 7 6 5 4 3 2 1

I dedicate this book to my wife, Sharon, and five daughters, who have encouraged and supported my efforts as a professor and author.
—Thomas R. Weirich

I dedicate this book to my family and friends who have supported me throughout my career.
—Natalie T. Churyk

I dedicate this book to future professionals, such as my daughter, Alicia Rose Pearson.
—Thomas C. Pearson

Contents

Preface   xiii

Acknowledgments   xv

Chapter 1   **An Introduction to Applied Professional Research**   **1**

What Is Research?   2

Research Questions   4

The Nature of Professional Research   7

Critical Thinking and Effective Communication   9

The Economic Consequences of Standard Setting   14

The Role of Research in the Accounting Firm   15

Remaining Current in Knowledge and Skills   27

International Complexities in Practice   29

Summary   29

Notes   30

Appendix: Abbreviations Commonly Used in Citations   31

Chapter 2   **The Environment of U.S. Research—**
                the SEC and the FASB   **37**
                The Accounting Environment   37
                SEC Accounting for Public Companies   38
                American Institute of Certified Public
                  Accountants (AICPA)   47
                U.S. Generally Accepted Accounting
                  Principles (U.S. GAAP)   49
                The Financial Accounting Standards Board,
                  Advisory Boards, and the Emerging Issue
                  Task Force   52
                The Levels of U.S. GAAP and FASB
                  Accounting Standards Codification   61
                Locating U.S. GAAP   65
                The FASB Accounting Standards Codification
                  Research System (the Codification)   65
                Codification Access   66
                Navigating the Codification   68
                The Research Process   73
                Email, Print, and Copy/Paste Functions   81
                Summary   85
                Notes   85

Chapter 3   **The Environment of International Research**   **87**
                The International Accounting Environment   87
                Other Regional and National Standard-Setting
                  Bodies and Organizations Influencing IFRS   94
                IASB Authorities   95
                The IASB's Conceptual Framework   101
                IFRS Funding, Regulation, and Enforcement   103
                International Financial Reporting Standards
                  (IFRS) Research   106
                Summary   119
                Notes   120

Chapter 4   **Other Research Databases and Tools**   **121**
                Governmental Accounting Sources
                  (FASAB and GASB)   121

Other Databases for Accounting Authorities   127
Researching Industries and Companies   131
Industry Research   133
Major Databases   135
Researching Corporate News   149
Research Tools   154
Research Strategies   156
Summary   157
Appendix 1: Checklist for Industry Research   158
Appendix 2: Checklist for Company Research   159
Appendix 3: Websites   160

**Chapter 5   Tax Research for Compliance
and Tax Planning   163**
Tax Research Databases   164
The Internal Revenue Code   170
Treasury Regulations   172
Other Administrative Authorities   174
Judicial Sources   180
Original Jurisdiction Courts   183
Steps in Conducting Tax Research   185
The Tax Research Environment   196
Regulation of Tax Professionals   211
Summary   212
Notes   213
Appendix: Selected Tax Websites   213

Chapter 6   Assurance/Auditing Research   215
Introduction   215
Assurance Services   216
Consulting Services and Standards   217
Auditing Standard-Setting Environment   218
Auditing Standard-Setting Process   228
AICPA Code of Professional Conduct   231
Auditing Standards in the Public Sector   236
Compilation and Review Services   238
Role of Judgment in Accounting
and Auditing   239

Economic Consequences   240
Summary   241
Notes   241

About the Authors   243
Index   247

Preface

*A*ccounting & Auditing Research and Databases: Practitioner's Desk Reference is an easy-to-use, do-it-yourself reference book on accounting and auditing research and databases. The treatise focuses on practical aspects of professional accounting and auditing research and databases.

The need for this treatise has arisen from an accounting and auditing environment in the United States that has recently encountered dramatic changes: U.S. GAAP is now consolidated in the FASB Accounting Standards Codification. Other accounting, auditing, and tax standards are quickly changing. Mastery of international financial reporting standards is also needed because of recognition of its standard setter, the International Accounting Standards Board (IASB), by the U.S. Securities and Exchange Commission. Finally, research databases are constantly evolving with new interfaces and technologies.

Practitioners must increasingly perform all types of research: accounting, auditing, tax, and business research. The ability to research effectively and efficiently is a major determinant of success in the profession. Therefore, *Accounting & Auditing Research and Databases: Practitioner's Desk Reference* is an invaluable guide to practical professional research. Through understanding the governing authorities and research methodologies, one is much better prepared for the future.

This work is focused on online databases, supplemented with information on essential tools for research and analysis. The subtitle, *Practitioner's Desk Reference*, synthesizes the treatise's teaching abilities. The book enables practitioners/researchers to discover justifiable authoritative solutions to accounting or auditing problems.

The professional book differs from the authors' textbook on the subject, with more extensive discussion of the FASB and IASB structures, including the advisory boards, detailed research methods for the Codification and eIFRS, tax research sources, and types of audits. Also, we provide a search example utilizing the SEC's EDGAR database.

This treatise was created as a comprehensive, stand-alone reference tool for those who wish to become skilled in various professional research techniques and sources. Nearly every reader can acquire some benefit from the discussion here. In summary, *Accounting & Auditing Research and Databases: Practitioner's Desk Reference* is indispensable for learning and polishing professional research.

Chapter 1 introduces professional research and provides an overview of the research process. Chapter 2 explores the environment of financial research in the United States through the impact of the FASB and the SEC. Chapter 3 discusses the environment of international research through the IASB. Chapter 4 discusses other accounting and business research databases and tools. Chapter 5 discusses tax research for compliance and tax planning. Chapter 6 concludes by exploring assurance and auditing research.

Acknowledgments

The authors greatly appreciate the feedback of former professionals who have helped shape the contents of this book. The authors wish to thank the numerous accounting firms that will incorporate this book into their staff training.

We applaud entities granting copyright permission to use screen images to enhance the readers' ability to understand, especially the AICPA, the Financial Accounting Standards Board, and the IASB Foundation. Various parts of this text have been adopted from *Accounting and Auditing Research: Tools and Strategies*, 7th edition, and *Mastering the FASB Codification and eIFRS* by the same authors. *Mahalo* is extended to the professional staff at John Wiley & Sons who have enhanced this desk reference.

Chapter 1

An Introduction to Applied Professional Research

P rofessional accountants, with their specialized knowledge and skills, attempt daily to solve a variety of complex client issues. However, the accounting profession, like other professions, is witnessing major changes due to developments in the law, new services, technologies, and an ever-increasing number of professional standards. In addition to accounting, auditing, and tax compliance services, accountants are involved in such services as attestation reviews, forensic accounting, fraud examinations, and tax planning. Even the types and nature of the problems facing accountants are changing and often becoming more complex. Professional accounting and auditing research is a critical skill for the practitioner. Knowledge of how to utilize major databases to gain an understanding of how to access the professional literature is essential in today's environment. The professional accountant must possess the knowledge to remain current and the skills to critically analyze various problems. Listening effectively, understanding opposing points of view, and applying professional judgment are also critical skills for accountants. Often one must present and defend his or her own views through formal and informal communications. Professional research and communication skills are vitally important in this environment.

Varying views and interpretations exist as to the meaning of the term *research*. In the accounting profession, research points to what the accounting practitioner does as a normal, everyday part of his or her job. Research in general is the means or methodology of systematically obtaining necessary information related to the issue or problem at hand. In today's environment, to become proficient in accounting, auditing, and tax research one must also possess the skills to use various professional databases, which are increasingly available on the Internet.

The professional accountant, whether in public accounting, industry, or government, frequently becomes involved with the investigation and analysis of an accounting, auditing, or tax issue. Resolving these issues requires a clear definition of the problem, using professional databases to search for the relevant authorities, reviewing the authoritative literature, evaluating alternatives, drawing conclusions, and communicating the results. This research process often requires an analysis of very complex and detailed issues. Therefore, researching such issues will challenge the *critical thinking* abilities of the professional. That is, the professional must possess the expertise to understand the relevant facts and render a professional judgment, even in some situations where no single definitive answer or solution exists. In such cases, the researcher would apply professional judgment in the development of an answer to the issue or problem at hand. This practitioner's desk reference will provide you with an overview of the steps in the research process (this chapter), and the major databases to access the professional literature (Chapters 2–6).

What Is Research?

The objective of conducting any type of research, including professional accounting, auditing, and tax research, is a systematic investigation of an issue or problem utilizing the researcher's professional judgment. Following are two examples of generalized research problems that can provide insight as to the types of research questions confronting the accounting practitioner:

1. A recent client has requested your assistance with the following issue: The client manufactures precision parts to customers' specifications. Parts that are produced by the client are inspected by a quality control representative and then held in a secured area in the plant. The client is entitled to full contract payment on parts inspected and held in the secured area. In the past, there has been a short time span between completion date and scheduled shipment. However, recently, production efficiency has improved to the extent that contracts are completed well in advance of scheduled shipment dates. Based on the recent experience of the client, what is the proper date for revenue recognition?

2. A controller for a construction contracting company faces the following problem: The company pays for rights allowing it to extract a specified volume of landfill from a project for a specified period of time. How should the company classify the payments for such landfill rights in its financial statements?[1]

Research is often classified as either theoretical research or applied research. *Theoretical research* investigates questions that appear interesting to the researcher, generally an academician, but may have little or no practical application at the present time. In conducting theoretical research, one attempts to create new knowledge in a particular subject. Sometimes theoretical research uses empirical data based upon experimentation or observation. For example, a theoretical researcher may conduct a controlled experiment to determine the relevance of fair value for financial instruments.[2] Thus, theoretical research adds to the body of knowledge in a particular field and may ultimately contribute directly or indirectly to practical problem solutions. Theoretical research using empirical research studies based on experimentation or observation are frequently reviewed and evaluated by standard-setting bodies in drafting authoritative accounting and auditing pronouncements.

Applied research, which is the focus of this text, investigates an issue of immediate practical importance. Professional accounting research is a process of carefully obtaining information from various sources that aid in the solution to a problem/issue. This process focuses on the identification of the issue, searching the authoritative literature, interpreting the standards, which often includes professional judgment, and finally communicating the results. One type of applied research is known as *a priori* (before the fact) research. This research is conducted before the client actually enters into the transaction. For example, assume that a public accounting firm needs to evaluate a client's proposed new accounting treatment for environmental costs. The client expects an answer within two days as to the acceptability of the new method and its impact on the financial statements. In such a case, a member of the accounting firm's professional staff would investigate to determine if the authoritative literature addresses the issue. If no authoritative pronouncement exists, the accountant would develop a theoretical justification for or against the new method.

Applied research relating to a completed event is known as *a posteriori* (after the fact) research. For example, a client may request assistance preparing his or her tax return for a transaction that was previously executed. Frequently, many advantages accrue to conducting a priori rather than a posteriori research. For example, if research reveals that a proposed transaction will have an unfavorable impact on financial statements, the client can abandon the transaction or possibly restructure it to avoid undesirable consequences. These options are not available, however, after a transaction is completed.

Society needs both theoretical and applied research. Both types require sound design to resolve the issue under investigation effectively and efficiently. No matter how knowledgeable a professional becomes in any aspect of accounting, auditing, or tax, he or she will always have research challenges. However, using a systematic research approach will greatly help in resolving the problem.

Research Questions

Individual companies and CPA firms conduct research to resolve specific accounting, auditing, and tax issues relating to a company or client. The results of this research may lead the firm to new policies or procedures in the application of existing authorities. In this research process, the practitioner (researcher) must answer the following basic questions:

1. Do I have complete knowledge to answer the question, or must I conduct research to consult authoritative references?
2. What is the law (tax law) or the authoritative literature?
3. Does the law or the authoritative literature address the issue under review?
4. Where can I find the law or authoritative literature and develop a conclusion effectively and efficiently?
5. Where can I find international accounting and auditing standards?
6. If there is no law or authoritative literature directly addressing the topic at issue, what approach do I follow in reaching a conclusion?
7. What professional databases or other sources on the Internet should I access for the research process?
8. If more than one alternative solution exists, which do I select?
9. How do I document my findings or conclusions?

The purpose of this text is to provide an understanding of the research process and skills needed to answer these questions utilizing various professional databases. The whats, whys, and hows of practical professional accounting, auditing, and tax research are discussed with emphasis on the following topics:

- How do I research effectively?
- How do I apply a practical research methodology in a timely manner?
- What are the generally accepted accounting principles, auditing standards, and tax authorities?
- What constitutes substantial authoritative support?
- What are the available sources of authority for accounting, auditing, and tax?
- What databases are available for finding relevant authorities or assisting in researching a particular problem?
- What role does the Internet have in the modern research process?

In conducting research for an issue or question at hand, one of the primary tools utilized in financial accounting research is the Financial Accounting Standards Board's (FASB) Codification System, which is discussed in detail in Chapter 2. Similar to understanding the Codification's structure, navigating through the authoritative literature is necessary to analyze a variety of questions or issues. A general guide to help focus or narrow your research would be a "navigation guide" as depicted in Exhibit 1-1.

In navigating through the literature, or the FASB's Codification, the researcher should first focus on the functional area(s) that will help guide one to the appropriate professional literature and/or database as well as the authoritative body that issued the related literature. For instance, is the problem or issue under review a financial accounting question, managerial accounting issue, or a technical SEC problem? Once the functional area is determined, the next step

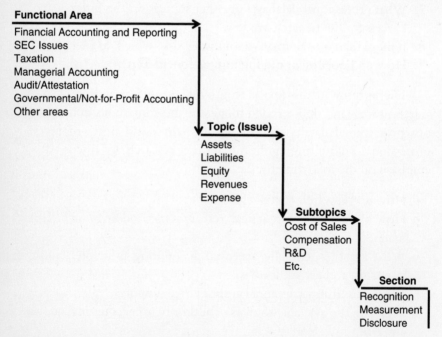

Exhibit 1-1 Research Navigation Guide
SOURCE: From *Accounting & Auditing Research: Tools & Strategies*, 7th ed. Reprinted with permission of John Wiley & Sons, Inc.

in the navigation is to determine the broad categorization of the topic such as an asset, revenue, or expense issue. Then focus on the subtopic that allows for further segregation and navigation of the issue. For example, if the topical area is an expense issue, the subtopic might relate to cost of sales, compensation, or research and development.

The final phase in the navigation process is to focus on the section or nature of the content, which is often a recognition, measurement, or disclosure issue. For instance, if the functional area is financial accounting, the topic is assets, the subtopic is financial instruments, the section or nature might address the proper measurement of the financial instrument either at cost or fair value. This navigation guide is explained in detail later in the text.

A practical research approach along with discussions of various research tools (databases) is presented in the text. The text also addresses the importance of critical thinking and effective writing skills that the researcher should possess in executing the research process.

The Nature of Professional Research

This text focuses on applied research, known as professional accounting research. Today's practitioner must conduct research effectively and efficiently to arrive at appropriate and timely conclusions regarding the issues at hand. Effectiveness is critical in order to determine the proper recording, classification, and disclosure of economic events; to determine compliance with authoritative pronouncements; or to determine the preferability of alternative procedures. Efficiency is needed to meet deadlines and manage research costs.

Additional examples of issues frequently encountered by the practitioner include such questions as:

- What are the accounting, auditing, or tax implications of a new transaction?
- Does the accounting treatment of the transaction conform with generally accepted accounting principles? Does the tax treatment conform with the law?

- What are the disclosure requirements for the financial statements or tax returns?
- What is the auditor's responsibility when confronted with supplemental information presented in annual reports but not as part of the basic financial statements?
- What responsibilities and potential penalties exist for tax accountants?

Responding to these often complex questions has generally become more difficult and time-consuming as the financial accounting and reporting requirements, auditing standards, and tax authorities increase in number and complexity. The research process often is complicated further when the accountant or auditor researches a practical issue for which no authoritative literature exists, or the authoritative literature does not directly address the question.

As a researcher, the accountant should possess certain characteristics that aid in the research process. These include inquisitiveness, open-mindedness, thoroughness, patience, and perseverance.[3] Inquisitiveness is needed while gathering the relevant facts to obtain a clear picture of the research problem. Proper problem definition or issue identification is the most critical component in research. An improperly stated issue usually leads to the wrong conclusion, no matter how carefully the research process was executed. Likewise, the researcher should avoid drawing conclusions before the research process is completed. A preconceived solution can result in biased research in which the researcher merely seeks evidence to support that position, rather than searching for the most appropriate solution. The researcher must carefully examine the facts, obtain and review authoritative literature, evaluate alternatives, and then draw conclusions based upon the evidence collected. The execution of an efficient research project requires thoroughness and patience. This is emphasized in both the planning stage, where all relevant facts are identified, and the research stage, where all extraneous information is controlled. Finally, the researcher must work persistently in order to finish the research on a timely basis.

Perhaps the most important characteristic of the research process is its ability to "add value" to the services provided. A professional auditor not only renders an opinion on a client's financial statements, but also identifies available reporting alternatives that may benefit the client. A professional tax accountant not only prepares the returns but also suggests tax planning for future transactions. The ability of a researcher to provide relevant information grows more important as the competition among accounting firms for clients becomes more intense and the potential significance and enforcement of penalties more common. Researchers who identify reporting alternatives that provide benefits or avoid pitfalls will provide a strong competitive edge for their employers. Providing these tangible benefits to clients through careful and thorough research is essential in today's accounting environment.

Critical Thinking and Effective Communication

The researcher needs to know "how to think." That is, he or she must identify the problem or issue, gather the relevant facts, analyze the issue(s), synthesize and evaluate alternatives, develop an appropriate solution, and effectively communicate the desired information. Such skills are essential for the professional accountant in providing services in today's complex, dynamic, and changing profession. In this environment, the professional accountant must possess not only the ability to think critically, which includes the ability to understand a variety of contexts and circumstances, but also apply and adapt various accounting, auditing, tax, and business concepts and principles to these circumstances to develop the best solutions. The development and nurturing of critical thinking skills will also contribute to the process of lifelong learning that is needed for today's professional.

Accountants must master critical thinking skills particularly because business organizations continue to evolve in response to new information technology and greater worldwide competition. Descriptions of critical thinking are summarized as follows:

1. Critical thinking is difficult because it is often complex.
2. Critical thinking applies multiple criteria.
3. Critical thinking requires an ability to tolerate ambiguity and uncertainty.

4. Critical thinking involves self-regulation of the thinking process.
5. Critical thinking may impose meaning and find structure in apparent disorder.
6. Critical thinking requires effort. It entails intense elaboration and careful judgment.
7. Critical thinking often yields multiple solutions and requires cost and benefit analysis.
8. Critical thinking involves making interpretations.[4]

Nothing is more important and practical to the accounting practitioner than developing critical thinking skills. Poor thinking will inevitably cause new problems, waste time, and ensure frustration. As you become more proficient in critical thinking, you also become more proficient in assessing issues and objectives, problems and solutions, information and data, assumptions and interpretations, different points of view, and frames of reference.

Critical thinking has many definitions. The *American Heritage Dictionary* defines *critical* as "characterized by careful and exact evaluation and judgment." Critical thinking points to a positive ability in those who possess it. It focuses on problem definition and problem solving; it is a rational response to questions that may lack definite answers or may be missing some relevant information. Its purpose is to explore situations to arrive at justifiable conclusions and optimal solutions, which rests on a willingness to take nothing for granted and to approach each experience as if it were unique. Although the purpose of critical thinking is to understand, its goal usually leads to evaluation, and therefore to judgment. Simply stated, critical thinking is the art of using your best thinking given your knowledge and skills.

Critical thinking is purposeful, goal-oriented, and creative, an active process involving rethinking the problem and refusing to merely consider the most obvious or easiest solutions. The qualities that lie behind rethinking are these:

- A willingness to say, "I don't know."
- An openness to alternative ways of seeing and doing—alternatives that are based on understanding how things work.
- An interest in the ideas of others shown by paying attention—even when the ideas conflict with your own.

- Thoughtfulness that is shown by genuine curiosity, not just idle curiosity.
- A desire to discover what other people have done and thought.
- An insistence on getting the best evidence before choosing between alternatives.
- An openness to your own intuition.[5]

Critical thinking is a process of understanding how thinking and learning work, using *higher-order* skills for comprehending issues, analyzing, synthesizing, and assessing those ideas logically. The higher-order reasoning skills include:

- **Analysis** of a problem, or breaking ideas into their component parts to consider each separately.
- **Synthesis** or the connection among different components or ideas in order to derive relationships that tie the parts of an answer together.
- **Critical assessment** of the conclusions reached, requiring an examination of the conclusions for sound logical reasoning.

The ability to reason critically is an essential, fundamental skill that enables one to acquire more knowledge more easily. To summarize, critical thinking includes:

1. Recognizing any explanatory relationship among statements.
2. Recognizing the structure of arguments (the premises, implicit assumptions, and conclusions).
3. Assessing consistency or inconsistency, equivalence among statements, and logical implications.
4. Formulating and identifying, deductively and inductively, justified conclusions based on the available evidence.

Critical thinking also depends on the ability to make certain specific decisions, such as

1. Deciding on the meaning (and intent) of a statement.
2. Deciding whether a definition is adequate.
3. Deciding whether an observation statement is reliable.

4. Deciding whether a statement is an assumption.
5. Deciding whether a statement made by an alleged authority is acceptable.
6. Deciding whether a conclusion follows necessarily from the underlying data.
7. Deciding whether an inductive conclusion is warranted.

In critical thinking, "you decide first what the words mean, then whether they make sense, and finally whether you believe them."[6] A simplified example that helps to reinforce the critical thinking process is presented in Exhibit 1-2.

The ability to communicate effectively, in both oral and written communications, is essential for today's practitioner. In the workplace, an accountant may write to a supervisor, a shareholder, a company's management, a government agency, or others. Strong communication skills are emphasized in the following personal statements shared by two leading business professionals:

> In accounting and all other professions, we must have the appropriate technical skills. But if we cannot communicate what we know, the value of technical skills is lessened. For example, knowing how to compute corporate income taxes is a valuable skill. Being able to tell others how to do it magnifies the value of that technical skill. Others can capitalize on your knowledge only if you can communicate it.
>
> —Dennis R. Beresford, former chair of the
> Financial Accounting Standards Board

> Learning to communicate well should be a top priority for anyone aspiring to lead or advance in a career. Strong technical skills are needed, but technical ability alone will not result in career advancement. Those who develop only technical skills always will work for people who have both technical and leadership abilities, and communication is the key ingredient in leadership.[7]
>
> —Hugh B. Jacks, former president, BellSouth Services

Purpose: To prepare a report based upon your research to answer the following client request.

Issue/Question: A major client, who maintains homes in both New York and Florida and uses both frequently throughout the year, asks you, from an economic standpoint, which state would be the best for her to establish residency in.

Answering this question quickly, intelligently, and accurately requires critical thinking to identify all the relevant factors regarding this decision and to develop proper conclusions, including focusing on such issues as (a) income tax rates of both states, (b) state sales tax rules and rates (e.g., buying and using such "discretionary" assets as a new car), (c) property taxes (e.g., buying or selling a home), unemployment/welfare taxes, municipal taxes, inheritance taxes (e.g., considering the client's age), and (d) costs of other essentials (e.g., food, clothing, and shelter).

After identifying the relevant factors, you should focus this analysis by asking specific questions to narrow the scope of this decision to such relevant issues as:

1. Does the client anticipate selling one of the homes? If so, which one?
2. Where will the client purchase and use her assets (e.g., the new car)?

The answers to these and other similar questions will affect how you proceed with this analysis, while fully considering all of the relevant factors. Considering relevant issues and eliminating irrelevant ones forms the crux of critical thinking.

This example can also help you better understand such critical thinking skills. For example, the researcher must analyze, synthesize, and critically assess the relevant factors. This process requires using the available evidence effectively. Specifically, the accountant should ascertain that the evidence is:

1. **Sufficient.** Does the accountant have adequate evidence to reach a proper conclusion or should he or she ask further questions (e.g., are state inheritance tax rates under review by the respective state legislatures)?
2. **Representative.** Is the evidence provided objective (e.g., will the client actually spend the requisite days in Florida to be considered a legal resident of that state)?
3. **Relevant.** Does the evidence relate directly to the provided assertion (e.g., will the client's plans to spend much time visiting her grandchildren in California impact her legal residence status)?
4. **Accurate.** Does the evidence come from reliable primary or secondary sources (e.g., can CPA firm employees observe the times spent in Florida or New York)?

Thus, the ability to reason critically is essential to the acquisition of knowledge in any discipline and may therefore be appropriately regarded as a fundamental skill, one that new accountants should acquire as soon as possible. Critical thinking includes:

1. Formulating and identifying deductively and inductively warranted conclusions from available evidence.
2. Recognizing the structure of arguments (premises, conclusions, and implicit assumptions).
3. Assessing the consistency, inconsistency, logical implications, and equivalence among statements.
4. Recognizing explanatory relations among statements.

Exhibit 1-2 Critical Thinking Accounting Example

Source: From *Accounting & Auditing Research: Tools & Strategies*, 7th ed. Reprinted with permission of John Wiley & Sons, Inc.

Accounting practitioners have ranked written communication as the most important skill out of 22 skills to develop in students, according to research conducted by Albrecht and Sack.[8] Similarly, writing skills are among the most important attributes in the hiring process, according to a survey of Fortune 500 senior tax executives.[9] Thinking and writing are somewhat related: Thinking determines what one wants to say, while writing records these ideas for future communication. However, effective writing is more than making a draft, jotting down isolated ideas, writing reminders to oneself, making outlines, or charting different sides of an issue. Writing is a process that enables one's knowledge to become more precise and effective, rather than merely relying on reading or discussion.

Certain research efforts may culminate in memos or work papers, letters to clients, journal articles, or firm reports. The dissemination of your research, in whatever form, will require *effective communication skills* for both oral presentations and written documents. One's research output must demonstrate coherence, conciseness, appropriate use of standard English, and achievement of the purpose for the intended reader.

The Economic Consequences of Standard Setting

Various accounting standards have produced far-reaching economic consequences. This was demonstrated by the Financial Accounting Standards Board (FASB) in addressing such issues as restructuring costs, financial instruments and fair value accounting, stock options, and post-employment benefits. Various difficulties sometimes arise in the proper accounting for the economic substance of a transaction within the current accounting framework.

Since financial statements must conform to generally accepted accounting principles, the standard-setting bodies, such as the FASB or the GASB (Governmental Accounting Standards Board), will conduct research on the economic impact of a proposed standard. For example, the handling of off-balance-sheet transactions has at times encouraged the selection of one business decision over another, producing results that may be less oriented to the users of financial statements.

In today's complex business and legal environment, the researcher conducting accounting and auditing research should understand the economic and social impacts that various accepted accounting alternatives may have on society in general and the individual entity in particular. Such economic and social concerns are becoming a greater factor in the evaluation and issuance of new accounting standards.

The Role of Research in the Accounting Firm

Although research is often conducted by accountants in education, industry, and government, accounting, auditing, and tax research is particularly important in a public accounting firm. As a reflection of today's society, significant changes have occurred in the accounting environment. The practitioner today requires greater knowledge because of greater complexity in many business transactions, the proliferation of new authoritative pronouncements, and advances in technology. As a result, practitioners should possess the ability to conduct efficient research. An accountant's responsibility to conduct accounting/auditing research is analogous to an attorney's responsibility to conduct legal research. For example:

> A lawyer should provide competent representation to a client. Competent representation requires the legal knowledge, skill, thoroughness, and preparation reasonably necessary for the representation.[10]

A California court interpreted the research requirement to mean that each lawyer must have the ability to research the law completely, know the applicable legal principles, and find "the rules which, although not commonly known," are discovered through standard research techniques.[11] Thus in the California case, the plaintiff recovered a judgment of $100,000 in a malpractice suit that was based upon the malpractice of the defendant in researching the applicable law.

The U.S. Securities and Exchange Commission (SEC) has also stressed the importance of effective accounting research through an enforcement action brought against an accountant. In Accounting and Auditing Enforcement Release No. 420, the SEC instituted a public administrative proceeding against a CPA. The Commission charged that the CPA failed to exercise due care in the conduct of an audit. The enforcement release specifically stated the following:

> In determining whether the [company] valued the lease properly, the [CPA] failed to consult pertinent provisions of GAAP or any other accounting authorities. This failure to conduct any research on the appropriate method of valuation constitutes a failure to act with due professional care.

Thus it is vital that the professional accountant possesses the ability to use relevant sources to locate applicable authoritative pronouncements or law and to ascertain their current status.

Due to the expanding complex environment and proliferation of pronouncements, many accounting firms have created a research specialization within the firm. Common approaches used in practice include the following:

1. The staff at the local office conducts day-to-day research, with industry-specific questions referred to industry specialists within the firm.
2. Selected individuals in the local or regional office are designated as research specialists and all research questions within the office or region are brought to their attention.
3. The accounting firm establishes at the executive office of the firm a centralized research function that handles questions for the firm as a whole on technical issues.
4. Computerized files of previous research maintained by the firm provide consolidated expertise on how the firm has handled various issues in the past.

The task of accurate and comprehensive research is often complex and challenging. However, one can meet this challenge by becoming familiar with the suggested research process to solve accounting, auditing, or tax issues.

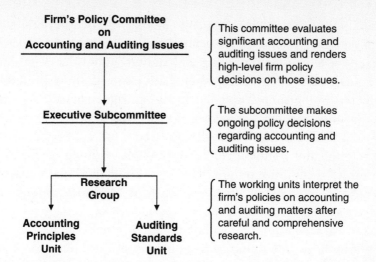

Firm's Policy Committee on Accounting and Auditing Issues — This committee evaluates significant accounting and auditing issues and renders high-level firm policy decisions on those issues.

Executive Subcommittee — The subcommittee makes ongoing policy decisions regarding accounting and auditing issues.

Research Group / **Accounting Principles Unit** / **Auditing Standards Unit** — The working units interpret the firm's policies on accounting and auditing matters after careful and comprehensive research.

Exhibit 1-3 Organizational Framework for Policy Decision Making and Research within a Typical Multioffice Accounting Firm
SOURCE: From *Accounting & Auditing Research: Tools & Strategies*, 7th ed. Reprinted with permission of John Wiley & Sons, Inc.

A more in-depth look at a typical organizational structure for policy decision making and research on accounting and auditing matters within a multioffice firm that maintains a research department is depicted in Exhibit 1-3. The responsibilities of a firm-wide accounting and auditing policy decision function include maintaining a high level of professional competence in accounting and auditing matters, developing and rendering high-level policies and procedures on accounting and auditing issues for the firm, disseminating the firm's policies and procedures to appropriate personnel within the firm on a timely basis, and supervising the quality control of the firm's practice. Research plays an important role in this decision-making process.

A CPA firm's policy committee and executive subcommittee, as shown in Exhibit 1-3, generally consists of highly competent partners with many years of practical experience. The policy committee's primary function is to evaluate significant accounting and auditing issues and establish firm-wide policies on these issues. The executive subcommittee's function is to handle the daily ongoing policy decisions (lower-level decisions) for the firm as a whole. The responsibility of the accounting and auditing research personnel is to interpret firm policies in the context of specific client situations. Frequently, technical accounting and auditing issues that arise during the course of a client engagement are resolved through research conducted by personnel assigned to the engagement. When a local office cannot resolve a research matter satisfactorily, assistance is requested from the firm's specialized research units. These units conduct careful and comprehensive research in arriving at the firm's response to technical inquiries. This response is then disseminated to the various geographic offices of the firm for future reference in handling similar technical issues.

Practical accounting and auditing research is not confined to public accounting firms. All accountants should possess the ability to conduct effective research and develop logical and well-supported conclusions on a timely basis. The basic research process is similar, whether the researcher is engaged in public accounting, management accounting, governmental accounting, auditing, or even taxation.

Overview of the Research Process

The research process in general is often defined as a scientific method of inquiry, a systematic study of a particular field of knowledge in order to discover scientific facts or principles. An operational definition of research encompasses the following process:[12]

1. Investigate and analyze a clearly defined issue or problem.
2. Use an appropriate scientific approach.
3. Gather and document adequate and representative evidence.
4. Employ logical reasoning in drawing conclusions.
5. Support the validity or reasonableness of the conclusions.

With this general understanding of the research process, practical accounting, auditing, and tax research is defined as follows:

Accounting, auditing, or tax research: A systematic and logical approach employing critical thinking skills to obtain and document evidence (authorities) underlying a conclusion relating to an accounting, auditing, or tax issue or problem.

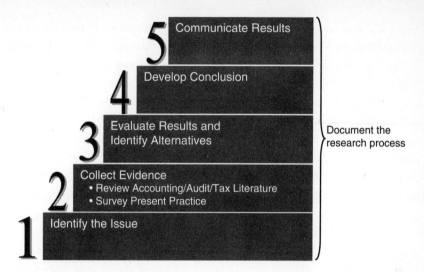

Exhibit 1-4 The Research Process
SOURCE: Modified from *Accounting & Auditing Research: Tools & Strategies*, 7th ed. Reprinted with permission of John Wiley & Sons, Inc.

The basic steps in the research process are illustrated in Exhibit 1-4, with an overview presented in the following sections. As indicated in the illustration, carefully document each step of the research process. When executing each step, the researcher may also find it necessary to refine the work done in previous steps.

Step 1: Identify the Issues and Establish the Facts. The researcher's first task is to gather the facts surrounding the particular problem. However, problem-solving research cannot begin until the researcher clearly and concisely defines the problem. One needs to analyze and understand the "why" and "what" about the issue in order to begin the research process. Unless the researcher knows why the issue was brought to his or her attention, he or she might have difficulty knowing what to research. The novice researcher may find it difficult to distinguish between relevant and irrelevant information. When this happens, it is advisable to err on the side of gathering too many facts rather than too few. As the researcher becomes more knowledgeable, he or she will become more skilled at quickly isolating the relevant facts.

In most cases, the basic issue is identified before the research process begins, that is, when a client requests advice as to the proper handling of a specific transaction. However, further refinement of the exact issue is often required. This process of refining the issue at hand is referred to as *problem distillation*, whereby a general issue is restated in sufficiently specific terms. If the statement of the issue is too broad or general, the researcher is apt to waste valuable time consulting sources irrelevant to the specific issue.

Factors to consider in the identification and statement of the issue include the exact source of the issue, justification for the issue, and a determination of the scope of the issue. To successfully design and execute an investigation, state the critical issue clearly and precisely. As explained in the following chapters, many research tools, especially computerized databases, are indexed by a set of descriptive words. Since keywords aid in reference identification, failure to use the appropriate keywords or understand the facts in sufficient detail can cause a researcher to overlook important authorities. Undoubtedly, writing a clear, concise statement of the problem is the most important task in research. Failure to frame all the facts can, and often will, lead to an erroneous conclusion.

Additional facts are often needed in research. Thus sometimes the problem requires one to go back and acquire more from one's manager or even the client. Certain types of facts, such as related-party situations and dates, are almost always relevant. Sometimes an important fact to clarify is exactly which entity or person is the client. Analyzing the problem is similar to an auditor conducting planning for an audit. The auditor will acquire more information about the business and potential risks. One might begin by going to a financial research database to acquire additional information about the company. Also, one might begin to address issues/problems by examining the relevant corporate websites. Usually, corporate websites offer an "About" link to the company, which explains more about the history and current structure of a company.

Step 2: Collect the Evidence.   As previously stated, problem-solving research cannot begin until the researcher defines the problem. Once the issues are adequately defined, the researcher is ready to proceed with step two of the research process, the collection of evidence. This step usually encompasses a detailed review of relevant authoritative accounting or auditing literature and a survey of present practice. In collecting evidence, the researcher should have familiarity with the various sources available, know which sources to use, and know the order in which to examine the sources and applicable authorities.

This early identification of the relevant sources will aid in the efficient conduct of the research. A number of research tools, including electronic databases and the Internet, that will aid in the collection of evidence are available and are discussed in detail in Chapters 2 through 6. With the Internet growing at an exponential rate as new web-sites are added on a daily basis, this tool provides an increasingly significant impact on the way people conduct business, including accountants, auditors, and tax professionals. The Internet permits an accounting professional to use various discussion groups or webinars whereby professionals discuss topics on accounting, auditing, or tax issues. Accountants use the Internet to search for federal and state legislation that may have an impact on clients and to retrieve financial statements from SEC filings. Exhibit 1-5 provides an example of how a small CPA firm might utilize the Internet. Many accountants also use the Internet to interact quickly and effectively with the client to assist in collecting the appropriate evidence, such as requesting additional facts that may influence the evidence needed or result from the relevant authorities.

In cases where authoritative literature does not exist on a specific issue, the practitioner should develop a theoretical resolution of the issue based upon a logical analysis of the factors or analogous authorities involved. In addition, the researcher needs to evaluate the economic consequences of the various alternatives in the development of a conclusion. Note that in practice, a solution is sometimes not readily apparent. Professional judgment and theoretical analysis are key elements in the research process.

Step 3: Analyze the Evidence and Identify the Alternatives. Once a practitioner has completed a thorough investigation of the facts and collection of evidence, the next step is to evaluate the results and identify alternatives for one or more tentative conclusions to the issue. Fully support each alternative by authoritative literature or a theoretical justification with complete and concise documentation. One cannot expect to draw sound conclusions from faulty information. Soundly documented conclusions are possible only when the information has been properly

Mark Jensen, CPA, states that the Internet has become the "greatest equalizer" because it provides his small practice with many of the research tools utilized by the big international accounting firms. "It lets me offer resources and services to my clients and future clients that the big firms have to offer," says Jensen.

Mark was asked by a would-be entrepreneur to help write a business plan to open a computer software store in southern New York. Both Jensen and the client were computer literate, but neither of them knew much about the software business. So Mark accessed the Internet, and within an hour was deluged with information about software stores.

A word search for "software" yielded more than 100 articles about computer stores, including one from the *Washington Post* about a software store start-up. Jensen also gleaned information about software stores from the small business forums on the Internet. Mark and his client used the information to prepare a business plan that helped secure financing for the business.

Being online via the Internet allows Jensen to search through news sources throughout the world. Publications and news services such as the *New York Times*, Associated Press, United Press International, Reuters, *Financial Times of London*, and the Dow Jones News Service are just a few of the sources available on the Internet.

Mark also retrieves news items for clients as an effective way to maintain relationships and attract new clients. One of his clients is involved in the machine tools industry and Mark frequently notifies the client when a major industry event takes place.

Besides tracking news, Jensen uses the Internet to exchange email with clients and associates. He also can access the SEC's website and obtain recent SEC filings of major public companies, such as their 10-K, 10-Q, or other filings.

Exhibit 1-5 An Example of a Small CPA Firm's Utilizing the Internet
SOURCE: From *Accounting & Auditing Research: Tools & Strategies*, 7th ed. Reprinted with permission of John Wiley & Sons, Inc.

collected, organized, and interpreted. Sometimes extending the search to insightful nonauthoritative literature or relevant standards may supplement one's understanding of the authoritative pronouncements under review.

Further analysis and research are sometimes needed as to the appropriateness of the various alternatives identified. This reevaluation may require further discussions with the client or consultations with colleagues. In discussing an issue with a client, the researcher should use professional skepticism and recognize that management is not always objective in evaluating alternatives. For example, the issue may involve the acceptability of an accounting method that is currently being used by the client. In such cases, the research is directed toward the support or rejection of an alternative already decided on by management. The possibility of bias should cause the researcher to retain a degree of professional skepticism in discussions with the client regarding a conclusion.

Exercise professional judgment in carefully reviewing the results and identifying potential alternative solutions. Evaluate the quality and amount of authoritative support for the research problem. Given a more principled approach to accounting standards, alternative solutions may have justification. Review the evidence and alternatives with other accountants knowledgeable in the field. One might check industry practices to verify any different possibilities for alternative reporting.

Step 4: Develop a Conclusion.   After a detailed analysis of the alternatives, including economic consequences, the researcher develops a conclusion and thoroughly documents the final conclusion selected from the alternatives identified. The conclusion should logically arise from well-reasoned analysis and be well supported by the evidence gathered. The conclusion and details of the proposed solution are then presented to the client.

Step 5: Communicate the Results.   The most important point in the communication is the conclusion reached. The communication often takes the form of a research memorandum, requiring an objective and unbiased analysis and report. The memorandum should contain a statement of facts, a clear and precise statement of the issue, a brief and straightforward conclusion, discussion of the authoritative literature, and explanation as to how it applies to the set of facts. The written communication should communicate clearly and follow the conventional rules of grammar, spelling, and punctuation. Particularly, because a client often cannot evaluate the quality of research, nothing diminishes a professional's credibility with the client faster than misspellings, incorrect grammar, or misuse of words. Sloppy communications may suggest sloppy research and analysis.

In drafting the appropriate written communication, avoid making common errors such as (1) excessive discussion of the issue and facts in a memo, which indicates that the memo was not drafted with sufficient precision; (2) excessive citations to authoritative sources—cite only the relevant authorities for the conclusion reached; and (3) appearing to avoid a conclusion by pleading the need for additional facts. Novice researchers too often include irrelevant information. This distracts from the fact that the proposed solution to the problem is appropriate.

After completing your research, adequate documentation of your results is essential. While the authors advocate as much precision as possible, given current practices in accounting research, the example documentation worksheet presented in Exhibit 1-6 provides the authors' view of the appropriate documentation needed for references to the accounting authorities related to the basic question of writing down goodwill. Such documentation is normally in electronic form for future reference.

A serious weakness in any part of the research and communication process undermines the entire effort. Therefore, address each segment of the process with equal seriousness as to its impact on the entire research project. A more refined diagram of the research process is presented in Exhibit 1-7.

Lessons Learned for Professional Practice

Many challenges exist to researching effectively and efficiently. By using the suggested five-step process discussed earlier, one is more likely to solve the problem accurately and in a timely manner. While research is both an art and a science, as one develops more experience in research, one will find it easier and exciting. Make sure the research work is well documented. One never knows when one's work will be tested within the firm's quality review program, reviewed by an auditor, perhaps in a peer review process, inspected by the PCAOB if one is part of a registered firm, or even defended in court.

Professional accounting research of accounting authorities based on codified principles is much easier than the old system in the United States of various rules-based pronouncements in the former five-GAAP hierarchy as Chapter 2 discusses. Recall that the FASB's accounting standards now use the more conceptual approach, similar to the IAS/IFRS, which the SEC is considering as a replacement, or convergence with U.S. GAAP, at some point in the near future.

SEC accounting research is important not only for its direct application to public companies, but also in learning to comprehend the potential regulatory environment that all accountants could face if additional crises arise in the profession.

Exhibit 1-6 Example Documentation Worksheet for Potential Write-Down of a Goodwill Issue

---

Client information

Name: Sony Corporation of America

I. Problem Identification or Statement of the Problems

Whether an annual write-down of goodwill under FASB ASC (IFRS/IAS) was necessary for an acquisition of a company with continued losses

Whether financial statement disclosures of only two industries when one industry had two businesses with different financial trends violated FASB ASC (IAS/IFRS) and was misleading under Securities Exchange Act § 13(a)

Contact person (Client):

A. Morita—Chairman

K. Tanaka—Administrative Assistant

II. Research Evidence (Keywords Utilized)

Disclosure goodwill impairment segment disclosure business Combination

References (citations):

ASC 280-10-50-various

ASC 805-30-30-1

ASC 350-20-35-4 and 28

ASC 350-20-50-1 and 2

IAS 36 and IFRS 8

IRC § 197

1934 Exchange Act § 13(a)

ASC 280-10-50-various

ASC 805-30-30-1

ASC 350-20-35-4 and 28

ASC 350-20-50-1 and 2

IAS 36 and IFRS 8

IRC § 197

1934 Exchange Act § 13(a)

Database (library resources) Utilized:

FASB Accounting Standards Codification

FASB CCH Accounting Research Manager

eIFRS for IFRS/IAS

RIA Checkpoint for tax

Websites for the entities involved

III. Alternatives Available

No other alternatives are permissible.

IV. Conclusions

The write-down of goodwill of an acquired entity with continuous losses is required. ASC 805-30-30-1 and 350-20-35-1 (IFRS 3.B12 and IAS 36.10). The financial statement disclosure of only two industries when one industry has two businesses with different financial trends is misleading under Securities Exchange Act § 13(a) and needs revising under ASC 280-10-50-various.

The write-down of goodwill of an acquired entity with continuous losses is required. ASC 805-30-30-1 and 350-20-35-1 (IFRS 3.B12 and IAS 36.10). The financial statement disclosure of only two industries when one industry has two businesses with different financial trends is misleading under Securities Exchange Act § 13(a) and needs revising under ASC 280-10-50-various.

Source: From *Accounting & Auditing Research: Tools & Strategies*, 7th ed. Reprinted with permission of John Wiley & Sons, Inc.

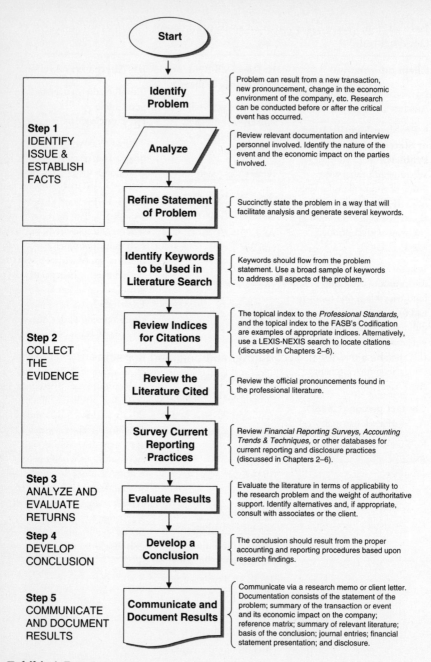

Exhibit 1-7 Refined Diagram of the Research Process

SOURCE: Modified from *Accounting & Auditing Research: Tools & Strategies*, 7th ed. Reprinted with permission of John Wiley & Sons, Inc.

Remaining Current in Knowledge and Skills

One should strive to remain current in knowledge by studying new updates of authorities or new pronouncements. A systematic plan to remain current usually achieves the best results. Regularly read accounting and business periodicals, newsletters, and other sources. Currency is essential with the typical expansion of accounting, auditing, and tax authorities. Consider adopting some of the following techniques in your plan to remain current in knowledge:

- **Use checklists.** Maintain a checklist of new developments to assist in remaining current. Accountants prepare listings of updates to the FASB's Accounting Standards Codification or new pronouncements and indicate which clients the change may affect. Pronouncements having no direct immediate effect on any client are often placed in a "rainy day" reading file.
- **Summarize new authorities.** Acquire or prepare summaries of new authorities at regular intervals. Such summaries identify and describe new legal, accounting, auditing, and tax authorities. Distribute the information to staff members through email, presentations within the firm, attendance at continuing education seminars, or by other means.
- **Read periodicals.** Read several accounting and business periodicals that summarize and explain new authorities. For example, read the *Wall Street Journal*, the AICPA's *Journal of Accountancy*, and leading professional publications in one's area of expertise, such as *Internal Auditor* or the *Tax Adviser*. Successful accountants regularly spend time reading about new professional standards, technological enhancements for practice, management concerns, and many other accounting and business topics.
- **Check database updates.** Check for news on a company of interest or specialized industry news of interest.
- **Browse websites.** Browse websites that capture relevant information on a timely basis, which is then reviewed by the practitioner. Use newsgroups on the Internet to discuss topics of interest to you and your clients.

- **Read accounting newsletters.** Take advantage of sophisticated newsletters that update practitioners on current events. Newsletters are distributed by standard setters, publishers, large accounting firms, and others. They are increasingly distributed via email. Major newsletters by standard setters include the following:
  - *Action Alert.* FASB summarizes board actions and future meetings in this weekly publication, available through email.
  - **The *GASB Report.*** GASB summarizes new statements, exposure drafts, interpretations, or technical bulletins in a quarterly publication.
  - **The *CPA Letter.*** AICPA produces this online newsletter to address such topics as AICPA board business, new pronouncements on auditing, disciplinary actions against members, upcoming events, and more. This newsletter is one of a number of newsletters created by the AICPA. Other newsletters are often targeted toward specialty areas in accounting.

Remaining knowledgeable on every detail of all new authorities is not possible. However, every practitioner must develop and consistently use various techniques to acquire current professional knowledge. Currency is especially important with authorities and pronouncements that directly affect one's clients. Participate in continuing professional education to help learn about new developments in a formal, structured setting.

Remain current in skills, whether by continued research practice or training. Accountants will need even more skills in the future for new research opportunities, analysis, communication, or other needs. Today's professional world is much different than the accountant experienced a generation ago, with advances in technology, increased complexities in business, expanded sources of authority, increased regulation, and other developments.

The professional accounting world will undoubtably continue to evolve as new business practices develop, changes in the economy occur, or financial scandals are discovered. Failure to remain current in either knowledge or skills is likely to violate one's professional responsibilities and increase the chances for loss of one's job, professional sanctions, costly malpractice lawsuits, or government action.

International Complexities in Practice

In a global economy, one may desire to research the data, professional authorities, or legal environment in other jurisdictions. For example, researching authorities enables one to have a more sophisticated discussion with accounting professionals in a foreign country and best represent multinational clients who conduct business in multiple countries. However, due diligence in understanding, researching, analyzing authorities and data, and communicating solutions is essential.

Increasingly, accountants are accessing foreign authorities or data to engage in collaborative work or to ask a foreign professional more sophisticated questions. Yet differences around the world both cultural and societal may lead to various interpretations or actions based on the same data or professional authorities. Foreign regulators sometimes provide formal or informal interpretations or guidance on International Financial Reporting Standards (IFRS). One should not assume that all parts of the world have the same degree of professional commitment in reporting or high enforcement standards. Reporting incentives are influenced by such factors as a country's legal system, strength of the auditors, and a company's financial compensation scheme. Chapter 3 presents an overview of an international accounting standards database.

Outsourced accounting work to low-cost jurisdictions is likely to continue to increase, especially as more countries adopt IFRS. The accountants overseeing any outsourced work need to exercise extra due care to assure that the foreign professionals meet the professional standards interpretations that are expected in the United States or other highly developed countries.

Summary

The research work of a practicing professional accountant is very important. Few practitioners ever experience a workweek that does not include the investigation and analysis of an accounting, auditing, or tax issue. Thus every professional accountant should possess the ability to conduct practical research in a systematic way. The goal of this text is to aid current and future practitioners in developing a basic framework or methodology to assist in the research process.

The emphasis of the following chapters is on practical applied research that deals with solutions to immediate issues rather than theoretical research that has little or no present-day application. Chapter 2 presents the environment of U.S. GAAP research and important databases with a focus on the FASB's Codification Research System. The sources of authoritative literature when dealing with international accounting issues is discussed in Chapter 3. Chapter 4 presents other available research tools that may aid in the effective and efficient conduct of practical research, with an emphasis on computerized research via various databases that exist. Chapter 5 provides the basic steps of tax research and valuable databases and websites. Chapter 6 concludes with a discussion of assurance services and related research databases.

The following Appendix presents an alphabetized list of organizations that promulgate professional or legal authorities and indicates the major accounting, auditing, and tax abbreviations for their sources. This list includes various FASB accounting authorities discontinued after the development of the FASB Accounting Standards Codification, as well as accounting authorities previously discontinued by the AICPA that are still referenced by many practitioners.

Notes

1. *AICPA Technical Practice Aids*, vol. 1 (Chicago: Commerce Clearing House, Inc.).
2. Lisa Koonce et al., "Judging the Relevance of Fair Value for Financial Instruments," *Accounting Review* 86, no. 6 (November 2011): 2075–2098.
3. Wanda Wallace, "A Profile of a Researcher," *Auditor's Report, American Accounting Association* (Fall 1984): 1–3.
4. Lauren B. Resnick, *Education and Learning to Think* (Washington, DC: National Academy Press, 1987).
5. Robert Boostrom, *Developing Creative and Critical Thinking: An Integrated Approach* (Chicago: National Textbook, 1992), 24–25.
6. *Ibid.*, 198.
7. From William C. Himstreet, Wayne M. Baty, and Carol M. Lehman, *Business Communications: Principles and Methods*, 10th ed. (Beverly, MA: Wadsworth, 1993).
8. W. S. Albrecht and R. J. Sack, *Accounting Education: Charting the Course through a Perilous Future*, Accounting Education Series, vol. 16 (Sarasota, FL; American Accounting Association, 2000).

9. G. Paice and M. Lyons, "Addressing the People Puzzle," *Financial Executive*, September 2001; available online at www.fei.org/magazine/articles/9-2001_corptaxes.cfm.
10. Model Rules of Professional Conduct of the American Bar Association, Rule One.
11. *Smith v. Lewis*, 13 Cal. 3d 349, 530 P.2d 589, 118 Cal. Reptr. 621 (1975).
12. David J. Luck, Hugh C. Wales, and Donald A. Taylor, *Marketing Research* (Englewood Cliffs, NJ: Prentice Hall, 1961), 5.

Appendix: Abbreviations Commonly Used in Citations

An alphabetized list of organizations creating professional or legal authorities shows the major accounting, auditing, or tax abbreviations for their sources.

Issuance Abbreviation	Title of Issuance	(Division of the Standard Setter or Comment)
AICPA	**American Institute of Certified Public Accountants**	
AAG	Audit and Accounting Guide	(add hyphen and three-letter abbreviation for each)
APBO	Accounting Principles Board Opinions	(predecessor to FASB)
APBS	Accounting Principles Board Statements	(predecessor to FASB)
ARB	Accounting Research Bulletin	(AICPA's predecessor to APB)
AT	Attestation part of codified AICPA Professional Standards	
AU	Auditing part of codified AICPA Professional Standards	
AUG	Industry Audit Guide	(add hyphen and three-letter abbreviation for each)

(Continued)

Issuance Abbreviation	Title of Issuance	(Division of the Standard Setter or Comment)
AUIJ	Auditing Interpretation	(Auditing Standards Board)
ET-INT	Ethics Interpretation of Rules of Conduct	(Professional Ethics Division)
ET-RULE	Code of Professional Conduct—Rules	
PRP	Standards for Performing and Reporting on Peer Reviews	(National PRC)
SARI	Accounting and Review Services Interpretations	(ARS Committee)
SAS	Statements on Auditing Standards	(Auditing Standards Board—ASB)
SECPS	SEC Practice Section Statement on Standards	
SOP	Statements of Position	(Accounting Standards Division, prior to ASB)
SSAE	Statement on Standards for Attestation Engagements	(ASB)
SSAEI	Attestation Engagements Interpretation	(Auditing Standards Board)
SSARS	Statements on Standards on Accounting and Review Services	
SSCS	Statements on Standards for Consulting Services	(Consulting Executive Committee)
SSTS	Statements on Standards for Tax Services	(Tax Executive Committee)
SSVS	Statements on Standards for Valuation Services	(Business Valuation Committee)
FASB	**Financial Accounting Standards Board**	
CON (SFAC)	FASB Statements of Financial Accounting Concepts	
EITF	FASB Emerging Issues Task Force Consensus	(EITF Abstracts)

FAS (SFAS)	FASB Statements of Financial Accounting Standards	
FIN	FASB Interpretations	
FTB	FASB Technical Bulletins	
FASAB	Federal Accounting Standards Advisory Board	
SFFAS	Statement of Federal Financial Accounting Standards	
SFFAC	Statement of Federal Financial Accounting Concepts	
GAO	**Government Accountability Office**	
GAGAS	Generally Accepted Government Auditing Standards	(Comptroller General)
GASB	**Government Accounting Standards Board**	
GAC	Statements of Financial Accounting Concepts	
GAS	Statements on Governmental Accounting Standards	
GASI	Interpretations	
GAST	Technical Bulletins	
IASB	**International Accounting Standards Board**	
IAS	International Accounting Standards	
IFRIC	International Financial Reporting Interpretations Committee	
IFRS	International Financial Reporting Standards	
SIC	Standing Interpretations Committee	

(*Continued*)

Issuance Abbreviation	Title of Issuance	(Division of the Standard Setter or Comment)
IFAC	**International Federation of Accountants**	
IAU	International Statements on Auditing	(IAASB—International Auditing and Assurance Standards Board)
IPSAS	International Public Sector Accounting Standards	(IPSAB—International Public Sector Accounting Board)
ISAE	International Standards of Attestation Engagements	(IAASB)
ISQC	International Standards of Quality Control (IAASB)	
IIA	**Institute for Internal Auditors**	
Standards	Standards for Professional Practice of Internal Auditing	
OMB	**Office of Management and Budget**	
CASB	Cost Accounting Standards Board Standards	(Office of Federal Procurement Policy)
CASB-I	Cost Accounting Standards Board Interpretations	(OFFP)
CIR	Circulars	(includes audit standards for state and local governments, and nonprofit organizations)
PCAOB	**Public Company Accounting Oversight Board**	
AS	PCAOB Auditing Standards	(interim standards use AICPA's SAS)
AT	Attest Engagement Standards	(interim standards use AICPA's SSAE)
AU	Codified Auditing Standards	
QC	Quality Control Standards	

| REL | Releases | (when approved by PCAOB) |
| Rules | Rules | (when approved by both PCAOB and SEC) |

	U.S. Congress	
33 ACT	Securities Act of 1933	
34 ACT	Securities Exchange Act of 1934	
IRC	Internal Revenue Code of 1986, Title 26 of the United States Code	
SOX	Sarbanes-Oxley Act of 2002	

U.S. SEC	**Securities and Exchange Commission**	
AAER (ER)	Accounting and Auditing Enforcement Releases	(Enforcement Division)
ASR	Accounting Series Releases	(stopped in 1982)
FRP	Codification of Financial Reporting Policies	
FRR (FR-#)	Financial Reporting Releases	(OCA—Office of Chief Accountant)
Reg. FD	Regulation Fair Disclosure	(17 CFR parts 240, 243, and 249)
Reg. S-K	Regulation S-K	(Integrated Disclosure Rules, 17 CFR part 229)
Reg. S-X	Regulation S-X	(Requirements for Financial Statements, 17 CFR part 210)
REL.	Releases 33-# Release interpreting Securities Act of 1933 34-# Release interpreting Securities Exchange Act of 1934	(various types including AAER and FRR)
SAB	Staff Accounting Bulletin	(Corporate Finance Division and Office of Chief Accountant)

(Continued)

Issuance Abbreviation	Title of Issuance	(Division of the Standard Setter or Comment)
	U.S. Treasury Department	
REV. PROC.	Revenue Procedure	(IRS)
REV. RUL.	Revenue Ruling	(IRS)
TREAS. REG.	Treasury Regulation	(26 CFR)
	Various Common Non–standard–setter Abbreviations	
10-K	Annual report by a public company filed with the SEC	
EPS	Earnings per Share	
GAAP	Generally Accepted Accounting Principles	
GAAS	Generally Accepted Auditing Standards	
MD&A	Management Discussion and Analysis of Financial Condition and Results of Operation	
XBRL	eXtensible Business Reporting Language	

Chapter 2

The Environment of U.S. Research—the SEC and the FASB

Research on accounting issues is conducted in a dynamic and complex environment (see Exhibit 2-1) where new professional standards are issued and existing standards are updated or deleted.

The Accounting Environment

A variety of factors influences accounting standard development, including:

1. Federal government and other regulatory requirements.
2. Various tax laws affecting the financial reporting process.

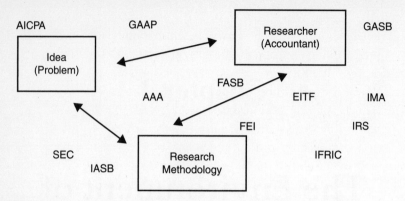

Exhibit 2-1 Accounting Research Environment
SOURCE: Modified from *Accounting & Auditing Research: Tools & Strategies,* 7th ed. Reprinted with permission of John Wiley & Sons, Inc.

3. Specialized industry practices, such as the motion picture and insurance industries.
4. Inconsistencies in practice.
5. Disagreements among constituents as to the objectives of financial statements.
6. Professional organizations.
7. International differences among countries in setting international accounting standards.
8. Increasing litigation concerns.

This chapter concentrates on U.S. financial accounting standard-setting bodies (the Securities and Exchange Commission [SEC] and the Financial Accounting Standards Board [FASB] along with its predecessors), U.S. standard-setting processes, and U.S. research processes (SEC's EDGAR and the FASB's Accounting Standards Codification Research System [the Codification]).

SEC Accounting for Public Companies

The U.S. SEC was established by the Securities Exchange Act of 1934. The law charged the SEC with the duty of ensuring full and fair disclosures of all material facts relating to publicly traded securities. Public companies, those with more than $10 million in assets whose securities are held by more than 500 owners, must comply with U.S. securities laws, such as filing annual and quarterly reports with the SEC. Congress empowered the SEC to specify the documents that public companies must file with the SEC and prescribe the accounting principles used in generating the financial data.

The SEC has the statutory authority to issue rules and regulations, interpretation releases, and staff policy. The SEC term *rules and regulations* refers to all rules and regulations adopted by the SEC, including the forms and instructions that are used to file registration statements and periodic reports. Interpretation releases include a variety of items such as Financial Reporting Releases that prescribe accounting principles to be followed and Accounting Enforcement Releases that announce enforcement actions. Staff policy appears in multiple locations such as Staff Accounting Bulletins (SABs) and no-action letters. A detailed discussion of each appears later in the chapter.

The SEC is comprised of five commissioners appointed by the president of the United States. All other SEC employees are accountants, lawyers, economists, and analysts. The commissioners are responsible for approximately 20 offices (e.g., the Office of Ethics Counsel and the Office of General Counsel). The Office of the Chief Accountant (OCA) works to establish the accounting policies followed by the SEC and is divided into three groups:

1. **Accounting** to develop accounting and disclosure requirements for domestic private companies.
2. **Professional Practice** to develop auditing policies and procedures.
3. **International Affairs** to develop international auditing and regulatory policies.

The SEC has five divisions that are consulted by the OCA groups:

1. **The Division of Corporation Finance** reviews the financial statements of all public companies at least once every three years. Their review sometimes leads to financial restatements.
2. **The Enforcement Division** investigates potential securities law violations, including those related to accounting, auditing, and financial

issues. Some believe that audit firms often respond to Division of Enforcement decisions by pressing the accounting standard setter to establish a rule on that issue to prevent further problems.

3. **The Division of Investment Management** reviews financial reporting by investment companies.
4. **The Division of Trading and Markets** examines stockbrokers and self-regulatory agencies, such as the stock exchanges.
5. **The Division of Risk, Strategy, and Financial Innovation** provides analysis across all SEC activities to help identify developing risks and trends.

The SEC has delegated the major responsibility for accounting standard setting to the FASB predecessors and the FASB, but has retained an oversight function. The SEC recognizes the use of these accounting principles as acceptable for use in filings with the SEC and has reaffirmed this position in 1973, when the FASB was formed, and again pursuant to the Sarbanes-Oxley Act of 2002. In monitoring the FASB's activities, the SEC has occasionally overruled the FASB or its predecessor, the AICPA Accounting Principles Board (APB), as in the issues of accounting for the investment tax credit, accounting for inflation, and accounting for oil and gas exploration.

Over time, accounting standards have emerged to meet the needs of financial statement users. The number of users of financial statements—primarily investors, lenders, and governmental entities—has increased enormously over the past 80 years, and the complexity of the business enterprise has increased with it. These changes have resulted in a greater demand by users for more uniformity in accounting standards to facilitate comparison of financial statements. Government agencies, legislative bodies, and professional organizations have gradually responded to this demand.

SEC accounting is not the same as U.S. GAAP accounting. SEC sources follow the traditional legal hierarchy. Securities laws generally appear under Title 15 of the United States Code (USC). Because there are relatively few major securities laws, these are more commonly cited just by the name of the particular law, such as the Securities Exchange Act of 1934. These laws are widely available both on the web and in legal databases, such as LexisNexis.

SEC Regulations and Sources

SEC rules and regulations refer to all rules and regulations adopted by the SEC. A comprehensive list is located within the Division of Corporation Finance on the SEC website. Some rules provide definitions of terms in certain statutes or regulations and are called *general rules*. Other rules are found in regulations, a compilation of rules related to a specific subject (for example, Regulation 14A on solicitation of proxies). Still other rules relate to procedural matters, such as the steps to be followed in proceedings before the SEC, where to file documents, and what font size to use in materials filed with the SEC. Regulations interpreting the statutory securities laws are codified in the Codification of Federal Regulations (CFR). Securities regulations issued by the SEC are placed under a different title number than the corresponding statutory law, CFR Title 17. Securities regulations include but are not limited to:

1. **Regulation S-X, Form and Content of Financial Statements.** Describes the types of reports that public companies must file and the forms to use.
2. **Regulation S-K, Integrated Disclosure Rules.** Prescribes the requirements for information presented outside the financial statements required under Regulation S-X.
3. **Regulation AB.** Describes disclosure requirements for and definitions of asset-backed securities.
4. **Regulation Fair Disclosure (FD).** Requires that all publicly traded companies disclose material information to all investors at the same time.
5. **Regulation S-T.** Prescribes rules and regulations for electronic filings.

As previously mentioned, Regulation S-X describes the types of reports companies must file and the forms to use. Common forms include:

1. **Schedule 14A**—proxy statement.
2. **Form S-1/F-1**—registration statement for all U.S./foreign companies.
3. **Form 10-K/20F**—annual report for U.S./foreign companies. In Form 20F, a reconciliation between U.S. GAAP and home-country

GAAP (e.g., IFRS) is required. The SEC now allows this reconciliation to be omitted if the foreign-based company follows IFRS as issued by the IASB.

4. **Form 10-Q**—quarterly reports.
5. **Form 8-K/6-K**—information about material events for U.S./foreign companies.

SEC Releases

Beyond regulations, the SEC administrative interpretations include various types of releases, which include the following:

1. **Financial Reporting Releases (FRRs)** prescribe the accounting principles that public companies must follow. FRRs update the SEC Codification of Financial Reporting Policies and Regulations S-K and S-X. A typical SEC Financial Reporting Release contains the following types of information:
   - The background of the topic
   - An evaluation of the comments received on the proposed rules
   - A discussion of the final rules
   - A discussion of transition provisions
   - The text of new rules
2. **Accounting and Auditing Enforcement Releases (AAERs)** announce enforcement actions of the SEC's reporting and disclosure requirements. AAERs generally include a summary of the enforcement action, a discussion of the facts, the SEC's conclusions, and any orders issued (for example, an order to restrict practice before the SEC by the accountant involved for a specific time period).
3. **Accounting Series Releases (ASRs)**, predecessors to the development of FFRs and AAERs, were issued from 1937 to 1982. The SEC has codified non-enforcement-related ASRs that are still in effect. The SEC has published a topical index to enforcement-related ASRs.

All releases are identified with release numbers: a prefix indicating the applicable statute or special type of release and a sequential number that is assigned in the order of issuance. Some common prefixes and their applicable statute or special type of release are:

Prefix	Applicable Statute or Special Type of Release
33	Securities Act of 1933
34	Securities Exchange Act of 1934
AS	(ASR) Accounting Series Release
FR	(FRR) Financial Reporting Release
ER	(AAER) Accounting and Auditing Enforcement Release

Some reference sources, however, replace the prefix with the applicable statute or special type of release. A release often has several release numbers because it applies to more than one statute. For example, Release Nos. 33-6483, 34-20186, and FR-14 represent the same release on an accounting matter that affects filings under the 1933 and 1934 Acts.

The Codification of Financial Reporting Policies is a compendium of the SEC's current published views and interpretations relating to financial reporting. It supplements the rules in Regulations S-K and S-X by providing background and rationale for certain of those rules. Generally, the Codification of Financial Reporting Policies is updated only for the discussion of final rules. While that information is generally adequate in that it provides the important views of the SEC, accountants occasionally refer to the original release for more detailed background information.

SEC Staff Interpretations

SEC staff interpretations (written and oral) provide guidance on accounting and legal matters. Staff interpretations are not legally binding and include the following;

1. **Staff Accounting Bulletins (SABs)** are unofficial interpretations of the SEC's prescribed accounting principles and relate to accounting and disclosure practices under the rules and regulations. SABs represent interpretations and practices followed by the SEC's staff in

the Chief Accountant's Office and Division of Corporation Finance in administering the disclosure requirements of the federal securities laws. The SEC maintains a codification of SABs to make them more useful to users.

2. **Staff Legal Bulletins** are a summary of the Commission staff's views with respect to SEC regulations and federal securities laws. Staff legal bulletins are interpretations and policies followed by the Divisions of Corporation Finance, Market Regulations, and/or Investment Management.

3. **Compliance and Disclosure Interpretations** are a summary of the views of the Division of Corporation Finance staff on various issues. They are considered highly informal and include interpretations of such items as the American Recovery and Reinvestment Act of 2009 and Regulations M-A and Related Rules.

4. **The Division of Corporation Finance Financial Reporting Manual** is an internal reference document including topics related to a registrant's financial statements, pro forma financial information, smaller reporting companies, and related-party matters, to name a few.

5. **CF Disclosure Guidance Topics** include topics such as European sovereign debt exposures, cyber security, and staff observations related to review of 8-K forms reporting reverse mergers.

6. **Staff No-Action, Interpretive, and Exemptive Letters** are published SEC staff responses to inquiries for interpretations of the application of statutes or rules and regulations to a particular transaction contemplated by a registrant or for a general interpretation of the statutes. These responses are related to the Divisions of Corporation Finance, Investment Management, and Trading and Markets as well as the Office of the Chief Accountant.

Given this extensive literature regarding SEC pronouncements, Exhibit 2-2 summarizes the hierarchy of the major SEC Authoritative Pronouncements and Publications.[1] Many of the previously discussed SEC administrative materials are available on its website (www.sec.gov). The SEC web page on information for accountants is also helpful, as shown in Exhibit 2-3.

Exhibit 2-2 Hierarchy of SEC Authorities and Publications

Level 1:	**Statutes**
	i.e., 1933 Securities Act
	Securities Exchange Act
Level 2:	**Regulations and Forms**
	i.e., Regulation S–X
	Regulation S–K
Level 3:	**Commission Releases**
	i.e., Financial Reporting Releases
	Accounting and Auditing Enforcement Releases
	Securities Releases
	Exchange Act Releases
Level 4:	**Staff Advice**
	i.e., No-Action Letters
	Staff Accounting Bulletins

SOURCE: Modified from *Accounting & Auditing Research: Tools & Strategies*, 7th ed. Reprinted with permission of John Wiley & Sons, Inc.

Exhibit 2-3 SEC web page on Information for Accountants
SOURCE: www.sec.gov.

The SEC influences accounting standards set by the FASB and actions within the profession. In December 2001, the SEC sought to remind professionals that

> the selection and application of the company's accounting policies must be appropriately reasoned. . . . Even a technically accurate application of U.S. GAAP may nonetheless fail to communicate important information if it is not accompanied by appropriate and clear analytical disclosures to facilitate an investor's understanding.

This release suggested, as the U.S. courts have repeatedly stated, that compliance with the technical professional standards in U.S. GAAP is not enough. A professional must comply with the underlying intentions of the law and regulations for financial information.

Accessing SEC Filings and Regulations

SEC filings and regulations can be accessed using several methods: the SEC website (www.sec.gov) including EDGAR, which is discussed later, company websites, the Codification (limited SEC guidance), and commercial databases such as Commerce Clearing House, Inc. In most databases, SEC accounting sources are located in a different part of the database from FASB sources.

The researcher can access company filings (for example, proxy statements, annual reports, 10-Ks, and 8-Ks) from several sources as well, including the SEC website via EDGAR, company websites, and Lexis-Nexis Academic. EDGAR is a portal to SEC filings that allows users (analysts, investors, and professionals) to extract data using customized searches. Documents can be retrieved in ASCII, HTML, or XBRL. XBRL filings set EDGAR apart from other databases because the XBRL format and format viewer allow the researcher to extract desirable information for analysis directly from filings without having to retype it. This removes human error in data extraction and retyping.

Example.   Assume the researcher is interested in locating recent Coca-Cola Co. filings. Where would the researcher begin?

The researcher can link to EDGAR from the SEC website, as shown in Exhibit 2-3. Once hyperlinked to the EDGAR search screen (Panel A of Exhibit 2-4), the researcher can search by company or fund name, ticker symbol, central index key, file number, state, country, or SIC. Panel B of Exhibit 2-4 shows the hyperlinked company search screen, and Panel C of Exhibit 2-4 shows the search results. A researcher may also subscribe to filing feeds (RSS, or Really Simple Syndication). The RSS will alert the researcher when a new filing becomes available.

To access regulations other than through the Division of Corporation Finance on the SEC website, use the FASB's Codification for general guidance or a securities law service such as the Commerce Clearing House, Inc. (CCH) Federal Securities Law Reporter. A securities law service reprints the statutes, regulations, abstracts of selective administrative authorities, case abstracts, and helpful practice aids, such as forms used in practice to communicate with the SEC. Other commercial databases include a securities law service. For example, the Research Institute of America (RIA) Checkpoint database has an SEC reference library.

American Institute of Certified Public Accountants (AICPA)

Before the establishment of the FASB in 1973, the AICPA was the recognized standard-setting body for the private sector. The AICPA Committee on Accounting Procedures published 51 ARBs from 1939 to 1959, dealing with a wide spectrum of accounting issues. Because of FASB approval and clearance, some of the ARBs from the AICPA still apply. However, FASB Statements have superseded some ARB pronouncements and modified the application of others.

In 1959, the APB became the standard-setting body. The APB issued 31 APBOs, binding on all CPAs. The APB also issued several unofficial interpretations and four nonauthoritative statements addressing broad concepts rather than specific accounting principles.

Following the formation of the FASB, the AICPA created an Accounting Standards Division to influence the development of

Search the Next-Generation EDGAR System

SEC Home » *Current Page*

Note: EDGAR Search Changes (see below)

Since 1934, the SEC has required disclosure in forms and documents. In 1984, EDGAR began collecting electronic documents to help investors get i improve how investors find and use information.

You can search information collected by the SEC several ways:

- Company or fund name, ticker symbol, CIK (Central Index Key), file number, state, country, or SIC (Standard Industrial Classification)
- Most recent filings
- Full text (past four years)
- Boolean and advanced searching, including addresses
- Key mutual fund disclosures
- Mutual fund voting records
- Mutual fund name, ticker, or SEC key (since Feb. 2006)
- Variable insurance products (since Feb. 2006)

Custom searches:

- Confidential treatment orders
- Effectiveness notices
- SEC Central Index Key (CIK)
- Daily filings

Other Resources

- Researching Public Companies Through EDGAR: A Guide for Investors

A

Enter your search information.   I

Company name:	[_____]
	⦿ Starts with ◯ Contains
or CIK or Ticker Symbol:	[KO]
	Tickers for 10,000 largest publicly traded companies
or File Number:	[_____]
State:	[_____ ▾]
Country:	[_____ ▾]
and/or SIC:	[_____]
and Ownership Forms 3, 4, and 5.	◯ Include ⦿ Exclude ◯ Only
[Find Companies]	

B

COCA COLA CO CIK#: 0000021344 (see all company filings)

SIC: 2080 - BEVERAGES
State location: GA | State of Inc.: DE | Fiscal Year End: 0417
(Assistant Director Office: 9)
Get insider transactions for this issuer.
Get insider transactions for this reporting owner.

Filter Results:	Filing Type: [_____]	Prior to: (YYYYMMDD) [_____]	O C

Items 1 - 40 🔊 RSS Feed

Filings	Format	Description
8-K	(Documents)	Current report, items 5.02 and 9.01 Acc-no: 0001104659-12-010168 (34 Act) Size: 468 KB
8-K	(Documents)	Current report, items 2.02 and 9.01 Acc-no: 0001104659-12-007148 (34 Act) Size: 1 MB
NO ACT	(Documents)	[Paper]No Action Letter Acc-no: 9999999997-12-000606 (34 Act) Size: 1 KB
NO ACT	(Documents)	[Paper]No Action Letter Acc-no: 9999999997-12-000553 (34 Act) Size: 1 KB
8-K	(Documents)	Current report, item 5.02 Acc-no: 0000021344-11-000015 (34 Act) Size: 216 KB

C

Exhibit 2-4 SEC's EDGAR

SOURCE: www.sec.gov.

accounting standards. The Accounting Standards Executive Committee (AcSEC) of the Accounting Standards Division became the spokesperson for the AICPA on financial accounting matters. AcSEC responds to FASB and SEC accounting pronouncements by issuing comment letters and preparing issues papers (financial accounting and reporting issues for the FASB to consider). AcSEC also often publishes brief notes and news releases in the AICPA's monthly online publication, the *CPA Letter*, which reaches more than 340,000 members.

In the past, AcSEC also issued Statements of Position (SOPs) to propose revisions of AICPA-published Industry Audit and Accounting Guides. However, due to changes in the profession, authority for issuing SOPs resides with the FASB.

Various committees of the AICPA also publish materials, including *Accounting Research Monographs* and *Accounting Trends and Techniques* that are applicable to special concerns, such as business valuation. The annual *Accounting Trends and Techniques* publication summarizes current accounting practices of over 600 publicly owned companies. It presents tabulations of the numbers of surveyed companies that use particular practices; it also presents excerpts of actual reports issued by the surveyed companies.

U.S. Generally Accepted Accounting Principles (U.S. GAAP)

U.S. GAAP is "a technical accounting term which encompasses the conventions, rules, and procedures necessary to define accepted accounting practice at a particular time."[2] This definition implies two points:

1. U.S. GAAP is a fluid set of principles based on current accounting thought and practice. It changes in response to changes in the business environment. Therefore, the researcher must review the most current authoritative support, recognizing that recent Accounting Standards Updates (ASUs) sometimes supersede or modify older standards.

2. U.S. GAAP allows alternative principles for similar transactions and the alternatives are considered equally acceptable. Therefore, the researcher must keep searching for alternatives rather than quitting after locating one acceptable principle.

Major U.S. GAAP functions include:

1. **Measurement.** U.S. GAAP requires recognizing or matching expenses of a given period with the revenues earned during that period (for example, depreciating fixed assets and recognizing stock option compensation expense and bad debt allowances). Besides attempting to measure periodic income objectively, the measurement principle focuses on the valuation of financial statement accounts (for example, adjusting trading securities each reporting period to fair value).

2. **Disclosure.** U.S. GAAP provides information necessary for the users' decision models (for example, methods to aggregate accounts and descriptive terminology, as in reporting lease obligations in the footnotes). However, U.S. GAAP does not require disclosure of certain macroeconomic factors (for example, interest rates and unemployment rates) that may interest competitors, bankers, and other financial statement users.

CPAs may not express an opinion that the financial statements are presented in conformity with U.S. GAAP if the statements depart materially from an accounting principle promulgated by an authoritative body designated by the AICPA Council, such as the FASB and the AICPA's APB. While opinions from these bodies previously provided the "substantial authoritative support" necessary to create U.S. GAAP, other sources of U.S. GAAP were available. Most notable were standard industry practices either when a practice addresses a principle that does not otherwise exist in U.S. GAAP or when a practice seems to conflict with U.S. GAAP. In either case, management must justify the practice, and the CPA must evaluate the case to ascertain whether the practice violates established U.S. GAAP. In addition, if unusual circumstances would make it misleading to follow the normal procedure, management must disclose departures from the authoritative guidelines and justify the alternative principle.

The FASB uses the following guiding principles[3] to establish and improve standards:

1. To be objective and ensure neutrality.
2. To solicit and weigh stakeholders' views.
3. To examine costs versus benefits before issuing a standard.
4. To issue high-quality standards.
5. To manage the standard improvement process.
6. To provide clear and timely communications.
7. To review effects of past decisions.

It arrives at U.S. GAAP by considering objectives of financial reporting set out in Statement of Financial Accounting Concepts No. 8. Financial reporting should provide information that:

1. Is useful to present and potential investors, creditors, and other users in making rational investment, credit, and similar decisions. The information should be comprehensible to those who have a reasonable understanding of business and economic activities and are willing to study the information with reasonable diligence.
2. Helps present and potential investors, creditors, and other users in assessing the amounts, timing, and uncertainty of prospective cash receipts and disbursements from dividends or interest, as well as the proceeds from the sale, redemption, or maturity of securities or loans.
3. Provides information about the economic resources of an enterprise; the claims to those resources (obligations of the enterprise to transfer resources to other entities and owners' equity); and the effects of transactions, events, and circumstances that change its resources and claims to those resources.
4. Is useful for assessing financial performance as reflected by accrual accounting. Accrual accounting better enables users to assess past and future performance of an entity compared to cash flows alone.
5. Helps assess changes in economic resources and claims to those resources not reflected in financial performance.
6. Provides investors and creditors with cash flows related to enterprise cash flows. Financial reporting should provide information to help investors, creditors, and others assess the amounts,

timing, and uncertainty of prospective net cash inflows to the related enterprise.[4]

The Financial Accounting Standards Board, Advisory Boards, and the Emerging Issue Task Force

The role of the FASB in today's capital markets is to develop high-quality financial reporting standards that result in credible and transparent financial information in order to service the investing public. The FASB's financial accounting standard-setting process actually involves several entities: the Financial Accounting Foundation (FAF), the FASB Board itself, the FASB staff, and the Emerging Issues Task Force (EITF), as noted in Exhibit 2-5.

The seven-member FASB Board represents a broad spectrum of the financial community. It might include partners from large and small CPA firms, corporate executives, financial analysts, and an academic. The FASB pursues its investigative activities with a full-time research staff of approximately 60 to 70 professionals from various backgrounds.

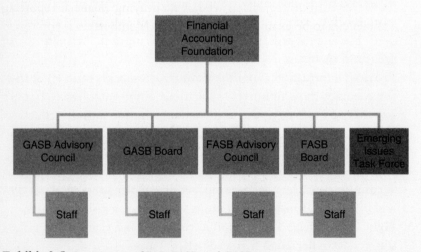

Exhibit 2-5 Organization of FAF, FASB, and GASB
SOURCE: Modified from *Accounting & Auditing Research: Tools & Strategies*, 7th ed. Reprinted with permission of John Wiley & Sons, Inc.

The FASB acquires advice from the Financial Accounting Standards Advisory Council (FASAC) on the priorities of its current and proposed projects, selecting and organizing task forces, and any other matters that the FASB requests. In addition to the regular FASB staff, the Board has several formal channels for gathering information in the standard-setting process, including various advisory councils and project resource groups. These information channels aid the Board when considering the appropriateness of current standards or conducting research for creating new accounting standards and include the:

1. **Financial Accounting Standards Advisory Council (FASAC).** Established in 1973 to advise the FASB on issues related to the FASB's agenda (current and new), priorities, and other matters. Membership can include CEOs, CFOs, executive directors, academics, senior partners, and analysts.
2. **Investor Task Force (ITF).** Established in 2005 to provide the FASB with sector-specific insight and expertise. Membership is comprised of the nation's largest institutional asset managers.
3. **Investors Technical Advisory Committee (ITAC).** Established as a strong technical accounting standing resource for the FASB. It aids with current projects as well as identifying financial reporting deficiencies to be examined by the FASB. Membership is comprised of investment professionals.
4. **Not-for-Profit Advisory Committee (NAC).** Established in 2009 as a strong not-for-profit standing resource for the FASB. Membership is comprised of individuals with financial accounting and reporting and expertise in the not-for-profit sector.
5. **Private Company Financial Reporting Committee (PCFRC).** Established in 2006 to represent all nonpublic business entities as to how the standard-setting process affects them. Membership includes four users, four preparers, and four CPA practitioners.
6. **Small Business Advisory Committee (SBAC).** Established in 2004 as a standing resource to represent the small business community with respect to FASB financial accounting and reporting standard development. Membership includes users, preparers, and auditors in the small business community.

7. **Valuation Resource Group (VRG).** Established in 2007 as a resource to the FASB with respect to fair value measurement implementation issues. Membership includes a broad spectrum of the accounting community.

8. **Private Company Council (PCC).** Established in 2012 to work in conjunction with the FASB to "determine whether exceptions or modifications to existing nongovernmental U.S. Generally Accepted Accounting Principles (U.S. GAAP) are necessary to address the needs of users of private company financial statements." Membership includes users, preparers, and practitioners with private company financial statement experience.

To help practitioners and their clients implement the provisions of FASB Standards, the FASB staff periodically issued Technical Bulletins to provide timely guidance on implementation issues. These Technical Bulletins allowed conformity with FASB pronouncements without the need for the entire FASB Board to issue a new authoritative statement.

The EITF was established in 1984 to help answer questions by financial statement preparers and users about issues not clearly covered by an existing set of authoritative pronouncements. Chaired by the FASB director of Research and Technical Activities, the EITF consists of highly knowledgeable individuals with the foresight to identify issues before they become prevalent and conflicting practices regarding them become well established. The EITF normally addresses industry-specific issues rather than those encompassing accounting and financial reporting as a whole. For example, update No. 2011-07—"Health Care Entities (Topic 954): Presentation and Disclosure of Patient Service Revenue, Provision for Bad Debts, and the Allowance for Doubtful Accounts for Certain Health Care Entities" (a consensus of the FASB Emerging Issues Task Force) is specific to the health care industry.

If the EITF is unable to reach a consensus on an issue under consideration and decides that the problem merits further action, it will forward the file to the FASB Board for further deliberation. Conversely, if the EITF can reach a consensus on an issue, the FASB can usually infer that no Board action is necessary. Thus EITF's consensus positions are still included in the levels of U.S. GAAP for financial and state and local government reporting, and are now issued in sequential order along with other FASB authorities.

The FASB staff often receives questions regarding the appropriate application of FASB literature. Prior to the Codification (July 2009), the FASB staff issued application guidance through FASB Staff Positions (FSP) in order to more quickly and consistently respond to practitioners' and users' needs. After receiving approval from FASB Board members, a 30-day exposure period existed for interested parties to comment on a proposed FSP. The FSPs were posted on the FASB website (www.fasb.org) and remained there until incorporated into printed FASB literature. Prior to 2003, the FASB issued Staff Implementation Guides in response to such issues. Firms may still submit questions to the FASB regarding application of FASB literature through a Technical Inquiry Service form located on the FASB website. However, a staff member's response to a firm is not authoritative since the response is the staff member's opinion based upon submitted facts.

Statements of Financial Accounting Concepts Nos. 1–8

The conceptual framework project seeks to establish objectives and concepts (Statements of Financial Accounting Concepts [SFACs]) for the development of accounting standards and in the preparation of financial statements, especially where no published standards exist. The project's focus is to produce a constitution for accounting, resulting in a coherent set of accounting standards. SFACs are not considered authoritative. However, the researcher normally utilizes these pronouncements when no authoritative pronouncement is directly on point to the issue under consideration. In such cases, the researcher needs to develop a theoretical foundation for the solution to the problem.

The first eight Concept Statements issued under the conceptual framework project are as follows:

1. SFAC No. 1 was superseded by SFAC No. 8.
2. SFAC No. 2 was superseded by SFAC No. 8.

3. SFAC No. 3 was superseded by SFAC No. 6.

4. **Objectives of Financial Reporting of Nonbusiness Organizations.** SFAC No. 4 establishes the objectives of general-purpose external financial reporting by nonbusiness organizations.

5. **Recognition and Measurement in Financial Statements.** SFAC No. 5 establishes recognition criteria and guidance regarding what information should be incorporated into financial statements. It also describes and defines the concept of earnings and what should be included in a full set of an entity's financial statements.

6. **Elements of Financial Statements.** SFAC No. 6 redefines the 10 interrelated elements of financial statements: assets, liabilities, equity, investment by owners, distributions to owners, comprehensive income, revenues, expenses, gains, and losses. It also defines three classes of net assets for nonprofit organizations as well as accrual accounting and other related concepts. Besides amending portions of SFAC No. 2, SFAC No. 6 also supersedes SFAC No. 3.

7. **Using Cash Flow Information and Present Value in Accounting Measurements.** SFAC No. 7 provides a framework for using future cash flows as the basis for accounting measurements and for the interest method of amortization. It also provides general principles that govern the use of present value.

8. **Conceptual Framework for Financial Reporting—Chapter 1, "The Objective of General Purpose Financial Reporting," and Chapter 3, "Qualitative Characteristics of Useful Financial Information."** SFAC No. 8 sets forth the objectives of general-purpose external financial reporting by business enterprises (e.g., financial reporting should provide financial information about the reporting entity) and examines the characteristics of accounting information that make the information useful (e.g., relevance and faithful representation).

FASB SFASs and ASUs

The FASB Codification of accounting standards has superseded most accounting authorities.[5] However, standards, now known as

Accounting Standards Updates (ASUs), are still issued in a similar format with an additional section containing Codification update instructions. The previously issued standards themselves are no longer authoritative, nor are the ASUs, but both contain background information the practitioner may find of interest. ASUs amend the Codification but in and of themselves are not authoritative.

The FASB previously issued pronouncements labeled Statements of Financial Accounting Standards (SFASs) and Interpretations of Financial Accounting Standards, which interpret the FASB's own statements as well as predecessor authorities from the AICPA, Accounting Research Bulletins (ARBs), and Accounting Principles Board Opinions (APBOs). Changes to authoritative U.S. GAAP, labeled ASUs, include all prior forms of authoritative U.S. GAAP (e.g., FASB Statements and EITF Abstracts) and are issued in the format of year-sequential update number (for example, 2011-01, the first pronouncement issued in 2011). Typical archived SFAS standard content is as follows:

1. A summary
2. A table of contents
3. Introduction and other narrative
4. The actual standard
5. A list of the FASB members actually voting
6. The basis for a qualifying or dissenting vote of a FASB member
7. Appendices containing background information, a glossary of terms, numerical and other examples of applying the standard, and other ancillary information

Typical ASU content is as follows:

1. A summary including:
   a. Why the update is being issued,
   b. Who is affected,
   c. The main provisions,
   d. How the main provisions differ from current U.S. GAAP,
   e. The effective date, and
   f. How the main provisions compare to IFRS.
2. The specific amendments to the Codification including implementation guidance.

3. A list of voting members along with the basis for any dissentions.
4. Background information and basis for conclusions.
5. Amendments to the XBRL Taxonomy.

These basic elements are not necessarily presented as separate sections of the pronouncement. Those that are relatively short may combine the introduction and background information and eliminate the illustration of applications section if it is not a complicated principle. However, there is always a separate section designated as the Standard of Accounting or Amendments to the Codification. Codified FASB Statements include Codification Update Instructions. SFASs are archived and accessible through a navigation panel at the FASB Codification website (http://asc.fasb.org).

The introductory/summary section of a pronouncement defines the accounting issue that necessitated the pronouncement. This section gives the scope of the pronouncement, that is, it defines the type of entity affected. It can also limit the application of the pronouncement to companies of specific size (for example, sales exceeding $250 million). The introduction also gives the effects of the new pronouncement on previously issued standards. It specifies which pronouncements or sections of prior pronouncements are superseded by the new standard. Generally, within the introduction, there is a summary of the standard so the researcher can see quickly if the standard applies to the specific situation under investigation. ASUs also contain a comparison to IFRS.

The background information section describes in more detail the business events and related accounting treatments presented in the pronouncement. This section develops the various arguments supporting alternative approaches to resolving the issue. The underlying assumptions for these alternatives are defined, and the different interpretations of the economic impact of the business event are presented. The FASB generally places the background information in an appendix to the official pronouncement.

The basis for conclusion of the authoritative standard is described in the opinions, statements, and ASUs. This section explains the rationale for the accounting principles prescribed in the pronouncement, indicating which arguments were accepted and which were rejected. The FASB incorporates dissenting viewpoints at the end of its main section,

Standards of Financial Accounting and Reporting, and positions the basis for conclusion in a separate appendix. The background information and basis for conclusion provide the researcher with a description of the business events and transactions covered by the pronouncement. These sections can help in determining if the pronouncement addresses the specific issue under investigation. If the researcher is in the early stages of investigation, these sections can help in defining the business transactions, determining their economic impact, and relating them to the proper reporting format.

The opinion, standard, or amendment to the Codification section prescribes the accounting principles for the business transactions described in the pronouncement. This section represents the heart of the official pronouncement. Accountants must follow it when concluding that the standard applies to the business transactions under investigation. The length of this section will depend upon the complexity of the business events involved. For example, the standard length varies from short, as in the case of ASU 2011-02, "Receivables (Topic 310): A Creditor's Determination of Whether a Restructuring Is a Troubled Debt Restructuring," to very long and complicated, as in FASB ASU 2011-04, "Fair Value Measurement (Topic 820): Amendments to Achieve Common Fair Value Measurement and Disclosure Requirements in U.S. GAAP and IFRSs."

The Effective Date section states when the new pronouncement goes into effect. It also identifies any transition period that a company might use to implement a new standard. For example, FASB Statement No. 13, "Accounting for Leases," had a four-year transition period to permit companies to gather data for retrospective application of this complicated pronouncement. While some standards may take effect retrospectively, others take effect shortly after their issuance. If the Board prescribes the method of implementation, retrospective application, or prospective application, this section of the pronouncement will indicate the permissible method.

FASB Due Process

Given the importance of FASB standards, the Board uses an extensive due process. The standard-setting process followed by the Board appears

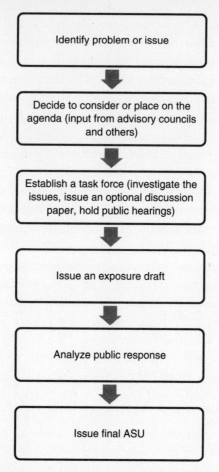

Exhibit 2-6 The FASB Due Process

in Exhibit 2-6. The FASB is held to a fixed procedure, and before issuing an ASU, it must take the following steps:

1. **Identify the issue.** The FASB identifies the problem or issue via a number of sources and takes into account legal or SEC pressures.
2. **Issue consideration.** The FASB decides whether to consider the issue and place it on the agenda. The board generally seeks opinions from the FASAC, advisory councils, project resource groups, and professional organizations such as the Financial Executives International (FEI), the Institute of Management Accountants (IMA), and the Risk Management Association.

3. **Set up a task force.** This step involves establishing a task force (usually about 15 people) to study the problem, investigate the issues, issue a discussion paper to interested parties (optional), hold public hearings, and request written comments on the issue. Several hundred responses are usually received.
4. **Issue an exposure draft (ED).** If action is appropriate, the FASB issues an ED, a preliminary ASU. The normal exposure period is at least 60 days but can be as short as 15 days for urgent matters.
5. **Hold public hearings and analyze responses.** The FASB holds public hearings and may request additional comments on the ED. Constituent responses (e.g., comment letters and public roundtable discussions) are analyzed to determine if a second ED is required or if an ASU should be issued.
6. **Issue a final ASU.** The last step in the FASB due process is to issue a final ASU that describes amendments to the Codification.

Having gone through this due process procedure, the FASB's final pronouncement is placed in the "authoritative" level of U.S. GAAP. ASUs and pre-codification SFASs are issued in a standard format as previously discussed and can be located at the FASB website (www.fasb.org), reprinted in the Official Release section of the *Journal of Accountancy*, and available in the FASB Accounting Standards Codification database.

The Levels of U.S. GAAP[6] and FASB Accounting Standards Codification

A five-level hierarchy existed for the components of U.S. GAAP prior to the FASB Accounting Standards Codification Research System (the Codification). To create a single authoritative source of U.S. GAAP, the FASB flattened the five-level hierarchy to two levels (authoritative and nonauthoritative) via the Codification.[7]

Authoritative guidance is founded on the basic assumption and principles of financial accounting and reporting. The fundamental assumptions underlying financial reporting include the assumptions of economic entity, going concern, monetary unit, and periodicity. The fundamental principles relate to measurement, revenue recognition, expense recognition, and full disclosure. The assumptions and principles are constrained by cost/benefit and industry practices. Qualitative characteristics identify the types of information to be included in financial accounting and reporting. The fundamental characteristics are relevance and faithful representation. Information is relevant (capable of making a difference) if it has predictive value, confirmatory value, or both. It is constrained by materiality. Information has faithful representation if it is complete, neutral, and free from error. In addition to fundamental characteristics, the enhancing characteristics of comparability, verifiability, timeliness, and understandability improve the quality of information. As described next, the authoritative level is based on reference sources containing established accounting principles. Nonauthoritative U.S. GAAP is comprised of other accounting literature not necessarily based on accounting principles, such as notable industry practices, or other literature not adopted by the FASB, such as International Financial Reporting Standards.

The following additional information about the levels of the Codification should enhance understanding of the items within each level.

Authoritative Level

This level is based on literature issued by the following standard setters:

1. FASB
   a. Statements (FASs) and ASU Codification amendments: Original pronouncements
   b. Interpretations (FIN): Clarify, explain, or elaborate on prior FASB, APB, and ARB statements
   c. Technical Bulletins (FTB): Provide guidance in applying pronouncements
   d. Staff Positions (FSP): Offer application guidance
   e. Staff Implementation Guides (Q&A)
   f. Statement No. 138 Examples: Accounting for Certain Derivative Instruments and Certain Hedging Activities
2. EITF: Research resulting from unclear original pronouncements
   a. Abstracts

    b. Topic D: Other technical matters and implications and imple-
       mentation of Abstracts
3. Derivative Implementation Group (DIG) Issues: 189 originally
   issued
4. APB Opinions: 31 opinions of the AICPA APB
5. ARB: 51 ARBs, issued by the Committee on Accounting Procedures (CAP) of the AICPA
6. Accounting Interpretations (AIN)
7. AICPA
    a. SOP
    b. Audit and Accounting Guides (AAG): Only incremental
       accounting guidance, normally reviewed by the AICPA AcSEC
       and cleared by the FASB
    c. Practice Bulletins (PB): Include the Notices to Practitioners ele-
       vated to Practice Bulletin status by Practice Bulletin 1
    d. Technical Inquiry Services (TIS): Only for Software Revenue
       Recognition

Nonauthoritative Level

This level provides other accounting literature and industry practice that the researcher could reference in the absence of a higher-level authority. Examples include textbooks, journal articles, AICPA Issue Papers, and International Financial Reporting Standards.

    While reference to an authoritative pronouncement (now the Codification) usually provides adequate support for an accounting decision, accountants forced to rely on lower levels of support must often build a case involving multiple references. Exhibit 2-7 provides a division between primary, self-supporting references (now included in the Codification) and secondary, non–self-supporting references.

    In researching an issue, the question often arises: Where does the researcher start and when can he or she stop the research process? To begin, the researcher would focus on the primary authoritative support, which has the highest level of authority. If no primary sources are cited, the researcher would then drop down and review the secondary support.

    If the researcher determines that the answer to the question is located in a primary authoritative support, he or she can stop the research

Exhibit 2-7 Primary and Secondary Support

Primary Authoritative Support: Sources that provide sufficient authoritative support for including a particular accounting principle within U.S. GAAP

Post-Codification
A. The Codification

Pre-Codification
A. General application to the field of accounting

1. FASB, FASAB, and GASB Statements of Financial and Governmental Accounting Standards and ASU Codification amendments
2. FASB, FASAB, and GASB Interpretations
3. Opinions of the AICPA Accounting Principles Board
4. Accounting Research Bulletins of the Committee on Accounting Procedures
5. Consensus Positions of EITF of the FASB

B. Special application to certain entities

1. Regulations of the Securities and Exchange Commission
2. AICPA Industry Accounting Guides
3. AICPA SOPs
4. Statements of the CASB
5. Interpretations of the CASB

Secondary Authoritative Support (Pre- and Post-Codification): Sources that support inclusion of particular accounting principles within U.S. GAAP, but individually are not sufficient authoritative support

A. Official publications of authoritative bodies

1. FASB Statements of Financial Accounting Concepts
2. GASB Concept Statements
3. FASB Technical Bulletins*
4. APB Statements of the AICPA
5. Interpretations of APB Opinions*

B. Other sources of information

1. Pronouncements of industry regulatory authorities
2. Substantive industry practices
3. Published research studies of authoritative professional and industrial societies
4. Publications of recognized industry associations
5. Accounting Research Monographs of the AICPA
6. SEC Staff Accounting Bulletins
7. Pronouncements of the IFAC and other international accounting bodies
8. Accounting textbooks and reference books authored by recognized authorities in the field

---

*After July 1, 2009, Secondary Support Items A3 and A5 became primary support.

SOURCE: Modified from *Accounting & Auditing Research: Tools & Strategies*, 7th ed. Reprinted with permission of John Wiley & Sons, Inc.

process because these sources are sufficient for a conclusion. However, if the researcher cited secondary support, additional research is needed because any secondary source individually is insufficient authority. The researcher must recognize that many research questions will not have clear-cut answers. Therefore, professional judgment is a key element in deciding when to stop the research process.

Locating U.S. GAAP

The Codification is the major source for finding essential U.S. GAAP authorities. As previously discussed, the Codification includes all authoritative U.S. GAAP. For example, it incorporates the principles from FASB Statements and Interpretations and the predecessor AICPA ARBs and APBOs, FASB Technical Bulletins, AICPA SOPs that are cleared by the FASB, Abstracts of EITF Statements, FASB Staff Positions, and limited AICPA Audit and Accounting Guidance.

A mixture of authoritative and nonauthoritative U.S. GAAP authorities is located in the AICPA Online Professional Library database discussed in Chapter 6. For instance, the full AICPA Industry and Audit Guides and the AICPA SOPs are available from the AICPA Online Professional Library database. These guides are more fully discussed in the text concerning the auditing authorities. Similarly, the researcher can use the Codification or AICPA Online Professional Library database to access the AICPA Practice Bulletins. Industry practices that are widely recognized and prevalent in the industry are left to the individual accountant's analysis, which one should document by using some of the accounting and business databases described in Chapter 4.

The FASB Accounting Standards Codification Research System (the Codification)

The Codification enables comprehensive, but not complete, research on accounting issues for the private sector. The Codification includes essential[8] content and implementation guidance from the highest four (levels A–D) of the five-level GAAP hierarchy previously referenced and organizes it into approximately 90 topical areas described later in this chapter. A master glossary is also contained in the Codification.

To provide users with a more comprehensive database, the Codification team included limited SEC content (Regulation S-X, Financial Reporting Releases, Accounting Series Releases, Interpretive Releases, Staff Accounting Bulletins, EITF Topic D, and SEC Staff Observer comments) in the Codification. SEC Codification content is labeled with the letter "s." The included SEC literature is for user convenience only and the researcher should be aware that SEC sources follow a traditional legal hierarchy.

Upon adoption, the Codification superseded all preexisting nongovernmental accounting and reporting standards. The Codification replaced the prior five-level GAAP[9] hierarchy with two levels: authoritative and nonauthoritative. Thus the Codification supersedes the previously discussed standards and implementation guidance issued by the FASB and prior standard setters.

Codification Access

Access the Codification from the FASB website (www.fasb.org) as shown in Exhibit 2-8 or go directly to www.asc.fasb.org as shown in Exhibit 2-9. From left to right and top to bottom, the user will see three available subscriptions, a login option, an ordering option, and an academic user option.

1. **Professional view.** The professional view provides full access to the Codification for a fee. The user can browse by topic, keyword search, advanced search, or glossary. Additionally, the user can proceed directly to a code section, join content, cross-reference from archived standards, print with or without references, and access archived/legacy standards. Each of these functions is discussed later in the chapter.
2. **Academic view.** The academic subscription provides faculty and students access to the professional view of the Codification at a reduced rate through the American Accounting Association.
3. **Basic view.** The basic view is free to users who register with a valid email address. It has limited functionality. The user can browse by

Exhibit 2-8 Access to the Codification
SOURCE: www.fasb.org.

topic, locate legacy (archived) standards, and utilize basic print functions.

4. **Login.** This area allows registered users to log in.

5. **Order professional or basic view.** Clicking on this box will provide registration options for two types of subscriptions, basic and professional. Once subscribed, the user will click on "Login" to access the Codification.

6. **Academic user.** This area provides academic users access to the Codification.

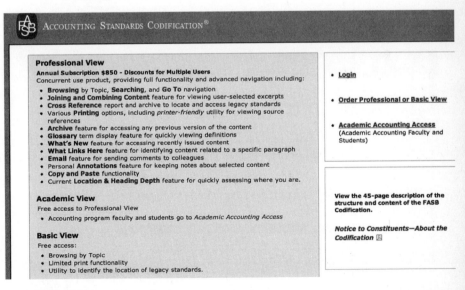

Exhibit 2-9 Registration Options
SOURCE: www.asc.fasb.org.

Navigating the Codification

The Codification opening screen appears in Exhibit 2-10. There are five tabs: "Browse," "What's New," "Recently Issued," "Cross Reference," and "Join Sections." The "Browse" tab is presented last since it leads into a detailed discussion following this section.

1. "What's New" includes information by date, topic, or document for various time periods, up to one year.
2. "Recently Issued" organizes recently issued content by date.
3. "Cross Reference" allows the researcher to cross-reference between the original archived standards and the Codification. This is very useful for researchers familiar with prior GAAP levels. For instance, as demonstrated in Exhibit 2-11, the researcher selects a Standard Type (APB, EITF, FIN, etc.) from a drop-down menu. The Standard Number drop-down menu is populated based upon the Standard Type selection. The researcher then left-clicks the "Generate Report" button to produce a report cross-referencing each standard paragraph to the Codification.

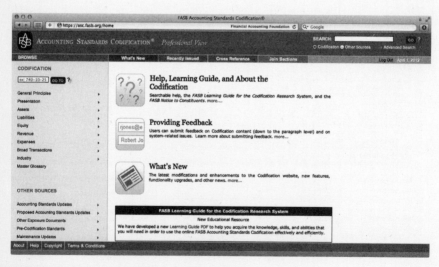

Exhibit 2-10 The Codification Opening Screen
SOURCE: www.asc.fasb.org.

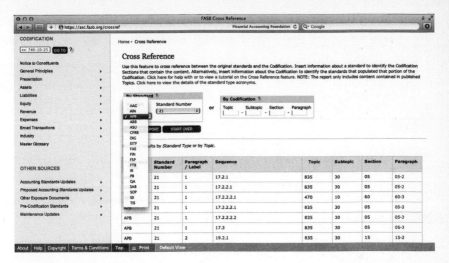

Exhibit 2-11 Cross Reference
SOURCE: www.asc.fasb.org.

4. "Join Sections" allows the researcher to select multiple topics and display those choices in one document. For instance, the researcher can select a Topic and Section utilizing a drop-down menu as displayed in Panel A of Exhibit 2-12. The researcher can choose to include or exclude intersection subtopics and choose between FASB, SEC, or all material. By left-clicking the "Get Sections" button, a report is generated as shown in the bottom half of Panel A of Exhibit 2-12. The researcher then selects the desired sections, left-clicks the "Join Sections" button, and a report similar to Panel B in Exhibit 2-12 is generated. The researcher has the option to expand or collapse the joined material once the report is generated.

5. "Browse" is the opening screen and is a powerful research tool further divided into three areas: the left navigation panel providing access to the Codification and other sources, the middle screen area providing access to items such as "Help" and "Providing Feedback" links, and the top right screen search area. Each item appearing on the "Browse"/opening screen tab is briefly discussed below from left to right, and top to bottom. Some items are discussed in detail later in the chapter when covering research topics.

Join Sections

The Join Sections function allows you to select Codification content that spans multiple Topics and Subtopics. You must select a Topic AND a Section. Click here for help with or to view a tutorial on the Join Sections feature.

	Topic	Subtopic	Section	Title
☐	810	10	05	810 Consolidation > 10 Overall > 05 Background
☐	810	20	05	810 Consolidation > 20 Control of Partnerships and Similar Entities > 05 Background
☐	810	30	05	810 Consolidation > 30 Research and Development Arrangements > 05 Background

JOIN SECTIONS

A

Table of Contents
Collapse | Expand

- ☐ 810 Consolidation
  - ☐ 10 Overall
    - ☐ 05 Overview and Background
      - ■ General
      - ⊞ Variable Interest Entities
      - ■ Consolidation of Entities Controlled by Contract
  - ⊞ 20 Control of Partnerships and Similar Entities
  - ⊞ 30 Research and Development Arrangements

810 Consolidation
10 Overall

810-10-05 Overview and Background

General Note: The Overview and Background Section provides overview and background material for the guidance contained in the Subtopic. It does not provide the historical background or due process. It may contain certain material that users generally consider useful to understand the typical situations addressed by the standards. The Section does not summarize the accounting and reporting requirements.

General

⊕ COMBINE SUBSECTIONS ?   ⊠ RELATED EXPOSURE DRAFT ?

05-1 The Consolidation Topic provides guidance on entities subject to consolidation as well as on how to consolidate. Paragraph 810-10-10-1 discusses the objectives of consolidation.

B

Exhibit 2-12 Join Sections

SOURCE: www.asc.fasb.org.

Browse Tab—Left Navigation Panel

The left navigation panel is divided into two areas: the Codification and Other Sources. This panel remains on the screen regardless of which tab or which heading the researcher clicks on. Each heading in the left navigation panel is discussed below. Search strategies utilizing topical categories and the master glossary are discussed later in the chapter.

The Codification.

1. **"Go To" box.** If the researcher is familiar with a desired code section, the researcher can type the Codification Section number in the box and be hyperlinked to that particular Section.
2. **Topical categories.** Topical categories (described below) include general principles, presentation, financial statement accounts (assets, liabilities, equity, revenue, expenses), broad transactions, and industry.
   a. General principle topics are assigned codes 105–199. The topics cover conceptual matters such as generally accepted accounting principles. As of July 2012, much of the content is still pending.
   b. Presentation topics are assigned codes 205–299 and include items such as comprehensive income (220), notes to the financial statements (235), and segment reporting (280).
   c. Financial statement accounts numbered from 305–705 appear in the left navigation panel separately: assets (305–399), liabilities (405–499), equity (505–599), revenue (605–699), and expenses (705–799). Examples of items located within the financial statement accounts include inventory (330), contingencies (450), and research and development (730).
   d. Broad transactions topics are assigned codes between 805 and 899. Because some items, such as business combinations (805) and interest (835), affect more than one financial statement, they are considered to be transactions-oriented and are included in this area.
   e. Industries topics are assigned codes 905–999 and include unique accounting topics such as development-stage enterprises (915).
      The topical categories follow a three-two-two numbering scheme (XXX-YY-ZZ). Topics are assigned three-digit codes between 105 and 999 as described above. Subtopics are subsets (type

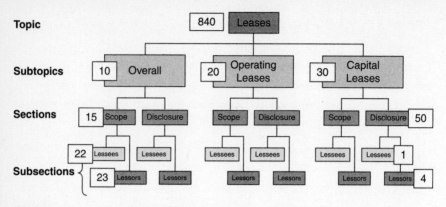

Exhibit 2-13 The Codification Coding Structure
SOURCE: Modified from Codification Notice to Constituents, www.asc.fasb.org/ (2008).

or scope) of topics. For example, 15 (products) and 20 (services) are subtopics of revenue (605). The subtopics are further refined into sections from 00 to 99. For consistency, section numbers do not change. For instance, section 05 refers to "Overview and Background" and section 20 refers to the "Glossary" whether the researcher is examining the business combination subtopic of overall (10) or reverse acquisitions (40). Subsections refine sections in a limited number of cases. Exhibit 2-13 provides a visual representation of the numbering schematic used by the Codification. When citing the Codification, the researcher will preface the code numbers with ASC (Accounting Standards Codification). For instance, the citation for capital lease disclosures for lessees is ASC 840-30-50-1.

3. **Master glossary.** The master glossary provides a list of all glossary terms contained in each topic.

Other sources.   "Other Sources" appearing in the left navigation panel includes five items: "Accounting Standards Updates," "Proposed Accounting Standards Updates," "Other Exposure Documents," "Pre-Codification Standards," and "Maintenance Updates." "Accounting Standards Updates" links the researcher to current ASUs organized by year. "Other Exposure Documents" is also organized by year. "Pre-Codification Standards" links the researcher to FASB and AICPA archived standards. Researchers more familiar with superseded authoritative literature will find this link useful for input into the cross-reference function described earlier. Maintenance updates are editorial-type corrections to the Codification.

Browse Tab—Middle Screen

The middle screen area of the "Browse" tab contains the following headings: "Help," "Learning Guide," and "About the Codification"; "Providing Feedback"; and "What's New." Each area is discussed below.

1. "Help," "Learning Guide," and "About the Codification" contain several useful links. Help pages exist for navigation methods and help on other features such as annotations, archived content, copy and paste, feedback, glossaries, joining content, location, pending content, printing, SEC content, and XBRL.
2. The *FASB Learning Guide for the Codification Research System* contains 17 lessons for working with the Codification. The Notice to Constituents is a 45-page document describing the Codification in detail. It provides discussions on the Codification in general, its goals, its content, its functionality, its structure, future standard setting, and background material.
3. "Providing Feedback" links to information about how to provide content feedback and general feedback.

The Research Process

The Codification database enables researchers to obtain authoritative evidence to help solve their research questions more efficiently than they could using manual hardbound tools. In addition to the cross-reference search discussed previously, search processes in the Codification include using the master glossary, performing a topical category search, and utilizing keyword search inquiries. The location of each search process is shown in the prior-referenced Exhibit 2-10, the Codification opening screen. The master glossary and topical categories options are located in the left navigation panel, and the search function is located in the top right screen area. Each search process is discussed in detail next. Note that the Codification may

Glossary

Use the quick find feature at the end of this page, or use the alphabetic index to browse the terms beginning with that letter.

General Note: The Master Glossary contains all terms identified as glossary terms throughout the Codification. Clicking on any term in the Master Glossary will display where the term is used. The Master Glossary may contain identical terms with different definitions, some of which may not be appropriate for a particular Subtopic. For any particular Subtopic, users should only use the glossary terms included in the particular Subtopic Glossary Section (Section 20).

A | B | C | D | E | F | G | H | I | J | K | L | M | N | O | P | Q | R | S | T | U | V | W | X | Y | Z | 0-9 | View All

Glossary Term Quick Find

variable interests

Variable Interests

A

The investments or other interests that will absorb portions of a variable interest entity's (VIE's) expected losses or receive portions of the entity's expected residual returns are called variable interests. Variable interests in a VIE are contractual, ownership, or other pecuniary interests in a VIE that change with changes in the fair value of the VIE's net assets exclusive of variable interests. Equity interests with or without voting rights are considered variable interests if the legal entity is a VIE and to the extent that the investment is at risk as described in paragraph 810-10-15-14. Paragraph 810-10-25-55 explains how to determine whether a variable interest in specified assets of a legal entity is a variable interest in the entity. Paragraphs 810-10-55-16 through 55-41 describe various types of variable interests and explain in general how they may affect the determination of the primary beneficiary of a VIE.

B

Exhibit 2-14 Master Glossary
SOURCE: www.asc.fasb.org.

not contain guidance for the researcher's question, requiring the researcher to examine nonprimary support.

Master Glossary

The master glossary provides a list of all glossary terms contained in each topical category. To use the master glossary, left-click on the "Master Glossary" heading. As illustrated in Exhibit 2-14, the alphabet will appear in the center screen along with a glossary term quick-find option. Left-click the desired letter or type in a term in the "Quick Find" area. If a letter is clicked, scroll down to the area of interest and click on the term to display its definition. If a term is entered in the quick-find area, the center screen will display results of all definitions with the term of interest.

Example.   Assume the researcher is interested in the definition of variable interests. How would the researcher find the definition using the quick-find option?

Glossary Term Usage

The glossary term is used in the following locations.

Variable Interests

810 Consolidation > 10 Overall > 20 Glossary
- 810 Consolidation > 10 Overall > 20 Glossary

810 Consolidation > 10 Overall > 25 Recognition
- 810 Consolidation > 10 Overall > 25 Recognition > Variable Interest Entities , paragraph 25-20

810 Consolidation > 10 Overall > 50 Disclosure
- 810 Consolidation > 10 Overall > 50 Disclosure > Variable Interest Entities , paragraph 50-12

810 Consolidation > 10 Overall > 55 Implementation
- 810 Consolidation > 10 Overall > 55 Implementation > Variable Interest Entities , paragraph 55-16

Exhibit 2-15 Master Glossary Incoming Links
SOURCE: www.asc.fasb.org.

The researcher would left-click on the "Master Glossary" heading, at which point a glossary term quick-find option would appear. Type the term "variable" and such terms as "variable annuity," "variable interest entity," "variable interests," and so on will appear in the center screen. As the researcher continues to type, the results will be narrowed to that demonstrated in Panel A of Exhibit 2-14. Click the desired term to display the definition as shown in Panel B of Exhibit 2-14. Once in the definition, left-click on the incoming links heading to produce the location of the term within the Codification (Exhibit 2-15).

Topical Categories

As previously mentioned, the topical categories ("Presentation," "Assets," "Liabilities," "Equity," "Revenue," "Expenses," "Broad Transactions," and "Industry") are always displayed in the left navigation panel. Because most researchers have an idea of which topic is of interest to them, this tends to be the favorite search method and thus is utilized more than the other search functions. To search within the topics, move the cursor over the category of interest to open the subtopic window (see Exhibit 2-16). Keep moving the cursor to the right to open new windows until reaching the final area of interest, at which point left-clicking will allow access to the desired information in the center screen.

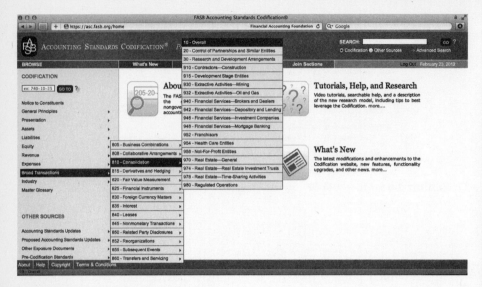

Exhibit 2-16 Topical Category Search
SOURCE: www.asc.fasb.org.

Example.   Assume the researcher is interested in how to consolidate variable interests. Where would he or she begin to search using the topical category method?

Consolidation is located in the Broad Transactions topic. As illustrated in Exhibit 2-16, highlight "Broad Transactions," "Consolidation" (810). Since this topic is new to the researcher, the researcher might try clicking on "Overall." Left-click subtopic 10 to display sections, as illustrated in Panel A of Exhibit 2-17. The researcher is interested in variable interests, so he or she would most likely left-click on section 05, "Overview and Background," which contains information about variable interests. Once in section 05, the researcher scrolls down to paragraph 8 (ASC 810-10-05-8) as illustrated in Panel B of Exhibit 2-17 to examine consolidation criteria.

Keyword Search: Basic and Advanced

Basic.   A keyword search utilizes the search bar appearing at the top right screen area of the database as illustrated in Panel A of Exhibit 2-18. Enter a single keyword or multiple keywords and left-click "Go." The search results appear in the center screen with short excerpts under each

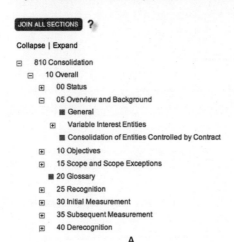

810 Consolidation
10 Overall

To join all Sections within this Subtopic, click JOIN ALL SECTIONS.

JOIN ALL SECTIONS   **?**

Collapse | Expand

⊟   810 Consolidation
   ⊟   10 Overall
      ⊞   00 Status
      ⊟   05 Overview and Background
         ■ General
         ⊞ Variable Interest Entities
         ■ Consolidation of Entities Controlled by Contract
      ⊞   10 Objectives
      ⊞   15 Scope and Scope Exceptions
      ■ 20 Glossary
      ⊞   25 Recognition
      ⊞   30 Initial Measurement
      ⊞   35 Subsequent Measurement
      ⊞   40 Derecognition

A

Variable Interest Entities

⬤ COMBINE SUBSECTIONS **?**   ■ RELATED EXPOSURE DRAFT **?**

> **Consolidation of VIEs**

05-8   The Variable Interest Entities Subsections clarify the application of the General Subsections to certain **legal entities** in which equity investors do not have the characteristics of a controlling financial interest or do not have sufficient equity at risk for the legal entity to finance its activities without additional **subordinated financial support**. Paragraph 810-10-10-1 states that consolidated financial statements are usually necessary for a fair presentation if one of the entities in the **consolidated group** directly or indirectly has a controlling financial interest in the other entities. Paragraph 810-10-15-8 states that the usual condition for a controlling financial interest is ownership of a majority voting interest. However, application of the majority voting interest requirement in the General Subsections of this Subtopic to certain types of entities may not identify the party with a controlling financial interest because the controlling financial interest may be achieved through arrangements that do not involve voting interests.

Pending Content: ?

Transition Date: *Various* | **Transition Guidance: 810-10-65-2**

The Variable Interest Entities Subsections clarify the application of the General Subsections to certain **legal entities** in which equity investors do not have sufficient equity at risk for the legal entity to finance its activities without additional **subordinated financial support** or, as a group, the holders of the equity investment at risk lack any one of the following three characteristics:

   a. The power, through voting rights or similar rights, to direct the activities of a legal entity that most significantly impact the entity's economic performance

   b. The obligation to absorb the expected losses of the legal entity

   c. The right to receive the expected residual returns of the legal entity.

B

Exhibit 2–17 Topical Category Hyperlink
SOURCE: www.asc.fasb.org.

A

1 - 10 of **20** Results for: **variable interests**   (Refine Search)

810 Consolidation > 10 Overall > 25 Recognition

Variable Interest Entities

...a legal entity is a variable interest entity (VIE) and would need to be consolidated by the reporting entity, specifically: a Determining the variability to be considered b Initial involvement with a legal entity c Consolidation based on variable interests 1 The effect of related parties 2 Sufficiency of equity at risk 3 Implicit variable interests 4 Variable interest and interests in specific assets of a VIE.   Determining the ...

General

...is appropriate if a reporting entity has a controlling financial interest in another entity and a specific scope exception does not apply (see Section 810-10-15). The usual condition for a controlling financial interest is ownership of a majority voting interest, but in some circumstances control does not rest with the majority owner.   The Effect of Noncontrolling Rights on ...

Consolidation of Entities Controlled by Contract

...Subsection addresses various considerations related to whether an entity is controlled by contract that is not a variable interest entity (VIE) (see the Variable Interest Entities Subsection of Section 810–10–15), specifically: a General guidance b Term c Control d Financial interest e Determining whether an employee is an employee of the consolidating entity f Consideration recorded in the period consideration is provided.   General Guidance 25-61 The information necessary to evaluate the requirements in paragraph 810-10-15-...

810 Consolidation > 10 Overall > 05 Overview and Background

Variable Interest Entities

    Consolidation of VIEs 05-8 The Variable Interest Entities Subsections clarify the application of the General Subsections to certain legal entities in which equity investors do not have the characteristics of a

B

Narrow

By Related Term: ?

- fair value
- cash flow
- reporting entity
- gain or loss
- interest rate
- derivative instrument

By Area: ?

☐ Presentation(1)
☐ Broad Transactions(18)
☐ Industry(1)

GO

Exhibit 2-18 Basic Keyword Search
SOURCE: www.asc.fasb.org.

heading as shown in Panel B of Exhibit 2-18. Left-click the desired heading to produce the related literature. Note that whenever the researcher uses the search button, a box to the right of the results helps narrow the search by related terms or by area.

Advanced. An advanced search option is located beneath the search bar. As illustrated in Panel A of Exhibit 2-19, this feature allows the search to be narrowed by search area (all areas or specific categories with topic/subtopic choices as shown with the revenue subtopic), keyword (all, any, exact, or within so many words), Codification reference, document/title heading, area (all areas or specific categories without topic/subtopic choices), source type (the Codification or other), and number of results to display. As with the

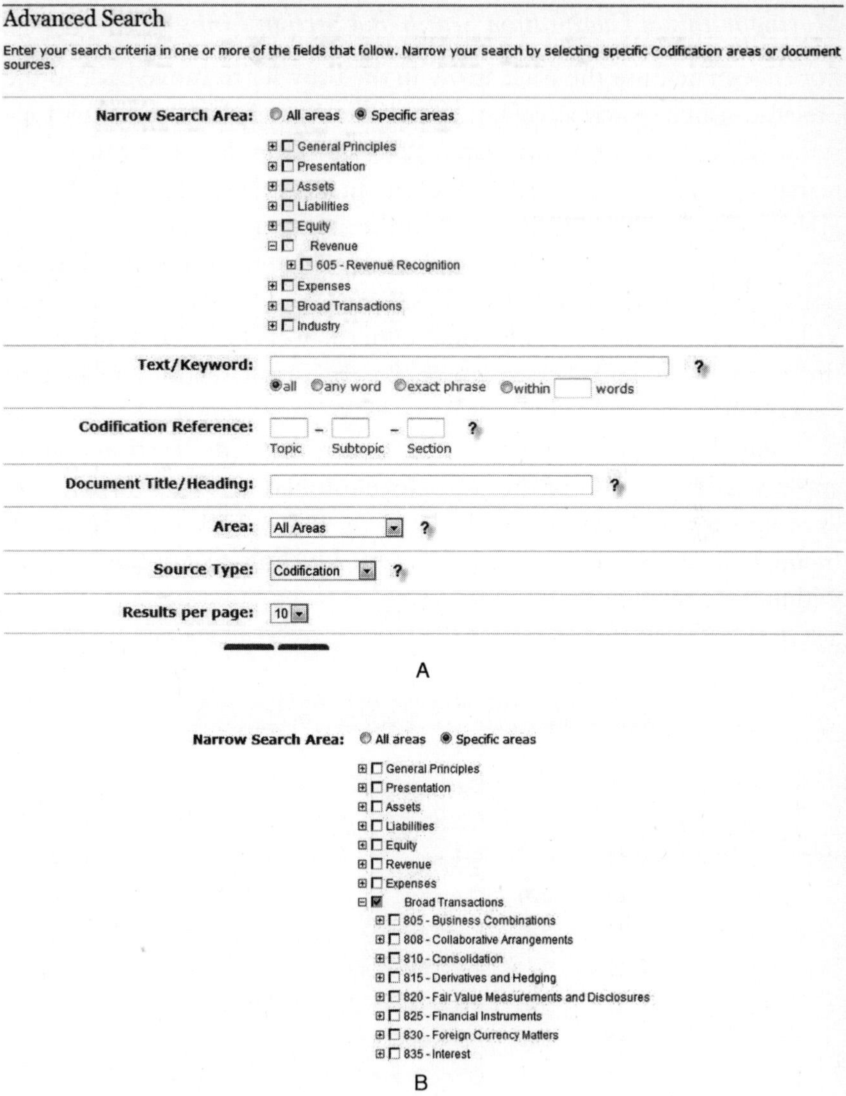

Advanced Search

Enter your search criteria in one or more of the fields that follow. Narrow your search by selecting specific Codification areas or document sources.

Narrow Search Area: ○ All areas   ● Specific areas

- ⊞ ☐ General Principles
- ⊞ ☐ Presentation
- ⊞ ☐ Assets
- ⊞ ☐ Liabilities
- ⊞ ☐ Equity
- ⊟ ☐ Revenue
  - ⊞ ☐ 605 - Revenue Recognition
- ⊞ ☐ Expenses
- ⊞ ☐ Broad Transactions
- ⊞ ☐ Industry

Text/Keyword: [   ] **?**
● all   ○ any word   ○ exact phrase   ○ within [   ] words

Codification Reference: [   ] – [   ] – [   ] **?**
Topic   Subtopic   Section

Document Title/Heading: [   ] **?**

Area: [All Areas ▼]   **?**

Source Type: [Codification ▼]   **?**

Results per page: [10 ▼]

A

Narrow Search Area: ○ All areas   ● Specific areas

- ⊞ ☐ General Principles
- ⊞ ☐ Presentation
- ⊞ ☐ Assets
- ⊞ ☐ Liabilities
- ⊞ ☐ Equity
- ⊞ ☐ Revenue
- ⊞ ☐ Expenses
- ⊟ ☑ Broad Transactions
  - ⊞ ☐ 805 - Business Combinations
  - ⊞ ☐ 808 - Collaborative Arrangements
  - ⊞ ☐ 810 - Consolidation
  - ⊞ ☐ 815 - Derivatives and Hedging
  - ⊞ ☐ 820 - Fair Value Measurements and Disclosures
  - ⊞ ☐ 825 - Financial Instruments
  - ⊞ ☐ 830 - Foreign Currency Matters
  - ⊞ ☐ 835 - Interest

B

Exhibit 2-19 Advanced Keyword Search
SOURCE: www.asc.fasb.org.

simple search function, the search terms appear in the center screen with the suggested narrowing subtopics window to the right. Once a search is performed, the advanced search function reappears below the potential results. Panel B of Exhibit 2-19 displays the narrow search area function.

Moving within a Codification Search and Section Links

For all searches, use the back arrow in the browser to move back to the previous search. Alternatively, the researcher can click on the larger topical area, and the previous search results will display. For instance, a search on "goodwill" results in topic and subtopic 350-20 ("Intangibles—Goodwill and Other)." A further refinement results in section 05, "Overview and Background," or 15, "Scope and Scope Exceptions." A researcher who left-clicks section 05 and then wants to return to the previous search results could either left-click the back button in the browser or left-click subtopic 20 to list all sections related to "goodwill."

Once in a section-related area, a box labeled "Section Links" appears at the bottom of the page. As illustrated in Exhibit 2-20, left-clicking on the "Section Links" heading will open up a drop-down menu that allows the researcher to quickly link to another section within the same subtopic.

FASB	SEC	Section
00	S00	Status
05		Background
10		Objectives
15		Scope
20	S20	Glossary
25	S25	Recognition
30		Initial Measurement
35	S35	Subsequent Measurement
40	S40	Derecognition
45	S45	Other Presentation
50	S50	Disclosure
55		Implementation
60		Relationships
65		Transition
75	S75	XBRL Elements
	S99	SEC Materials

FIGURE 2-20 Sections Links Menu
Source: www.asc.fasb.org.

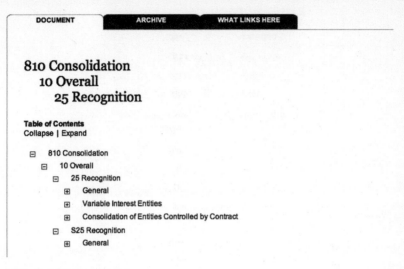

Exhibit 2-21 "Archive" Tab
SOURCE: www.asc.fasb.org.

The Section Tabs: "Document," "Archive," and "What Links Here"

Once in a section-related area (e.g., 810-10-25, "Consolidation," "Overall," "Recognition"), three tabs appear at the top of the center screen area: "Document," "Archive," and "What Links Here" (Exhibit 2-21). The document area is the default tab in the center screen area containing the table of contents, which can be collapsed or expanded.

The "Archive" tab contains links to the current and superseded literature related to the section. As demonstrated in Exhibit 2-22, the archived literature is organized by versions, with the highest version number linking to the most recent literature and the smallest version number (1) linking to the content in effect upon Codification adoption (July 1, 2009).

The "What Links Here" tab provides links to related Codification content. As demonstrated in Exhibit 2-23, Paragraph 25-2 links to seven content areas.

Email, Print, and Copy/Paste Functions

The content of a standard can be emailed, printed, or copied and pasted. To email the content, simply left-click on the email option and fill out

Archived FASB Content

General

Version 3 (current)

Version 2 superseded on 2010-07-01

Version 1 superseded on 2010-02-02

Variable Interest Entities

Version 4 (current)

Version 3 superseded on 2010-02-25

Version 2 superseded on 2009-12-23

Version 1 superseded on 2009-10-05

Exhibit 2-22 Section-Related Tabs
SOURCE: www.asc.fasb.org.

the form appearing in Exhibit 2-24. Once there is printable content-related output, a page/print function box will appear at the bottom of the content. Left-click on the heading and, as illustrated in Panel A of Exhibit 2-25, a menu window will appear.

To print a particular record, click the page/print functions box appearing at the bottom center of the screen once a search is performed and there is printable content. A menu window will appear, as illustrated in Panel A of Exhibit 2-25. Choose "Printer Friendly" to print or copy the record shown to another program (Panel B of Exhibit 2-25).

Links To FASB Content

Links to Section: 810 Consolidation > 10 Overall > 25 Recognition

Links To Subsection General

Links To Paragraph 25-1

- 810 Consolidation > 10 Overall > 25 Recognition > General, paragraph 25-3

Links To Paragraph 25-2

- 810 Consolidation > 10 Overall > 00 Status > General, paragraph 00-1
- 810 Consolidation > 10 Overall > 15 Scope > General, paragraph 15-10
- 810 Consolidation > 10 Overall > 15 Scope > Variable Interest Entities, paragraph 15-14
- 810 Consolidation > 10 Overall > 25 Recognition > General, paragraph 25-2
- 810 Consolidation > 10 Overall > 25 Recognition > General, paragraph 25-4
- 810 Consolidation > 10 Overall > 25 Recognition > General, paragraph 25-14
- 958 Not-for-Profit Entities > 810 Consolidation > 55 Implementation > General, paragraph 55-4A

Exhibit 2-23 "What Links Here" Tab
SOURCE: www.asc.fasb.org.

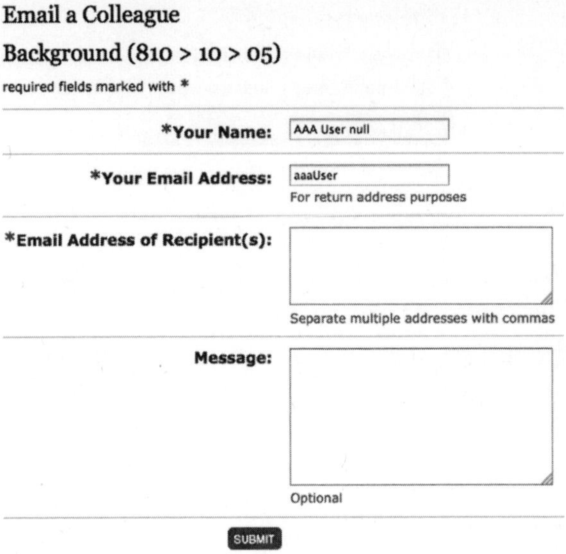

Email a Colleague

Background (810 > 10 > 05)

required fields marked with *

*Your Name:	AAA User null
*Your Email Address:	aaaUser
	For return address purposes
*Email Address of Recipient(s):	
	Separate multiple addresses with commas
Message:	
	Optional

SUBMIT

Exhibit 2-24 Email Option
SOURCE: www.asc.fasb.org.

Choose "Printer Friendly with TOC" to print or copy the content along with the associated table of contents (Panel C of Exhibit 2-25). Choose "Printer Friendly with Sources" to print or copy the content along with the corresponding archived standard and references (Panel D of Exhibit 2-25). Selecting any of the print options opens a new window. Alternatively, the researcher can choose to print or copy the content of that window using the print or copy functions within the browser. The copy function is explained in more detail next.

There are two approaches to copying a record. The first is to highlight the results from any of the search methods. Use the copy function within the browser and paste into another document using either the paste function within the location (Word, Excel) or right-clicking the mouse to use its paste function. This approach only provides the section and paragraph numbers, not the entire citation. Therefore, following the second approach is a better option. Select any of the print options from the page/print function menu discussed previously. This will open a new window from which the researcher can copy and paste the entire output (including citation) using the mouse or the browser functions.

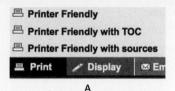

A

Variable Interest Entities

> **Consolidation of VIEs**

810-10-05-8 The Variable Interest Entities Subsections clarify the application of the General Subsections to certain **legal entities** in which equity investors do not have the characteristics of a controlling financial interest or do not have sufficient equity at risk for the legal entity to finance its activities without additional **subordinated financial suppo** Paragraph 810-10-10-1 states that consolidated financial statements are usually necessary for a fair presentation if one of the entities in the **consolidated group** directly or indire has a controlling financial interest in the other entities. Paragraph 810-10-15-8 states that the usual condition for a controlling financial interest is ownership of a majority voting interest. However, application of the majority voting interest requirement in the General Subsections of this Subtopic to certain types of entities may not identify the party with a controlling financial interest because the controlling financial interest may be achieved through arrangements that do not involve voting interests.

B

[810-10-05] Overall - Overview and Background
General
Variable Interest Entities
> Consolidation of VIEs
Consolidation of Entities Controlled by Contract

General Note: The Overview and Background Section provides overview and background material for the guidance contained in the Subtopic. It does not provide the historical background or due process. It may contain certain material that users generally consider useful to understand the typical situations addressed by the standards. The Section does summarize the accounting and reporting requirements.

General

810-10-05-1 The Consolidation Topic provides guidance on entities subject to consolidation as well as on how to consolidate. Paragraph 810-10-10-1 discusses the objectives of consolidation.

810-10-05-2 This Topic includes the following Subtopics:

a. Overall

b. Control of Partnerships and Similar Entities

c. Research and Development Arrangements.

810-10-05-3 [Paragraph not used]

810-10-05-4 The guidance in this Subtopic is presented in the following three Subsections:

a. General

C

Variable Interest Entities

> Consolidation of VIEs

810-10-05-8 [The Variable Interest Entities Subsections clarify the application of the General Subsections to certain **legal entities** in which equity investors do not have the characteristics of a controlling financial interest or do not have sufficient equity at risk for the legal entity to finance its activities without additional **subordinated financial supp** Paragraph 810-10-10-1 states that consolidated financial statements are usually necessary for a fair presentation if one of the entities in the **consolidated group** directly or indi has a controlling financial interest in the other entities. Paragraph 810-10-15-8 states that the usual condition for a controlling financial interest is ownership of a majority voting interest. However, application of the majority voting interest requirement in the General Subsections of this Subtopic to certain types of entities may not identify the party with a controlling financial interest because the controlling financial interest may be achieved through arrangements that do not involve voting interests. [FIN 46(R), paragraph 1, sequence 5

D

Exhibit 2-25 Page/Print Functions
SOURCE: www.asc.fasb.org.

Summary

This chapter has presented an overview of the bodies that set standards in accounting, the process of standard setting, the types of authoritative pronouncements, and the Financial Accounting Standards Codification System. Because U.S. GAAP is a fluid set of principles based on current accounting thought and practice, and not a static, well-defined set of accounting principles, accountants must research updates to the Codification or changes in the pronouncements. Accounting research is challenging. The Codification has consolidated U.S. GAAP down to two levels, but there are still many sources. One needs to use the Codification to find relevant authorities. Thus one must understand how the databases are structured, their contents, and search techniques. One sometimes needs to research SEC accounting rules and regulations for publicly traded companies and use other databases and websites to acquire those authorities. Practice developing research and analytical skills to meet the standards of the accounting profession and the public's expectations.

Notes

1. Paul B. W. Miller and Jack Robertson, "A Guide to SEC Regulations and Publications: Mastering the Maze," *Research in Accounting Regulation* 3 (July–August 1989): 239–249.
2. Auditing Standards Board AU Section 411.
3. FASB Rules of Procedure, Amended and Restated through February 28, 2011; www.fasb.org.
4. FASB, Statement of Financial Accounting Concept No. 8, "Conceptual Framework for Financial Reporting" (2010).
5. The FASB Accounting Standards Codification Notice to Constituents provides a list of the following grandfathered material: paragraph B217 of FAS 141; paragraphs 25 and 341 of FAS 140; paragraph 77 of FAS 87; paragraphs 97 and 102 of SOP 93-6; paragraph 24 of FAS 118; paragraph 83 of FAS 124(R); and paragraph 1.05 of the Investment Company Audit and Accounting Guide.
6. FASB, Statement of Financial Accounting Standards No. 162, "The Hierarchy of Generally Accepted Accounting Principles" (2008).
7. FASB, Proposed Statement of Financial Accounting Standard, "The Hierarchy of Generally Accepted Accounting Principles—a replacement of FASB Statement No. 162" (2009).

8. While developing the Codification Research System, the Codification team organized literature into essential and nonessential literature. Nonessential content includes items such as the basis for FASB dissension, summary, background information, and other, like content. Essential content includes items such as implementation guidance and the actual standard. Only essential content is codified. Nonessential content is located in an archived standard available by means of the left navigation bar of the Codification.

9. FASB, Statement of Financial Accounting Standards No. 162, "The Hierarchy of Generally Accepted Accounting Principles" (2008).

Chapter 3

The Environment of International Research

International competition has forced many firms to look to new markets to remain competitive. Internationalized capital markets result in a need for internationally comparable financial statements and accounting standards.

The International Accounting Environment

Efforts have increased during the past decade to move nations toward using international standards. The movement toward harmonization and convergence has included the activities of supranational groups and individual scholars. Harmonization moves toward reducing the overall number of alternatives but still allows for them as long as the alternatives do not conflict with IFRS. On the other hand, convergence moves toward adoption of one set of standards. Exhibits 3-1[1] and 3-2[2] depict the significant global and U.S. IFRS convergence efforts since inception, respectively. Included in the global category are the International Federation of Accountants (IFAC), the International Accounting Standards Board (IASB), the Organisation for Economic Co-operation and Development (OECD), and the European Union (EU).

The IASB, through a due process procedure described later in this chapter, has issued a number of International Financial Reporting Standards (IFRS) that incorporate the previously issued International Accounting Standards (IAS) by the International Accounting Standards Committee (IASC).

The IASB independently issues standards for financial reporting, although it works closely with the International Federation of Accountants (IFAC). The IASB has received support from organizations such as the International Organization of Securities Commissions, the World Trade Organization, and the European Financial Reporting Advisory Group (EFRAG) to create acceptable accounting standards for multinational securities and other international offerings.

U.S. convergence milestones with IFRS include the 2002 Norwalk Agreement and the subsequent reaffirmed Memorandum of Understanding and "roadmap," as shown in Exhibit 3-2. The Norwalk Agreement was the first Memorandum of Understanding (MOU) between the IASB and the FASB, whereby they agreed to work on both short- and long-term projects removing differences (convergence) between IFRS and U.S. GAAP and to continue coordinating activities. Reaffirmation of the MOU occurred in 2006 and 2008. In 2007, the SEC issued a "roadmap" to remove U.S. GAAP reconciliations for non-U.S. IFRS filers. A Work Plan, issued in 2010, outlined the process the SEC will follow to make an IFRS adoption determination. During 2011, the SEC issued several staff papers related to IFRS (adoption, practice, and comparison to U.S. GAAP) and is continuing to collect data to be able to make an informed IFRS adoption determination.

Research on international accounting issues is as dynamic as that of local environments. New professional standards and interpretations are constantly issued. The updating of existing standards through joint efforts between the IASB and the FASB helps to minimize the

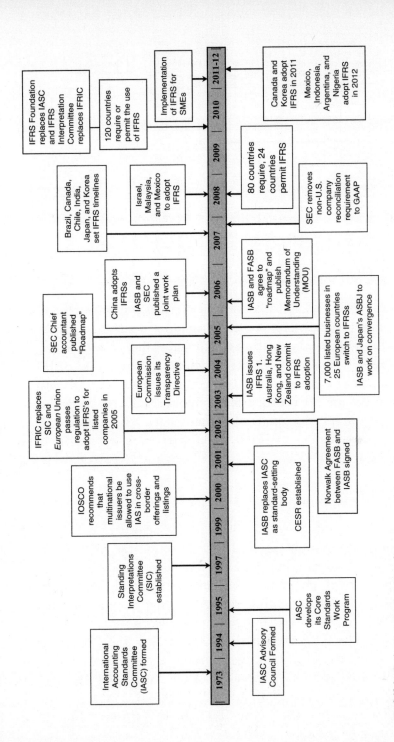

Exhibit 3–1 Global IFRS Timeline

SOURCE: *Mastering the FASB Codification and eIFRS: A Case Approach*, 1st ed.

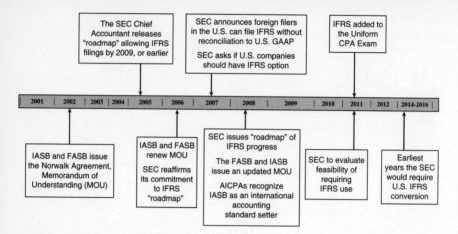

Exhibit 3-2 U.S. IFRS Timeline
SOURCE: *Mastering the FASB Codification and eIFRS: A Case Approach*, 1st ed.

differences between national boundaries. Various constituents and advisory bodies (for example, preparers, auditors, academics, investors, financial analysts, and regulators) influence the development of accounting standards. This chapter examines the adoption of IFRS globally and domestically in the United States, the IASB's standard-setting process, the IASB Board and committees, the standards themselves, the Conceptual Framework, other recognized standard setters, funding and regulation of IFRS, IFRS hierarchy, and research in electronic IFRS (eIFRS).

International Accounting Standards Board (IASB)

The IASB's objectives are to develop high-quality, enforceable, global financial reporting standards; promote the use of those standards while considering the needs of small and medium-sized entities; and work toward national accounting standards convergence. The IASB's financial accounting standard-setting process is similar to the FASB's process in that it involves several entities, as noted in Exhibit 3-3. The IFRS Foundation's Constitution (the Constitution) describes the name, objectives, membership, and governance of each of the following entities or committees: the Monitoring Board, the International Financial Reporting Standards Foundation (IFRS Foundation) Trustees, the IASB, the IFRS Interpretations Committee

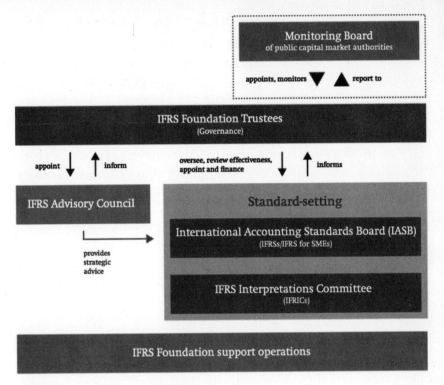

Exhibit 3-3 Organization of the IASB
SOURCE: IASB, "Who We Are and What We Do," www.ifrs.org.

(the Interpretations Committee), the IFRS Advisory Council (the Advisory Council), and the Small and Medium-sized Entities (SME) Implementation Group. The Constitution was approved in 2000 and has been revised several times.

The Monitoring Board oversees the IFRS Foundation by approving trustee appointments to the IFRS Foundation, reviewing the IFRS Foundation's annual written report regarding its activities, and meeting with the trustees of the IFRS Foundation at least on an annual basis. The Monitoring Board includes representation from regulators of major capital markets and leading global organizations. More specifically, as of March 2012, the Monitoring Board is comprised of: the commissioner of the Financial Services Agency, Japan; the chairman of the U.S. SEC; the commissioner for Internal Market and Services, European Commission; the chair of the IOSCO Technical Committee, who is also the vice commissioner for International Affairs, JFSA; the vice chair of the IOSCO (International Organization of Securities Commission) Technical Committee, who is also the vice chairman of the Comisión Nacional del Mercado de Valores of Spain; the vice chair of the IOSCO Emerging Markets Committee, who is also the chairman of the Securities Commission, Malaysia; an observer; and the chairman of the Basel Committee on Banking Supervision.

The IFRS Foundation's role is to develop a single set of global high-quality standards; promote the use of those standards; consider its constituents (small to large and stable to emerging); and initiate convergence of IFRS with other national accounting standards. Empowered to carry out the tasks of the IFRS Foundation are 22 financially knowledgeable trustees: 6 members each from Europe, North America, and Asia/Oceania; 1 from Africa; 1 from South America; and 2 from other geographic regions. The trustees are responsible for appointing, monitoring, and reviewing the effectiveness of the IASB members. The trustees also develop the IFRS Foundation's strategy and budget, amend the Constitution, raise funds, and appoint members to the Advisory Council and Interpretations Committee (discussed later in this chapter).

The IASB was created by the IASC Foundation (now IFRS Foundation) in 2001 to create a single set of high-quality global standards. The IASB holds public meetings during most months for a three- to five-day period, which are archived on the IASB website (www.iasb.org or www.ifrs.org). Membership of the IASB is based on professional competence and practical experience such that auditors, preparers, users, and academics are represented. As of July 1, 2012, membership increased to 16 members, of which 3 may be part-time. The IASB's composition is similar to that of the trustees: four members each from Europe, North America, and Asia/Oceania; one from Africa; one from South America; and two from other geographic regions.

The Interpretations Committee consists of 14 highly knowledgeable individuals who are in a position to become aware of implementation issues before they become widespread and divergent practices regarding them become entrenched. The members are appointed by the trustees and are chaired by the IASB's director of technical activities (or another senior member of the IASB staff). The Interpretations Committee meets as required.

The Advisory Council meets with the IASB at least three times per year to provide input on the IASB's technical agenda, project priorities, and individual projects. The Advisory Council also helps the IASB promote IFRS throughout the world by publishing articles and supporting IFRS at various professional meetings. The Advisory Council is comprised of more than 30 members from geographically and professionally diverse backgrounds, such as preparers, auditors, academics, investors, financial analysts, and regulators. The Advisory Council reports both its activities and those of the IASB to the trustees. Other advisory bodies include but are not limited to the:

1. **Capital Markets Advisory Committee (CMAC).** An international user resource for the IASB that is independent of the IASB and the IFRS Foundation. Both the group and the IASB set the CMAC agenda and its members are chosen by the group. The members serve as individuals, not as representatives of their employers.

2. **Emerging Economies Group (EEG).** Created in 2011 by the IFRS Foundation to focus on application and implementation of IFRS issues. Both the group and the IASB set the EEG agenda and its members are chosen by the group although the committee is cochaired by the IASB. Members serve as individuals and/or as representatives of their employers.

3. **Financial Crisis Advisory Group (FCAG).** Established by the IASB to examine investor confidence in financial markets resulting from financial reporting improvements. Its work has been concluded. Members were chosen by the Trustees and public search.

4. **Global Preparers Forum (GPF).** An international preparer resource for the IASB. Both the group and the IASB set the GPF agenda and members are chosen by the group. Members serve as individuals, not as representatives of their employers.

5. **SME Implementation Group.** Comprised of 22 members from geographically diverse regions. It considers and develops guidance for IFRS implementation issues related to small and medium-sized enterprises as well as recommending IFRS amendments to the IASB. The agenda is set by the group and its members are

international area experts chosen by the trustees and public search. It is chaired by the IASB.

Other Regional and National Standard-Setting Bodies and Organizations Influencing IFRS

The IASB relies on other standard-setting bodies and organizations as a source of information to ensure that new IFRSs consider regional and country-specific financial reporting needs. These bodies also help educate constituents regarding new IFRSs. Below is a list of several regional and national bodies:

1. **Asian-Oceanian Standard-Setters Group (AOSSG).** Promotes the adoption of IFRS and its consistent application; works with the IASB and governments/regulators to improve financial reporting.
2. **European Financial Reporting Advisory Group (EFRAG).** It "provides advice to the European Commission on all issues relating to the application of IFRS in the EU."[3]
3. **Group of Latin American Standard Setters (GLASS).** A regional group promoting IFRS. Its initial meeting was held in March 2012.
4. **G20 Leaders.** Consists of 20 finance ministers and central bank governors representing 19 countries plus the European Union and 80 percent of the global gross national product. It examines policy issues related to international financial stability.
5. **International Federation of Accountants (IFAC).** A global organization for international accountants contributing to and promoting the development, adoption, and implementation of high-quality international standards. It was founded in 1977 and is comprised of professional accountancy organizations. Currently, there are 164 members and associates from 125 different countries.
6. **International Organization of Securities Commissions (IOSCO).** Develops, implements, and promotes adherence to internationally recognized standards of regulation, oversight, and

enforcement. Its structure includes the Presidents Committee, comprised of all the presidents of member agencies; the Executive Committee, comprised of 19 members; and four Regional Standing Committees (Africa/Middle-East Regional Committee, Asia-Pacific Regional Committee, European Regional Committee, and Interamerican Regional Committee).

7. **National Standard Setters Group (NSS).** Supports the IASB's mission with respect to financial reporting by carrying out research projects, commenting on the IASB agenda and proposals, and providing a forum related to financial reporting.

8. **Public Interest Oversight Board (PIOB).** Improves the quality and public interest focus of international standards by providing independent oversight. It was created in 2005 and oversees the activities of the Public Interest Activity Committees (PIACs) and the Compliance Advisory Panel (CAP). The PIACs include the International Auditing and Assurance Standards Board (IAASB), the International Education Standards Board (IAESB), and the International Ethics Standards Board for Accountants (IESBA). The CAP evaluates member body compliance with IFAC membership rules.

IASB Authorities

The IASB issues pronouncements labeled International Financial Reporting Standards (IFRS) and interpretations labeled IFRICs. IFRICs interpret the IASB's own statements. The IASB also recognizes predecessor authorities from the IASC titled International Accounting Standards (IAS) and Standards Interpretations Committee interpretations (SIC). As of July 2012, the IASB follows 28 of the 41 previously issued IASs and has issued 13 new IFRSs. Most IFRSs contain:

1. An introduction
2. A table of contents
3. An objective
4. A scope
5. Definitions
6. The actual standard

7. A list of the IASB members actually voting
8. The basis for a qualifying or dissenting vote of an IASB member
9. Appendices containing background information, a glossary of terms, examples of applying the standard, and other ancillary information

IFRSs are used as a basis of financial reporting for many companies, stock exchanges, and regulatory authorities that allow presentation of financial statements using IFRS. IFRSs are also used by supranational bodies to produce results that meet the needs of capital markets, by many countries having national accounting requirements, and as international benchmarks by countries that develop their own accounting requirements.[4]

The Standards Interpretations Committee (SIC) was established in 1997 to timely answer questions by financial statement preparers and users about issues not clearly covered by an existing set of authoritative pronouncements. As of July 2012, 8 of its 33 interpretations are still followed.

The Interpretations Committee replaced the International Financial Reporting Interpretations Committee (IFRIC) and the SIC. It produces interpretations labeled IFRICs, and 16 of the 20 previously issued interpretations are in use. The Interpretations Committee can address industry-specific issues rather than those encompassing accounting and financial reporting as a whole. For example, IFRIC No. 20, "Stripping Costs in the Production Phase of a Surface Mine," applies primarily to the mining industry. To prevent divergence, clarification may be necessary, such as in IFRIC No. 10, "Interim Financial Reporting and Impairment," which addresses whether an entity should reverse impairment losses recognized on goodwill in an interim period.

When lack of consensus exists on an issue under consideration by the Interpretations Committee, and the Interpretations Committee decides that the problem merits further action, it will forward the file to the IASB for further deliberation. Conversely, if the Interpretations Committee can reach a consensus on an issue, the IASB can usually infer that no Board action is necessary. Approved Interpretations Committee interpretations have the same authority as IASB Standards. The interpretations (IFRICs and SICs), along with the original pronouncements, are collectively known as IFRS(s).

IASB Due Process

Given the importance of IASB Standards, an extensive due process was adopted in order to address transparency, accessibility, extensive consultation, responsiveness, and accountability. Additionally, a Due Process Oversight Committee (DPOC) was created to:

- Review and update the due process handbooks;
- Oversee (1) the IASB with respect to due process compliance and (2) the trustee's function with respect to operating in accordance with the Constitution; and
- Approve the working group composition.

The IASB's six-stage due process, as depicted in Exhibit 3-4 and set out in the Constitution, is as follows:

1. **Input from working groups and item evaluation.** Before a potential agenda item is set, the IASB receives input from working groups within the IASB, the Interpretations Committee, and the Advisory Committee. The IASB considers the potential agenda item's relevance, existing accounting guidance, the possibility of increased convergence, the potential quality of any proposed standard, and the resources needed to examine the potential agenda item.

2. **Plan a research project.** The IASB plans the research project to determine whether to work with other accounting standard setters, such as forming working groups comprised of staff and/or members from the various standard-setting bodies. The IASB's working groups are chaired by the director of technical activities or director of research.

3. **Issue a discussion paper (optional), allow public comment, and analyze comment letters.** Developing and publishing a discussion paper is not a mandatory stage, but the action is usually taken to obtain early feedback from constituents. If the discussion paper is omitted, the IASB will explain why. Typically, a discussion paper includes an examination of the topic, the alternative accounting treatments, the standard setters' views, and an invitation for comment. If another standard setter initiated the discussion paper, the IASB requires a simple majority vote before publication. If the

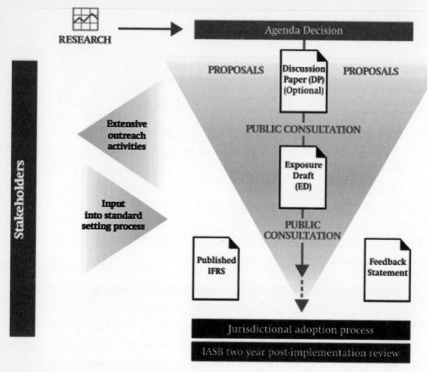

Exhibit 3-4 IASB Due Process
SOURCE: IASB, "Who We Are and What We Do," (www.ifrs.org).

IASB or one of its working groups initiated the research, the discussion paper is published because all IASB sessions are public. Analysis is performed on the comment letters received during the usual 120-day comment period, and the results are posted to the IASB website.

4. **Publish an exposure draft (ED).** Developing and publishing the ED is mandatory and is based on IASB staff research, discussion paper comments, Advisory Council input, working groups, and other standard-setter input. Before the ED is issued for comment, a ballot takes place requiring approval by 9 of the 14 IASB members (the number of members needed for approval will increase when IASB membership increases to 16 members in mid-2012). ED periods are usually 120 days or longer for major projects; if a matter is urgent, the ED period is 30 days. Once comments are received, they are summarized and posted to the IASB website.

5. **Draft an IFRS or a second ED.** The IASB then decides whether to draft an IFRS or publish a second ED. If IFRS is drafted, the IFRIC reviews the draft before it goes to the IASB for a vote. A version of the IFRS draft is also posted for paid subscribers. An IFRS is issued only after any outstanding issues are resolved and the IASB members have voted in favor of the standard.

6. **Provide implementation guidance.** The IASB and its staff periodically hold meetings with constituents with respect to implementation guidance and any unforeseen standard shortcomings. The IFRS Foundation promotes educational seminars and events to ensure proper application of IFRS.

Interpretations Committee Due Process

IFRICs are issued to clarify IFRSs or prevent diverging viewpoints. A seven-stage due process is followed for issuing interpretations. During the process, the Interpretations Committee ensures that its focus remains principle-based, it considers potential international convergence, and it ensures that its guidance does not change or conflict with existing IFRSs or the Framework. The Interpretations Committee seven-stage due process, as depicted in Exhibit 3-5 and set out in the Constitution, is as follows:

1. **Identify the issue.** A detailed description and evaluation of an issue may be put forward by individuals or an organization, by email or regular mail. The IASB staff assesses the issue and determines if it can be put on the agenda or requires additional input.

2. **Set the agenda.** The Interpretations Committee holds a public debate and decides whether to add the issue to the agenda. The issue is examined for relevance, divergence, improved financial reporting, scope, ability to reach a consensus, and if related to a current or planned IASB project. A comment period of at least 30 days is set, at which time a simple majority of Interpretations Committee members can choose to add an issue to the agenda.

3. **Meet and vote.** Public meetings are held in which the Interpretations Committee debates items proposed and actual agenda

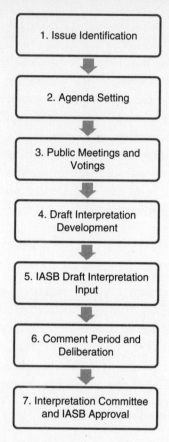

Exhibit 3-5 Interpretations Committee Due Process

items. A quorum consists of 10 voting members (in person or by teleconference).

4. **Develop a draft interpretation.** IASB staff members present papers with information describing the issue along with background information such as a description of the issue, the specific issue to be considered by the Interpretations Committee, any relevant Conceptual Framework concepts, alternatives, relevant IASB pronouncements, and a recommendation. The Interpretations Committee then develops and votes publicly on the draft interpretation, which includes a summary of the issue, the consensus reached (no more than four members voting against a

proposal), references (IFRSs and/or Conceptual Framework), and an effective date.

5. **Allow for IASB input.** The IASB plays a role in the release of a draft interpretation. IASB members comment on all Interpretations Committee agenda papers and are informed when the Interpretations Committee reaches a consensus. A draft interpretation is released for public comment.

6. **Allow a comment period.** Draft Interpretations are publicly available for at least 60 days. Comment letters are examined and summarized. At this time, the Interpretations Committee determines whether to finalize the interpretation or reexpose it.

7. **Approve the Interpretation.** An interpretation is approved by the Interpretations Committee and the IASB. After there is a consensus, the interpretation is put forth for IASB ratification in a public meeting.

Having completed a due process procedure, the IASB's or Interpretations Committee's final pronouncement is placed at an equal level in the IFRS hierarchy. All throughout the due process, IFRSs and IFRICs are summarized in nontechnical language in the IFRS Foundation's *Insight* journal. Final technical summaries are posted on the IASB website and the full standard is placed in eIFRS, discussed later in this chapter.

The IASB's Conceptual Framework

The IASB's Conceptual Framework (the Framework) establishes objectives and concepts for the development of accounting standards. The Framework is also useful in the preparation of financial statements by listing the objectives and the qualitative characteristics of the financial statements and providing the definition and measurement concepts of the elements of financial statements and capital maintenance.

Ideally, the Board uses the Framework in the development of future standards. The Framework should also assist users and preparers in applying and interpreting standards and financial statements. For instance, preparers may need to look to the Framework in the absence of a published standard, and auditors may want to ensure clients' financial statements are in compliance with IFRS to form an opinion on those statements. However, occasionally a conflict arises between the Framework and previously issued IASs or IFRSs. In conflict situations, the standards override the Framework.

The Framework is to provide information regarding the objectives of financial reporting, the qualitative characteristics of financial reporting, the definition, recognition, and measurement of the elements of financial statements, and the concepts of capital and capital maintenance. It does this through four chapters: 1. *The Objectives of General Purpose Financial Reporting*, 2. *The Reporting Entity* (yet to be added), 3. *Qualitative Characteristics of Useful Financial Information*, and 4. *The 1989 Framework: The Remaining Text*. Chapters 1 and 3 are converged with U.S. GAAP. A discussion of each existing chapter appears next.

The first chapter, *The Objective of General Purpose Financial Reporting*, contains information regarding the objective, usefulness, and limitations of general financial reporting and information about reporting entities' economic resources, claims to those resources, and changes in those resources and claims. The converged objective is to "provide financial information about the reporting entity that is useful to existing and potential investors, lenders, and other creditors in making decisions about providing resources to the entity."[5]

The third chapter, *Qualitative Characteristics of Useful Financial Information*, includes a discussion of the fundamental qualitative characteristics (relevance, materiality as it relates to relevance, and faithful representation) along with their application; enhancing qualitative characteristics (comparability, verifiability, timeliness, and understandability) along with their application; and the cost constraint on useful financial reporting. Information is useful if it is relevant and faithfully represented. Timeliness, comparability, verifiability, and understandability enhance the usefulness of information. Relevant information predicts or confirms prior expectations and surpasses a materiality threshold. Information with faithful representation is complete, neutral, and free from error.

The fourth chapter, *The 1989 Framework: The Remaining Text*, includes a discussion of all other items such as assumptions of financial reporting, going concern, the elements of the financial statements, measurement of these elements, and concepts for capital and capital maintenance. Elements of financial statements include assets, liabilities, equity, income, and expenses. Assets are future economic benefits owned by the entity, resulting in resource inflows. Liabilities are current obligations as a result of a past transaction resulting in resource outflows. Equity is the residual interest in an entity. Income is an inflow or economic benefit whereas an expense is a decrease in an economic benefit or outflow. Capital maintenance refers to return on capital and return of capital. In the process of examining global firms, revaluations of assets and liabilities occur and would appear as capital transactions.

Although the Framework is quite extensive, it is not as comprehensive as the IASB or the FASB would like. Therefore, the IASB and the FASB are continuing to work jointly to publish a new conceptual framework that will provide a principles-based, consistent, converged framework for developing future accounting standards. As previously discussed, in 2010 the IASB issued the Conceptual Framework, which superseded the Framework for the Preparation and Presentation of Financial Statements. The Conceptual Framework includes Chapter 1, *The Objective of General Purpose Financial Reporting*, and Chapter 3, *Qualitative Characteristics of Useful Financial Information*, as well as the remaining text from the prior Framework not covered in Chapters 1 or 3. As of 2012, the IASB and the FASB are at various stages of due process on the remaining Framework chapters.

IFRS Funding, Regulation, and Enforcement

Long-term funding commitments to the IFRS Foundation and the IASB from over 30 countries and/or organizations are shown on the IASB website. The Foundation's goal is to have broad-based funding that is open-ended (no strings attached), compelling (shared by all), and country-specific (measurement based on GDP). As of 2012, a majority of the Foundation's funding is voluntary. However, levy systems and regulatory contributions have been introduced in various countries. Presently, the most significant sources of funding include: 48 percent from publicly sponsored/nationally administered financing regimes, 26 percent from international accounting firms, and 15.5 percent through publications and related activities.

The IASB and the IOSCO have agreed to a list of necessary accounting issues to address in a core set of international accounting standards for use in cross-border offerings and multiple listings. Ideally, establishing a core set of international accounting standards should reduce the costs of doing business and help companies raise capital across borders, streamline internal accounting and auditing functions for multinational companies, increase the efficiency of market regulations, and decrease the costs of international financial statement analysis and investment.

The SEC has expressed three conditions for accepting international accounting standards for all public companies:

1. IASB standards should include a core set of accounting pronouncements that constitute a comprehensive, generally accepted basis of accounting.
2. IASB standards must have high quality, result in comparability and transparency, and provide for full disclosure.
3. Rigorous interpretations and applications must exist for IASB standards.[6]

As previously discussed, during 2011, the SEC issued several staff papers related to the 2010 Work Plan outlining the process the SEC will follow to make an IFRS adoption determination. The SEC continues to make progress toward the Work Plan completion.

Because local regulations govern the preparation and issuance of financial statements in most countries, differences of form and content persist among countries. The following provides a listing of organizations impacting the international environment, many of which are discussed throughout the chapter.

Organization	Website
Asian-Oceanian Standards-Setters Group (AOSSG)	www.aossg.org
Business Europe	www.businesseurope.eu
European Financial Reporting Advisory Group (EFRAG)	www.efrag.org
European Securities and Markets Authority (ESMA)	www.esma.europa.eu
European Union (EU)	europa.eu
Federation of European Accountants (FEE)	www.fee.be

Financial Accounting Standards Board (FASB)	www.fasb.org
International Accounting Standards Board (IASB)	www.ifrs.org
International Association for Accounting Education Research (IAAER)	www.iaaer.org
International Federation of Accountants (IFAC)	web.ifac.org
International Organization of Securities Commissions (IOSCO)	www.iosco.org
National Standard Setters (NSS)	www.frc.org.uk/asb/ about/nss.cfm
Organisation for Economic Co-operation and Development	www.oecd.org
Public Interest Oversight Board (PIOB)	www.ipiob.org
Securities and Exchange Commission (SEC)	www.sec.gov
World Trade Organization (WTO)	www.wto.org

Although the IASB does not have the authority to require compliance with IFRS, the success of international accounting harmonization and convergence will depend upon the recognition and support of interested groups such as the European Union (EU). The EU consists of 27 member states (Belgium, Germany, France, Italy, Luxembourg, the Netherlands, Denmark, Ireland, the United Kingdom, Greece, Spain, Germany, Austria, Finland, Sweden, the Czech Republic, Estonia, Cyprus, Latvia, Lithuania, Hungary, Malta, Poland, Slovenia, Slovakia, Bulgaria, and Romania). Two of the EU's objectives are to create a single market for goods in the EU and to have the EU become a world power.

The EU has taken several measures to ensure consistency with IFRS. For example, roundtables and forums such as the Europeans Enforcers Coordination Sessions (EECS) are utilized, and committees such as the European Securities and Markets Authority (ESMA) (formerly CESR) and the European Securities Committee (ESC) have been established to act as advisory groups. Roundtables identify potential IFRS application issues. The roundtable collects views from member states through the various audit firms, standard setters, and other interested bodies because membership includes the IASB, ESMA, the Interpretations Committee, EFRAG, FEE, Business Europe (formerly UNICE), audit firms, national standard setters, preparers, and the SEC. If divergence from an IFRS is identified, the roundtable makes a timely recommendation to the Interpretations Committee to eliminate the divergence.

In 2001, the CESR (now known as ESMA) and the ESC were established. These organizations have assisted the EU in adopting IFRSs. ESMA provides opinions as to the progress non-EU countries are making toward IFRS conversions and on agreements with the IASB. For instance, Japan has made two agreements with the IASB, as depicted in Exhibit 3-1. The CESR filed a report in March 2008 stating it had no reason to believe that Japan's Accounting Board (ASBJ) could not complete convergence in the time stated and that the EU should then consider Japanese GAAP as equivalent.

The SEC Office of International Affairs (OIA) works with a global network of securities regulators and law enforcement to promote cross-border regulatory compliance. The OIA advises the Commission with respect to SEC and non-U.S. initiatives on cross-border activities of U.S. issuers and U.S. financial service providers. The OIA also examines the impact of SEC rules on foreign market participants.

The IOSCO regulates international markets through its working committees: the Technical Committee, for developed markets, and Emerging Markets Committee, for less developed markets. Each IOSCO committee is further divided into the following functional groups: disclosure, regulation, enforcement, and investment.

International Financial Reporting Standards (IFRS) Research

International accounting research is complex, with numerous accounting standards, rules, and recommended practices. Although all IFRSs are considered to be of equal authority, there is a hierarchy when applying them to a situation.

IFRS Hierarchy

As previously discussed, the IASB issues pronouncements labeled IFRSs and the IFRS Interpretation Committee issues interpretations of pronouncements known as IFRICs. The IASB recognizes predecessor pronouncements and interpretations known as IASs and SICs. Collectively, all pronouncements and interpretations are known as IFRS or IFRSs. A hierarchy exists among the standards issued within and related to IFRS. This hierarchy shows the researcher where to begin the search for a solution to a problem or issue under review. Although all IFRSs, IASs, IFRICs, and SICs have the same authority, IFRS *application* is hierarchical, and the researcher may find that an IFRS does not contain the needed information to address the question. International Accounting Standards (IAS) No. 8, "Accounting Policies, Changes in Accounting Estimates and Errors," establishes a hierarchy for choosing IFRS accounting policies.

1. Apply specific IFRSs and consider relevant implementation guidance. If specific IFRSs do not apply, choose the relevant and reliable accounting policy from the listed sources in the following order:
   a. Apply other IFRSs that involve similar or related issues.
   b. Apply the IASB Framework.
   c. Apply pronouncements of other standard-setting bodies that are consistent with the IASB Framework.

eIFRS Access

There are several subscription services for eIFRS access available through the IASB and the International Association for Accounting Education and Research (IAAER). The IASB subscription can be accessed through the products and services tab on the IASB home page, www.ifrs.org, as illustrated in Panel A of Exhibit 3-6. After clicking on the eIFRS heading, a login page appears (Panel B of Exhibit 3-6) with two options for subscribing to eIFRS.

1. The first option is to register for free, enabling access to free content on the IFRS Foundation website. This option will also allow the user to receive email alerts, access the unaccompanied standards, view IFRS for SMEs, register to observe meetings, and submit comment letters. Unaccompanied standards are the core standards in English without implementation guidance or basis for conclusion.

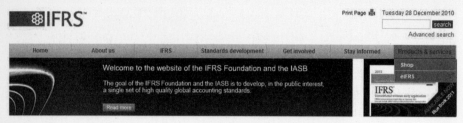

A

Welcome to the eIFRS pages

By logging into this service you agree to be bound by this website's Terms of Use. **Please read this document before proceeding.**

Your email address: [   ]

Password: [   ]

[Login]

Please use your existing IFRS Foundation Subscriber email address/password to access this site.
Register for free non-subscription content

Purchase **access to subscription-only content or view a** Preview **of eIFRS.**
Lost or forgotten your password? Click here.

B

Exhibit 3-6 eIFRS Access
SOURCE: *Mastering the FASB Codification and eIFRS: A Case Approach*, 1st ed. Original source: www .ifrs.org.

2. The second option is to purchase a subscription that includes online service with or without CD-ROMs and printed publications. At present, the online IFRS access offers English IFRSs, HTML, PDF versions, and IFRS PDF-translated versions in nine languages (English, German, Spanish, French, Greek, Dutch, Italian, Russian, and Slovak).

KPMG sponsors full access to the IASB's eIFRS online version for IAAER (www.iaaer.org) members (see Exhibit 3-7). Three subscriptions (individual, student, and university) are offered for varying rates (see Exhibit 3-8). Thus, individuals joining the IAAER greatly benefit from low-cost access to this database.

Entering eIFRS

After logging in (from any of the subscription options), the researcher is brought to a conditions of use page (Exhibit 3-9). From there, the researcher can click on the eIFRS heading to be brought to the opening

Exhibit 3-7 IAAER Access
SOURCE: www.iaaer.org.

screen of eIFRS (Exhibit 3-10). Note: Since the researcher is brought to the IFRS Foundation/IASB home page, the same seven tabs appear as in Panel A of Exhibit 3-6. eIFRS is located on one screen. Its home page is separated into three areas: the left navigation panel area, the center screen area, and the top right screen area located above the tabs. Each area is discussed in detail next.

Left Navigation Panel.   The left navigation panel is split into three areas: "Subscribers Only," "Registered Users," and "Other Information." The registered user area is a limited version of the subscriber-only version.

Subscribers Only.   There are five items in the subscribers-only area: "IFRSs," "IFRS for SMEs" (small and medium-sized entities), "Additional Material," "Search," and "Terminology."

1. "IFRSs (All Languages)" provides access to standards in HTML (English only) or PDF (all available languages). Choosing the HTML options allows the researcher to select between the latest published standards or the advanced search option to be discussed later. The latest published standards are an electronic version of the manual research materials issued by the IASB

INDIVIDUALS	**Join as an individual member** *One-year membership: US$25* Enjoy full, unlimited access to all eIFRSs! This includes the most up-to-date electronic html versions of all International Financial Reporting Standards including International Accounting Standards (IASs), Interpretations (IFRICs/SICs) and IASB-issued supporting documents-application guidance, illustrative examples, implementation guidance, bases for conclusions and all appendices. For a preview, visit http://eifrs.iasb.org/eifrs/Preview.
STUDENTS & PhD CANDIDATES	**Join as a student member or PhD candidate member** *One-year membership while enrolled: US$20* Download: Student Membership Flyer Enjoy full, unlimited access to all eIFRSs! This includes the most up-to-date electronic html versions of all International Financial Reporting Standards including International Accounting Standards (IASs), Interpretations (IFRICs/SICs) and IASB-issued supporting documents-application guidance, illustrative examples, implementation guidance, bases for conclusions and all appendices. For a preview, visit http://eifrs.iasb.org/eifrs/Preview.
UNIVERSITY MEMBERSHIP **(Universities & Colleges)**	**Join as a university member** *One-year membership: Varying rates* - Full, unlimited access to all eIFRSs hosted by the IASB. This includes the most up-to-date electronic html versions of all International Financial Reporting Standards including International Accounting Standards (IASs), Interpretations (IFRICs/SICs) and IASB-issued supporting documents-application guidance, illustrative examples, implementation guidance, bases for conclusions and all appendices. For a preview, visit http://eifrs.iasb.org/eifrs/Preview. - The IAAER website provides a link to all University members' websites and also enables search-engine support through the IFAC web search located at the bottom of each webpage.

Exhibit 3-8 IAAER Subscription Options
SOURCE: www.iaaer.org.

including the Framework; the standards (IFRSs, IASs, IFRICs, SICs); a glossary; a due process handbook for the IASB, IFRIC, and the Foundation; and the Constitution (original, revised, and Part 2). Additionally, the materials include contents, a preface to IFRS, an introduction, presentation of financial statements, an expert advisory panel statement on measuring fair value, and a judgment statement for measuring fair value.

2. "IFRS for SMEs" provides HTML and PDF standard access in English and PDF standard access in seven other languages. IFRS for SMEs is a single standard less than 250 pages and less complex than full IFRS due to option simplifications and fewer disclosure

<u>Update Profile</u>   <u>Change Password</u>   <u>Logout</u>

After clicking on the link below, if you are prompted to log in by eIFRS, please enter your IAAER username and password to successfully log in to eIFRS.

eIFRS (electronic International Financial Reporting Standards)
International Accounting Standards Board

By clicking on the above link, you are agreeing to the following terms & conditions of use:

- eIFRS access is restricted to academic members of the IAAER.
- The service takes the form of direct access to the IASB's online database service of International Financial Reporting Standards and related information.
- Members may reproduce works in unaltered form for personal, non-commercial use subject to the inclusion of an acknowledgement of IASCF's copyright in the works.
- Members may not reproduce in either hardcopy or electronic format the text of any individual standard or specific document, extract or combination thereof of the works for any seminar, conference, training or similar commercial event.
- Members are obligated to obtain the approval from the IASCF to use the Works for commercial purposes or public distribution.

Exhibit 3-9 Conditions of Use
SOURCE: *Mastering the FASB Codification and eIFRS: A Case Approach*, 1st ed. ORIGINAL SOURCE: www .ifrs.org.

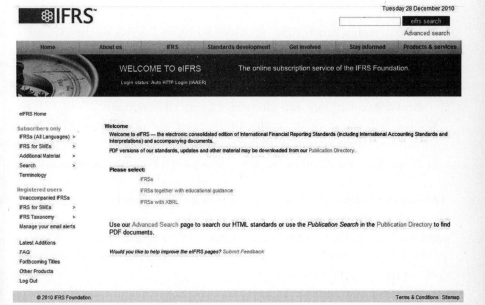

Exhibit 3-10 eIFRS Opening Screen
SOURCE: *Mastering the FASB Codification and eIFRS: A Case Approach*, 1st ed. ORIGINAL SOURCE: www .ifrs.org.

requirements. Clicking on this heading provides links to illustrative financial statements, contents, an introduction, the standard for SMEs, an appendix, board approval, the basis for conclusions, and a glossary.

3. "Additional Material" provides access to editorial corrections, educational material, IFRIC updates, IASB updates, IASB's *Insight*, IFRIC drafts, exposure drafts, discussion papers, near final drafts, IFRIC due process, revised standards, and versions in six other languages besides English.

4. "Search" provides access to an advanced HTML search or a PDF publication search. This will be discussed in detail later in the chapter.

5. "Terminology" provides a link to a terminology lookup for approximately 1,500 terms. Terms can be searched in 21 languages. This feature will be discussed in detail later in the chapter.

Registered Users. The registered users area is a limited version of the subscribers-only area and contains four items.

1. "Unaccompanied IFRSs" provides a link in English to the current year's core standards (without implementation guidance or basis for conclusion) and IFRS for SMEs.

2. "IFRS for SMEs" provides access in eight languages to the standard, basis for conclusion, and illustrative financial statements.

3. "IFRS Taxonomy" provides PDF access to full IFRS ordered by standard or report and IFRS for SMEs.

4. "Manage your email alerts" provides options for email notifications.

Other Information. This area contains links to the latest additions (the 10 most recent files that have been published); four frequently asked questions (FAQ) (subscriptions, logins, technical service, and access problems), forthcoming titles with notification of availability links, and links to partner publications.

Center Screen Area. The center screen starts with a welcome message and provides access to IFRSs, IFRSs together with educational guidance, IFRSs with XBRL, and the advanced search page to be discussed later in the chapter.

1. Clicking on the "IFRSs" heading provides access to collections from January 2005 to the present. Most collections provide both HTML and PDF versions. Links to non-English-language versions and the advanced search are also provided.
2. Clicking on "IFRSs together with educational guidance" provides access to HTML volumes from 2007 to the present. The educational volumes contain (in green italics) cross-reference and footnotes developed by the IFRS Foundation education staff. For instance, when examining the objective for IFRS 3—Business Combinations, the researcher sees green italicized links to the glossary (G) and to other paragraphs (link to paragraphs 10–31). The educational guidance is not part of IFRSs. As with the IFRS search, there is a link to the advanced search function.
3. Clicking on the "IFRS with XBRL" heading provides access to xIFRS (IFRSs and IASs with XBRL) and IFRS for SMEs with XBRL. xIFRS is a tool to aid in viewing and understanding the IFRS taxonomy (see Exhibit 3-11).

Top Right Screen Area.   The top right screen area contains two options: an eIFRS search that produces PDF/Word documents related to the search term, and an advanced search. Both are discussed in detail in the next section.

The IFRS Research Process

Search processes in eIFRS include using terminology lookup, searching the glossary, directly searching for a desired standard through collections/volumes found in IFRSs or IFRSs together with educational content, using a basic search inquiry, and using an advanced search inquiry. Each search process is located in multiple locations; however, access to each search process (except the glossary) is always available through the left navigation panel or top right screen area as previously referenced in Exhibit 3-10. Each search process is discussed in detail next.

106   An entity shall present a statement of changes in equity showing in the statement:
      (a)   total comprehensive income for the period, showing separately the total amounts attributable to owners of the parent and to non-controlling
            interests;

Comprehensive income, attributable to owners of parent	X	IAS 1.83 b (a)	410000, 420000
Comprehensive income	X	IAS 1.82 i	420000, 410000, 610000, 420005, 410005, 610005
Comprehensive income, attributable to non-controlling interests	X	IAS 1.83 b (i)	410000, 420000

First column
(concept label)

Second column
(disclosure format)

Third column
(IFRS cross-reference)

Fourth column
(IFRS Taxonomy component number/ELR)

Exhibit 3-11 XBRL Taxonomy
SOURCE: *Mastering the FASB Codification and eIFRS: A Case Approach*, 1st ed. ORIGINAL SOURCE: www
.ifrs.org.

Terminology Lookup.   The first method to search eIFRS is to use its
terminology lookup. The terminology lookup contains approximately
1,500 key IFRSs terms. As illustrated in Exhibit 3-12, the researcher has
the option of searching in 30 different languages (source language) and
the option of displaying the result in 30 different languages (target language). The search result provides a definition of the term, the standard
and paragraph number the term is referenced in, and a list of other

Terminology Lookup

This tool searches approximately 1,500 key terms used in the official translations of the International Financial Reporting Standards. This terminology has been
reviewed by a committee of accounting experts in each language. Languages are updated as and when changes are made. Please click here for more
information on when each language was last updated.

Source Term:

Term: [_____]   Source Language: [English   ▼]

Target Language(s): [select all] [clear]

Arabic: ☐	Bulgarian: ☐	Czech: ☐
Danish: ☐	German: ☐	Greek: ☐
English: ☐	Spanish: ☐	Estonian: ☐
Finnish: ☐	French: ☐	Hungarian: ☐
Italian: ☐	Japanese: ☐	Korean: ☐
Lithuanian: ☐	Latvian: ☐	Macedonian: ☐
Maltese: ☐	Dutch: ☐	Polish: ☐
Portuguese: ☐	Portuguese (Brazilian): ☐	Romanian: ☐
Slovak: ☐	Slovenian: ☐	Swedish: ☐
Turkish: ☐	Ukrainian: ☐	Chinese (Simplified): ☐
Chinese (Traditional): ☐		

[Find Terms]

Exhibit 3-12 Terminology Lookup
SOURCE: *Mastering the FASB Codification and eIFRS: A Case Approach*, 1st ed. ORIGINAL SOURCE: www
.ifrs.org.

similar terms. The researcher may need to click on one of the other similar terms in order to narrow the search term.

Example. Assume a researcher is interested in the definition of impairment. How would the researcher locate the definition?

The researcher would left-click the "Terminology" heading in the left navigation panel and be directed to a screen as illustrated in Exhibit 3-12. Type in the term "impairment" and the researcher is directed to other similar research terms to narrow the search (see Panel A of Exhibit 3-13). The researcher is concerned with the term "impairment loss" and left-clicks on that heading. The definition (along with the related standards) appears as illustrated in Panel B of Exhibit 3-13.

Glossary Search. A glossary is located once the researcher enters IFRSs by left-clicking on the "IFRSs" heading in the left navigation panel. The researcher will scroll down to just below the last standard and left-click on the glossary heading. An alphabetical list of all referenced IFRS terms appears along with a hyperlink to the related standard and paragraph, as illustrated in Exhibit 3-14.

Direct Search (Perusal of Standards). The third method of searching eIFRS is to proceed directly to the desired section by left-clicking

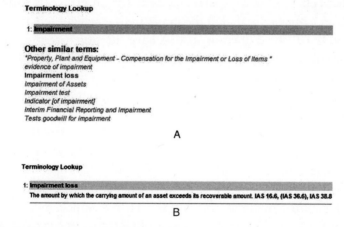

Terminology Lookup

1: **impairment**

Other similar terms:
"Property, Plant and Equipment - Compensation for the Impairment or Loss of Items "
evidence of impairment
Impairment loss
Impairment of Assets
Impairment test
Indicator [of impairment]
Interim Financial Reporting and Impairment
Tests goodwill for impairment

A

Terminology Lookup

1: **impairment loss**
The amount by which the carrying amount of an asset exceeds its recoverable amount. IAS 16.6, (IAS 36.6), IAS 38.8

B

Exhibit 3-13 Terminology Lookup Search
SOURCE: *Mastering the FASB Codification and eIFRS: A Case Approach,* 1st ed. ORIGINAL SOURCE: www .ifrs.org.

accounting policies	The specific principles, bases, conventions, rules and practices applied by an entity in preparing and presenting financial statements.	IAS 8.5
accounting profit	Profit or loss for a period before deducting tax expense.	IAS 12.5
accrual basis of accounting	The effects of transactions and other events are recognised when they occur (and not as cash or its equivalent is received or paid) and they are recorded in the accounting records and reported in the financial statements of the periods to which they relate.	F.22

Exhibit 3-14 Glossary Excerpt

SOURCE: *Mastering the FASB Codification and eIFRS: A Case Approach*, 1st ed. ORIGINAL SOURCE: www .ifrs.org.

on the standard once in "IFRSs" or "IFRSs together with educational guidance."

Example. Assume a client is interested in determining how to value year-end inventory. Which standard should be examined?

Left-click the "IFRSs" heading in the left navigation panel. A list of all IFRSs appears, as illustrated in Panel A of Exhibit 3-15. Scroll down until reaching the standard(s) of interest (IAS 2). Left-click on the "IAS 2" heading to reveal the contents of IAS 2 (Panel B of Exhibit 3-15). Left-click on the "IAS 2 Inventories" heading. Paragraph 1 (Panel C of Exhibit 3-15) explains the objectives of the standard and alludes to writing inventory down to net realizable value. The researcher continues to scroll down to find out how to calculate net realizable value (paragraphs 6–7, 28–33).

Basic Search.   A fourth search method within eIFRS is to use the eIFRS search button located in the upper right screen area. This method returns PDF or Word documents that have the search term in its title. Therefore the researcher will want to access the advanced search option, which provides searchable links.

Advanced Search.   The fifth search method within eIFRS is the advanced search function (illustrated in Exhibit 3-16) that can be accessed from multiple locations (the search subcomponent of the left navigation panel, the center screen area, and the upper right area). The researcher can refine a search by collection, standard issuance date, educational material, exact text, relative importance of words by use of the > and < symbols, exact phrases by using quotations, or word stems by use of the * symbol. The output can be refined by choosing to sort by relevance or by highlighting the search term.

elFRSs at 1 July 2010

Document
Contents
Preface to IFRS
Framework for the Preparation and Presentation of Financial Statements
Introduction to this edition
Presentation of Financial Statements
IFRS 1 First-time Adoption of International Financial Reporting Standards
IFRS 2 Share-based Payment
IFRS 3 Business Combinations
IFRS 4 Insurance Contracts
IFRS 5 Non-current Assets Held for Sale and Discontinued Operations
IFRS 6 Exploration for and Evaluation of Mineral Resources
IFRS 7 Financial Instruments: Disclosures
IFRS 8 Operating Segments
IFRS 9 Financial Instruments
IAS 1 Presentation of Financial Statements
IAS 2 Inventories
IAS 7 Statement of Cash Flows

A

Search Results

elFRSs at 1 July 2010

Document	Date of issue
IAS 2 Contents	
IAS 2 Introduction	
IAS 2 Inventories	2004-03-31
IAS 2 Appendix Amendments to other pronouncements	
IAS 2 Approval by the Board of IAS 2 issued in December 2003	
IAS 2 Basis for Conclusions	

B

1   The objective of this Standard is to prescribe the accounting treatment for inventories. A primary issue in accounting for inventories is the amount of cost to be recognised as an asset and carried forward until the related revenues are recognised. This Standard provides guidance on the determination of cost and its subsequent recognition as an expense, including any write-down to net realisable value. It also provides guidance on the cost formulas that are used to assign costs to inventories.

C

Exhibit 3-15 Search Directly Accessing Standards
SOURCE: *Mastering the FASB Codification and eIFRS: A Case Approach*, 1st ed. ORIGINAL SOURCE: www
.ifrs.org.

Choosing to highlight the search term is extremely beneficial since searches can return entire standards.

Example. Assume a U.S.-based client wants to expand into the United Kingdom. The client currently uses the LIFO cost flow method for inventory valuation purposes. Is that method allowed under IFRS?

Left-click the search heading in the left navigation panel and choose "Advanced Search" or left-click on the "Advanced Search" heading in

Advanced Search
All fields are optional

Collection	eIFRSs at 1 July 2010 ▼
Education Material	☐
Text	LIFO Exact Text? ☑ Sort by relevance ☐ (tips)
Highlight Terms?	☑
Standard	All ▼
Issued [YYYY-MM-DD]	[ ] to [ ] *(Standards only)*

[Search]

Search Tips for Text search (applicable to non-exact:match searches only)

- Enclose phrases in "double quotes"
- Sort by relevance only applicable when 'text' is used also
- Use '+' to indicate words, phrases or groups that must be present
- Use '>' to indicate important words
- Use '<' to indicate less important words
- Use '*' to indicate extensions to a word ie - 'financ*' matches 'financial', 'finance' and 'finances'
- Use '(' and ')' to group sub-expressions
- Searches are case-insensitive

A

Search Results

eIFRSs at 1 July 2010

Document	Date of Issue
IAS 2 Introduction	
IAS 2 Basis for Conclusions	
IAS 19 Employee Benefits	2004-12-16
IAS 19 Basis for Conclusions	

B

Prohibition of LIFO as a cost formula

IN13   The Standard does not permit the use of the last-in, first-out (LIFO) formula to measure the cost of inventories.

C

Exhibit 3-16 Advanced Search Function
SOURCE: *Mastering the FASB Codification and eIFRS: A Case Approach*, 1st ed. ORIGINAL SOURCE: www
.ifrs.org.

the top right screen area. As illustrated in Panel A of Exhibit 3-16, choose the most recent collection, type in "LIFO," and check the "Highlight Terms?" box. A list of all IFRS related to LIFO appears, as illustrated in Panel B of Exhibit 3-16. The researcher should click on the first option ("IAS 2 Introduction"). Scroll down until finding the term LIFO. Paragraph 13, as illustrated in Panel C of Exhibit 3-16, reveals that LIFO is not permitted under IFRS. The researcher may also try left-clicking on the second option ("IAS 2 Basis for Conclusions"). Scrolling down to the term LIFO, the researcher sees in BC 9 that the Board eliminated the LIFO method.

In deciding when to stop the research, consider the IFRS hierarchy. IFRSs, IASs, IFRICs, and SICs are primary authorities. If needed, use the Framework and other national GAAP in combination with other supporting authorities to support the research question when an answer does not exist within the highest levels.

Print and Copy/Paste functions

eIFRS does not contain special print or copy/paste functions. The researcher can conveniently use their browser's print and copy/paste functions to export results from eIFRS searches.

Summary

This chapter has presented an overview of the bodies that set standards in international accounting, the process of standard setting, the types of authoritative pronouncements, the meaning and hierarchy of IFRS, and the IFRS research process. Because the IFRS Foundation's objectives include promoting a single set of high-quality standards and promoting convergence, IFRS is continuing to evolve. The research process may involve judgment because IFRS employs a more principle-based approach than, for instance, U.S. GAAP. Additionally, although all IFRSs are equal, the researcher must follow a hierarchy when a specific IFRS does not address the research question. If the researcher is familiar with the research topic, the most expedient way to find a solution may be to examine the list of published IFRSs. For a comprehensive list of literature referencing a term or topic, the researcher wants to use a keyword search utilizing the term highlight option. The IASB is working independently and on joint projects with various international standard-setting bodies.

Therefore, accountants must research changes in pronouncements to keep abreast of current applications of principles.

Notes

1. Modified and updated "IASB and the IASC Foundation: Who Are We and What Do We Do?" (www.iasb.org), and "International Financial Reporting Standards (IFRS): An AICPA Backgrounder" (www.IFRS.org).
2. Adapted from "International Financial Reporting Standards (IFRS): An AICPA Backgrounder" (www.IFRS.com).
3. EFRAG website, www.efrag.org, EFRAG Facts.
4. *AICPA Professional Standards*, international volume (June 1, 2003).
5. The Conceptual Framework for Financial Reporting, www.ifrs.org.
6. M. Houston and A. Reinstein, "International Accounting Standards and Their Implications for Accountants and U.S. Financial Statement Users," *Review of Business* 22 (Spring/Summer 2001).

Chapter 4

Other Research
Databases and Tools

T his chapter provides insight into several major databases. They include GARS, CCH's Accounting Research Manager, Mergent Online, S&P NetAdvantage, and LexisNexis. Additional tools for accountants are also highlighted in the chapter. Database research strategies are discussed as applied to these other research databases.

Governmental Accounting Sources
(FASAB and GASB)

Remember that when researching U.S. federal government entities' accounting issues, use *The FASAB Handbook of Accounting Standards and Other Pronouncements, As Amended* (FASAB Handbook) by the Federal Accounting Standards Advisory Board (FASAB). This document is found

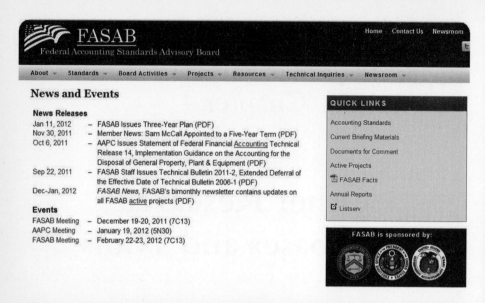

Exhibit 4-1 FASAB Website

at the FASAB's website under the "Standards" tab (see Exhibit 4-1 showing the FASAB's website).

While the FASAB Handbook is available for free downloading, the document is in a nonsearchable PDF file. However, it contains extensive cross-referencing and indexing. The current FASAB Handbook is the most authoritative source of generally accepted accounting principles (GAAP) for federal entities. The table of contents of the current FASAB Handbook is provided in Exhibit 4-2.

Federal GAAP consists of a four-level hierarchy of accounting authorities. The highest level consists of FASAB Statements of Federal Financial Accounting Standards (SFFASs) and interpretations. The interpretations are narrow in scope and attempt to clarify the original meaning of the Standards. FASAB Technical Bulletins and external sources cleared by the FASAB are in level B. Technical Bulletins are released when the nature of an issue does not warrant more extensive due process. They are generally presented in a

Table of Contents

Contents

Executive Summary

Federal Financial Reporting and the Role of the Federal Accounting Standards Advisory Board

The Federal Accounting and Financial Reporting Environment

Accountability and Users' Information Needs—the Foundation of Governmental Financial Reporting

Objectives of Federal Financial Reporting

Balancing Costs and Benefits in Recommending Standards

Qualitative Characteristics of Information in Financial Reports

How Accounting Supports Federal Financial Reporting

How Financial Reporting Supports Reporting on Operating Performance

Appendix A: Basis for Conclusions

Appendix B: Users' Information Needs Addressed by Federal Financial Reporting

Appendix C: Selected Federal Reports Prepared on a Recurring Basis

Exhibit 4-2 FASAB Codification

question-and-answer format. Level C includes technical releases of the FASAB's Accounting and Auditing Policy Committee and some AICPA materials. Level D, the lowest level, comprises implementation guides published by the FASAB staff and practices widely recognized in the federal government.

Realize that the FASAB Handbook (2011 version) incorporates six Statements of Federal Financial Accounting Concepts (Concepts), 38 Statements of Federal Financial Accounting Standards, seven Interpretations, Technical Bulletins, Technical Releases, and Staff Implementation Guidance. The Concepts are used to guide the FASAB as it deliberates on issues for new standards. Note that there are usually some additional statements issued after publication of the most recent FASAB Handbook.

Use the Government Accounting Standards Board (GASB) authorities for researching U.S. accounting issues for state and local governments. Acquire access to the Government Accounting Research System (GARS) on CD-ROM via the GASB website electronic store's subscription services tab.

GAAP for state and local accounting uses a five-level hierarchy of authorities that the accounting researcher must understand:

Category (a) is the highest level. GASB Statements and Interpretations comprise the category. Statement 62 incorporates the more than 120 FASB and AICPA pronouncements that were recognized as specifically made applicable to state and local governmental entities.

Category (b) includes GASB Technical Bulletins, AICPA Industry Audit and Accounting Guides, and AICPA Statements of Position made applicable to state and local governments by the AICPA and approved by GASB.

The remaining GAAP categories are less widely consulted: Category (c) consists of relevant AICPA Accounting Standards Executive Committee (AcSEC) Practice Bulletins. Category (d) includes GASB Implementation Guides published by GASB staff, as well as practices that are widely recognized and prevalent in state and local government. Category (e) allows consideration of other accounting literature in the absence of a pronouncement.

Included in GARS are the original pronouncements, codification of governmental and financial reporting standards, implementation guides, and a topical index. Exhibit 4-3 displays the contents of GARS. Original pronouncements present current accounting and financial reporting standards for state and local governments comprising GAAP as they were originally published. The opening screen of the original pronouncements is shown in Exhibit 4-4.

The Codification in GARS arranges currently effective government accounting standards by subject. The Codification's opening screen for the table of contents is shown in Exhibit 4-5.

Example

A question has arisen regarding the depreciation method for roads and bridges in the state.

Check the topical index in GARS for "depreciation," which refers to both the original GASB statement and the location in GASB's

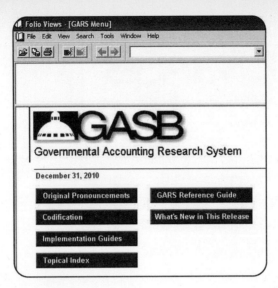

Exhibit 4-3 GARS Opening Screen

SOURCE: GASB material reproduced with permission from the Financial Accounting Foundation.

Original Pronouncements

Copyright 2010 Governmental Accounting Standards Board

> To search the entire infobase, click the **Query** button 📖 on the **Toolbar**. To directly access a segment of the infobase, click on any <u>green</u> <u>link</u> in the menu below.

<u>Foreword</u>

<u>Statements of the Governmental Accounting Standards Board (GASBS)</u>

<u>Interpretations of the Governmental Accounting Standards Board (GASBI)</u>

<u>Technical Bulletins of the Governmental Accounting Standards Board (GASBTB)</u>

<u>Concepts Statements of the Governmental Accounting Standards Board (GASBCS)</u>

<u>Statements of the National Council on Governmental Accounting (NCGAS)</u>

<u>Interpretations of the National Council on Governmental Accounting (NCGAI)</u>

<u>Concepts Statement of the National Council on Governmental Accounting (NCGACS)</u>

<u>Industry Audit Guide (ASLGU) and Statements of Position (SOP) of the American Institute of Certified Public</u>
<u>Accountants</u>

<u>Suggested Guidelines for Voluntary Reporting of the Governmental Accounting Standards Board (GASBSG)</u>

<u>Appendix A: Finding List</u>

<u>Appendix B: Effective Dates</u>

Exhibit 4-4 Original Pronouncements

SOURCE: GASB material reproduced with permission from the Financial Accounting Foundation.

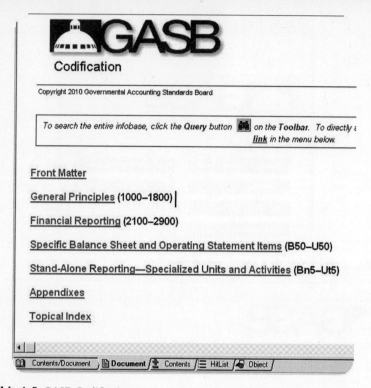

Exhibit 4-5 GASB Codification
SOURCE: GASB material reproduced with permission from the Financial Accounting Foundation.

Codification. One can use either location referenced, but if one uses the Codification one must also cite the date of the Codification since the Codification changes. Although the answer appears quickly that governments may use any established depreciation method, it is smart to read all of the information referenced. Thus one also learns that governments may depreciate dissimilar assets of the same class, such as state roads and bridges.

If one does not subscribe to a database that includes GARS, then use the online GASB store, which offers the pronouncement, implementation guide, and other documents. The pronouncements include GASB Statements, Interpretations, Technical Bulletins, and exposure drafts. Each statement is separately priced at slightly more than $20. If necessary, find summaries of GASB Statements and Interpretations at GASB's website under the "Technical Issues" tab and then down the menu to "Summaries/Status."

Other Databases for Accounting Authorities

Subscribe to at least one of the two major competing commercial accounting databases used to enhance the effectiveness and efficiency of accounting and auditing research. These databases are CCH's Accounting Research Manager (ARM) and Thomson Reuters's Checkpoint financial research library, commonly known as RIA Checkpoint.

RIA Checkpoint is primarily known as a tax database and is available at checkpoint.riag.com. However, it has an accounting and auditing research library available for a premium-cost subscription. This library provides standards by the FASB, IASB, and AICPA, as shown in Exhibit 4-6.

RIA Checkpoint helps to maintain one's currency in various topics with newsletters and financial news headlines on its website. Searching in RIA Checkpoint for accounting and auditing authorities is similar to that in tax. However, the browsing method is more widely used for the Codification. Keyword searches and access by citation are also possible.

RIA Checkpoint includes various ancillary AICPA materials, such as the AICPA Technical Practice Aids. This includes selected AICPA Technical Question and Answer; Trust Service Principles, Criteria, and Illustrations of the AICPA Assurance Services Executive Committee; a

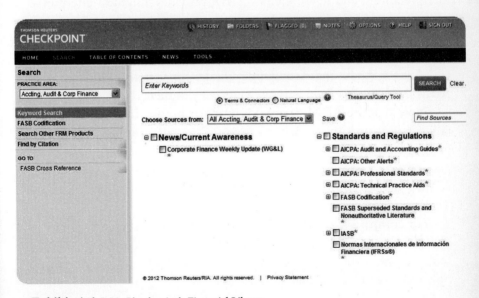

Exhibit 4-6 RIA Checkpoint's Financial Library

listing of issue papers of the AICPA Accounting Standards Division; and Statements of Position of the AICPA Audit and Attest Standards Division. The AICPA Technical Practice Aids also includes PCAOB Staff Guidance.

Example

A question has arisen about depreciating the cost of replaced cargo planes.

One may have to pursue several lines of inquiry. One might logically go first to search in the codification for "depreciation." An overwhelming result of more than 350 mentions appears. Thus one should browse by selecting a topic. While depreciation does not appear as a topic, one might suspect looking under assets for the topic of property, plant, and equipment. If one views the topic further, one will see that airlines is a specialized industry, under ASC 908. One might also try nonauthoritative sources such as Audit and Accounting Guides to see if a guide exists on the airline industry.

Available at www.accountingresearchmanager.com is CCH's Accounting Research Manager (ARM) database. This modular database provides accounting, auditing, and governmental accounting standards, interpretations, and news. CCH's ARM provides insightful interpretations on GAAP, GAAS, and SEC rules, as shown in Exhibit 4-7.

This database includes complete authoritative texts of major U.S. and international accounting standards, AICPA technical practice aids, and AICPA Audit and Accounting Guides for various industries. The ARM database also maintains one's currency in these topics.

Note that the ARM database is modular in subscription in order to tailor its information content to the user's needs at a more affordable price. ARM will show the organization for its entire database and then gray out the parts of the database that are not part of the subscription. ARM's organization for IFRS is shown in Exhibit 4-8. An index of accounting topics is also available in ARM.

For comparison, RIA Checkpoint's organization under the table of contents search method is shown for international accounting authorities in Exhibit 4-9. Other search methods, such as a search for international authorities, are shown in Exhibit 4-10.

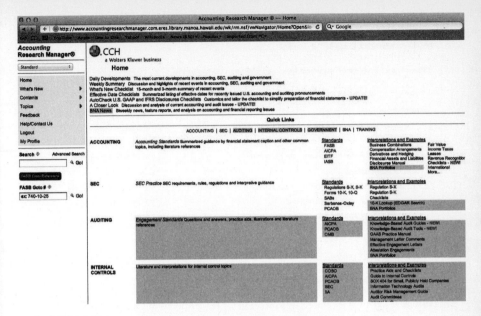

Exhibit 4-7 Accounting Research Manager's Opening Screen

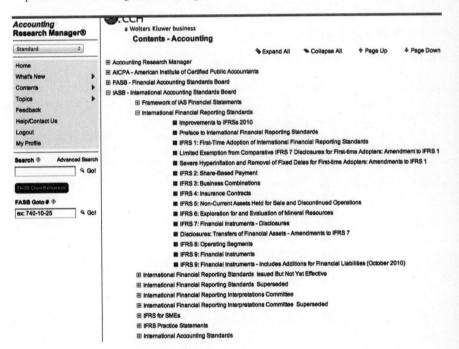

Exhibit 4-8 CCH ARM's Organization for IFRS

IASB Advanced Search*

Choose the sources and/or document types that you would like to search.

[Select All]   [Deselect All]

☐ IASB Standards
  ☐ International Financial Reporting Standards (IFRS)
  ☐ International Accounting Standards (IAS)
  ☐ International Accounting Standards Superseded
☐ IASB Interpretations
  ☐ International Financial Reporting Interpretations Committee (IFRIC)
  ☐ Standing Interpretations Committee
  ☐ Standard Interpretations Committee Superseded

☐ Proposal Stage Documents
  ☐ Exposure Drafts
  ☐ Discussion Papers
  ☐ IFRIC Draft Interpretations
☐ News
  ☐ IFRIC Meeting Materials
  ☐ Insight
  ☐ IFRIC Update
  ☐ IASB Update

[Next]

Exhibit 4-9 RIA Checkpoint's Organization for International Authorities
SOURCE: Checkpoint® screenshot, published online at http://checkpoint.riag.com. © 2011. Thomson Reuters/RIA. Reprinted with permission. All rights reserved. This information or any portion thereof may not be copied or disseminated in any form or by any means or stored in an electronic database or retrieval system without the express consent of Thomson/RIA.

IASB Advanced Search (cont.)

Enter additional search criteria in at least one of the fields below.

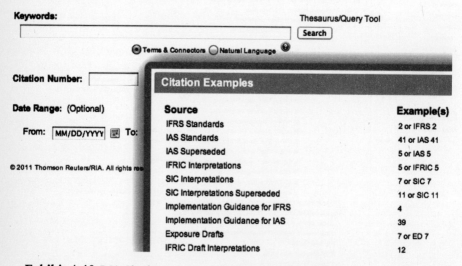

Keywords: Thesaurus/Query Tool
[   ] [Search]

   ● Terms & Connectors ○ Natural Language

Citation Number: [   ]

Citation Examples	
Source	**Example(s)**
IFRS Standards	2 or IFRS 2
IAS Standards	41 or IAS 41
IAS Superseded	5 or IAS 5
IFRIC Interpretations	5 or IFRIC 5
SIC Interpretations	7 or SIC 7
SIC Interpretations Superseded	11 or SIC 11
Implementation Guidance for IFRS	4
Implementation Guidance for IAS	39
Exposure Drafts	7 or ED 7
IFRIC Draft Interpretations	12

Date Range: (Optional)
From: [MM/DD/YYYY] To:

© 2011 Thomson Reuters/RIA. All rights re...

Exhibit 4-10 RIA Checkpoint's Search for International Authorities
SOURCE: Checkpoint® screenshot, published online at http://checkpoint.riag.com. © 2011. Thomson Reuters/RIA. Reprinted with permission. All rights reserved. This information or any portion thereof may not be copied or disseminated in any form or by any means or stored in an electronic database or retrieval system without the express consent of Thomson/RIA.

Register under "My Profile" to have email delivery of accounting news. Read weekly summaries of the news provided in the database. The news is organized by subject and standard setter.

Researching Industries and Companies

Company research may be needed for a variety of reasons, such as to determine whether potential customers are creditworthy, to determine whether a company would make a good prospect for a strategic business alliance, or as part of the due diligence on a company being acquired. Company research might also exist for investment planning decision making or as part of the process for researching an industry. Company comparisons based on asset or revenue size are often used for determining appropriate executive compensation for similarly sized organizations. The most famous ranking is the Fortune 500 companies.

Industry research can sometimes help member companies stay ahead of changing conditions in the industry. Industry research information varies depending upon the specific industry and database, websites, or hardbound sources used. Some industry reports exist on the web, often as a teaser to sell a full-length report on that industry. A true industry analysis requires compiling data from multiple sources: directories, statistics, government documents, corporate news, and trade publications. Start industry research by finding an industry code for the industry.

Industry Codes

To research an industry start by identifying the industry codes. Knowledge of the relevant industry codes enables one to gather more precise information for the various industries, as well as identifying companies within the industry. The industry codes are provided when looking up a company in a database. Some companies are often listed only under their primary code, so one might easily miss some major competitors in an industry.

Remember that two commonly used industry codes are the Standard Industrial Classification (SIC) and the newer North American Industry Classification System (NAICS). The SIC codes were created by the Office of Management and Budget. The governments of the

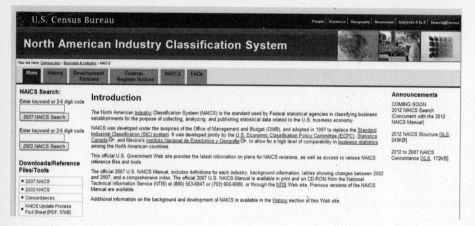

Exhibit 4-11 NAICS Code

United States, Canada, and Mexico developed NAICS to standardize industry classifications. The NAICS code is found at the Census Bureau's website (see Exhibit 4-11). A conversion table exists there between the two codes.

One should brainstorm the alternative classifications or names for an industry. For example, one can broaden the computer industry to the electronics industry or narrow it to the personal computer industry. It's important to find the right industry code or classification for a business.

Example.   Search for the industry codes appropriate to Amazon.com.

This online retailer business involves technology, retail, and information. The most relevant NAICS Code is 454111: Electronic Shopping. However, by checking a few sources, one might pull up additional relevant codes. For example, the Credit Risk Monitor website finds companies per state. Clicking on the name of the company provides several industry codes:

SIC

   5961 Catalog and Mail-Order Houses
   3577 Computer Peripheral Equipment

NAICS

   45411 Electronic Shopping and Mail-Order Houses
   334119 Other Computer Peripheral Equipment Manufacturing

NAICS divides industries into 20 sectors. The first two digits of NAICS refers to the broad economic sector, such as 45 for retail trade. The third digit designates a subsector. The fourth digit refers to a more specific industry. The process continues down the digits to get to very specific industries.

Various lesser used industry codes also exist. For example, international trade "harmonized tariff schedule codes" are available through the U.S. International Trade Commission. Another example is the Global Industry Classification Standard (GICS), which was developed by Standard & Poor's for the financial community. The GICS structure has 10 sectors, 24 industry groups, 68 industries, and 154 subindustries for classifying all major public companies.

Industry Research

After finding an industry code, read a few general overview articles or analyst reports on the industry in order to gain a big picture of the industry before going in-depth on a research topic in the industry. Try using industry and company databases or researching corporate news.

Among the common questions for an industry are identifying the leading companies in the industry, the market-leading products or services, the technologies that are impacting the industry, and the industry trends and areas of growth. Different databases will often provide different information on the various industries and companies.

Acquire general information about the industry and the companies within the industry, such as with Value Line Investment Surveys. These surveys evaluate the performance and economic outlook of industries and the major companies within them. The surveys are published weekly, tracking about 1,700 stocks in 90 industries.

For example, the Value Line website explains that "the Value Line Entertainment Industry is comprised of a set of diversified companies. They are mainly television network and station owners, and are typically involved in programming and production of content, including feature films. It is a constantly evolving group." The industry surveys are available at Value Line's website. The company advertises itself as the "Gold Standard in Investment Research."

Use websites that explain industry research, such as virtualpet. com. Such websites get into details about identifying trade organizations, learning about consumers of the products, examining patents, determining the legal issues in the industry, and examining regulatory issues affecting the industry. For instance, IPL2.org describes associations on the web.

Industry research sites also suggest finding information about specific compensation of executives in the industry, the type of competition in the industry, and acquiring an understanding of the international market. One could interview people familiar with the industry such as distributors, consumers, and those in the distribution chain.

Some specialized areas about an industry include its geography, history, and weather. The geography of the industry shows whether they are a local, regional, national, or international player. It identifies where their major competitors are located, as well as their wholesalers and end users. The history of an industry is valuable for identifying trends and significant events impacting the industry. Determine the importance of weather and climate on an industry, because some industries are seasonal. Weather might also have a major effect on suppliers or raw materials.

Government, a huge consumer of various goods and services, has a major impact on some industries. Knowing the government's role in an industry can help determine when the industry might prosper or when it might retract. A checklist of factors for industry research is provided in Appendix 1 at the end of this chapter.

Company Research

In acquiring initial information on a company, one might start by using the Internet to locate basic communications with the company: the address, telephone number, and corporate website of a business. Researching companies often proceeds with a review of a company's website.

Obtain an understanding of a company's major products or services. Determine a company's major competitors. One could use a database (described later) or websites, such as Canadian Company Capabilities. Note that a company's website might include a newsroom with recent press releases about the company. Verify the company's official name.

Acquire a variety of information on companies. To gather investment and financial information for public companies, review recent filings with the U.S. Securities and Exchange Commission or the equivalent abroad. For example, for Canadian companies check SEDAR for filings with the Canadian Securities Administrators.

A company's annual report (10-K) filing contains frank information about the business, risk factors, properties, and legal proceedings. The 10-K also describes submission of matters for shareholder vote, the company's markets, consolidated financial statements, and a Management's Discussion and Analysis (MD&A). The goal of the MD&A is to enable shareholders to see the events through the eyes of management.

Analyst reports and news articles about the company are also fertile ground for an in-depth investigation on a company. Analyst reports prepared by major-firm analysts will track companies over time. These reports are prepared mostly for large institutional investors.

Other helpful sources exist, such as ThomasNet, which provides information on American and Canadian manufacturers. *Forbes* provides information on the largest companies, such as the world's 2,000 largest companies (the Global 2000). Seeking Alpha is a free website indexing quarterly earning conference calls by company name or ticker. Fitch Ratings rates financial institutions, municipal bonds, sovereign debt, and more. Appendix 2 provides a checklist for company research.

While company research may not be as extensive as due diligence research on a potential corporate acquisition when one has access to internal corporate minutes, documents, and other sources of internal information, many of the concepts are the same, such as reviewing financial statements, major contracts, and business practices. Company research using major databases may yield valuable information in a relatively short amount of time.

Major Databases

Mergent Online

One database that is a good source for industry and company information is Mergent Online. See Exhibit 4-12 for the database's initial search screen. Note that the initial web page that one views of a company is

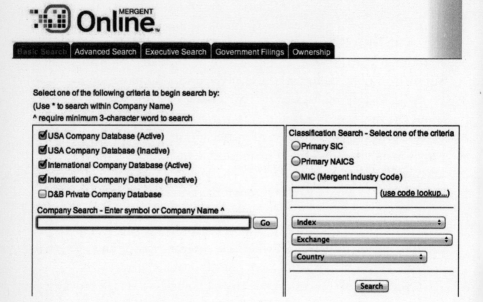

Exhibit 4-12 Mergent Online Opening Screen

only a summary of the detailed information available from other tabs in the database. Pull up a company in Mergent Online and the same summary information appears on the top of each page. This information includes the sector and the industry of the business, complete with the SIC and NAICS codes. Other summary items include the company's auditor, company website, PE ratio, and various other items.

When viewing a page in Mergent Online, scroll down to find other types of information that may be available. Note that the trick in maximizing the potential of Mergent Online is to understand that two levels of tabs exist at the top of the database. The top-level tabs include "Company Details," "Executives," "Ownership," "Competitors," and "Report Builder." Tabs of particular importance to financial analysts are "Financials," "Equity Pricing," "SEC Filings," and "News."

Use the second-level tabs for acquiring insightful information. "Ownership Information" includes identification of institutional holdings, insiders, and insider trading. "Competitors" views company competitors based on industry codes and financial highlights. "IT" also provides competitor news.

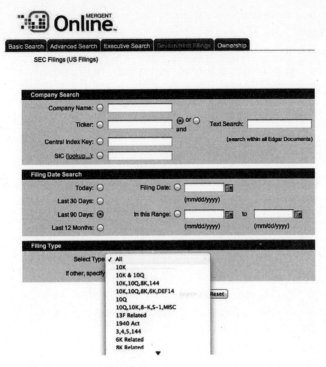

Exhibit 4-13 Mergent Online Government Filings

"Report Builder" views annual reports, industry reports, buy/sell/hold reports, and more. Note that the default shows only the information on the far left tab. For example, the initial default is company details, synopsis. Similarly, when the "Executives" tab is selected, the second-level tab appears showing officers, directors, and committees. Thus when selecting Executives, one is viewing only the company's officers. See Exhibit 4-13 for an alternative search by SEC filing.

Observe that the tabs on top of the public company snapshot information results screen provide access to specialized information, including company financials, company history, joint ventures, and property locations. The company financials have important drop-down boxes. These choices allow one to select from 3 to 15 years of annual and quarterly financial information, the particular financial statement of interest, and alternative currencies with which to view the financial statements.

Ratios are categorized profitability, liquidity, debt management, asset management, and per share.

Track daily stock prices of public companies for the most recent day of trading (close, high, and low). The yearly high and low are presented in Mergent Online after one selects a company and chooses "Quotes" on the left side of the screen.

Example.   Acquire financial information about Amazon.com, a public company headquartered in Washington State.

After inputting the name of the company, summary information appears. A one-paragraph business summary, five key executives, key financials, and pricing summary appear. Notice that the pricing summary graph is adjustable from one week to one year. Scrolling over the key executives raises a blurb with their executive work history. One can go to the second-level tabs to acquire financial statement highlights of the company, corporate history, a more detailed business description, information on the location and size of property, subsidiaries, long-term debt, and business segments.

Generate industry comparisons of companies in a customized report in Mergent Online. To perform such a comparison, on the research screen identify all companies. Use either the name or the stock ticker symbol, separating them by commas. The search results will display basic information about each company, such as the SIC code for its industry classification. After confirming that these are the desired companies for comparison, open the analyst list and select "Create Company Report."

To create a company report, criteria selections for categories and subcategories appear in drop-down boxes. Add the desired items to the report and select the years for the report before finishing by choosing "Create Report." One can select a popular format for the report, such as a PDF file, Microsoft Word document, or Excel spreadsheet.

Find financial ratios for an industry in Mergent Online under the "Company Financials" tab. Unlike some databases, Mergent Online provides only about 20 ratios over the default five-year period. This is far fewer ratios than some databases, such as the legal database LexisNexis.

The financial statements in Mergent Online are presented as either annual or quarterly statements. Similarly, one may change the numbers from the reported currency to a variety of other currencies. The analysis option shows a variance analysis between years. The "Equity Pricing" tab allows for index comparisons, such as the Fortune 500 and many others.

Realize that foreign companies (non-U.S. companies) included in Mergent Online actually outnumber U.S. companies. The 20,000 foreign companies included in the database represent 95 percent of non-U.S. global capital markets. However, one's subscription may be limited to just public companies.

Example. Acquire financial information about Koch Industries, a private company headquartered in Kansas.

Check the D&B Private Company Database, a subdatabase in Mergent Online. Enter the company. Four related companies appear. Select the main company, an oil refining company. It provides credit insight, such as "25% of trade experience indicate slow payment(s) are present." It also provides a family tree overview showing almost 900 related entities, the address and size of major entities within the corporate family.

LexisNexis

The LexisNexis database comes in various forms. LexisNexis has evolved to include various practice centers that attempt to provide links to all the resources needed in that area of professional practice.

The LexisNexis Mergers and Acquisitions Practice Center helps to get the deal done by providing for the life cycle of corporate mergers and acquisitions. Among the major tabs of work are researching for a deal, structuring a deal, conducting due diligence in the transaction with news and financial intelligence on the targeted entity, getting authoritative information and guidance on negotiating the deal, documenting and consummating the corporate transaction, and speed processing. Like each practice center, the Mergers and Acquisition Practice Center includes integrated access to LexisNexis resources.

The LexisNexis Bankruptcy Law Practice Center provides suggested solutions to track emerging issues such as pension issues or pending bankruptcy legislation, to interview and counsel clients with relevant forms and advice from Collier Commercial Bankruptcy Practice Guide, and to perform due diligence such as on bankruptcy filings and people. The site enables researching bankruptcy issues, including gathering company profiles from bankruptcy sources. Additional items especially of interest to attorneys are provided.

In the LexisNexis Corporate Business and Compliance Center, tools are designed to help practitioners meet organizational and operational demands more effectively. Additional LexisNexis Practice Centers include ones for Public Records, Real Estate, and Securities. Public records can include searching for Uniform Commercial Code liens, property and tax assessor records, legal judgments, articles of incorporation, and more.

LexisNexis has a Corporate Affiliations database. Use the database to learn about the corporate hierarchy. One can view company hierarchies by clicking on the company name link under "Hierarchy/Family Role." Secondary company details are shown such as the year founded, the state of incorporation, and whether they import or export. Basic information includes how to communicate with the company, company financials, and industry codes.

Further provided in the results of the LexisNexis Corporate Affiliations database are lists of competitors, executives, board of directors members, former executives and board members, and companies that board members are affiliated with. Comprehensive executive compensation is provided with columns for salary, bonus, other annual compensation, restricted stock awards, securities underlying options, and more.

The "Outside Service Firms" tab shows such relationships as advertising agency and auditors. Recent mergers and acquisitions activity is shown. Last and most importantly is the corporate hierarchy of related entities. The LexisNexis Corporate Affiliations database was recently enhanced to include in the corporate hierarchy shell companies, entities that are legal but nonoperating.

Various tools exist in the database. For example, the user's guide explains, "The background comparison tool allows you to select up to 20 executives to identify any connections in their biographical detail. Commonalities between individuals are highlighted for easy identification." The results produce a chart of person, companies, education, responsibilities, committees, industries, and accomplishments.

Use LexisNexis to acquire company dossiers that present extensive financial information on companies, including financial ratios and analyst reports. Note that company dossier results for a company will first present a snapshot summary. The introductory nonfinancial information shows contact information for the corporate headquarters, industry classification, business description, and current news.

Included in the snapshot's financial information is contact information for the corporate headquarters, industry charts, and issues of stock outstanding. The people and firms listed in the snapshot are the major executives, board of directors, key competitors, and the firm's auditor.

View important additional selections in LexisNexis that provide more detail on the company. Select the financial information to view five years of financial statements, financial ratios, growth estimates, insider trading activity, and analyst reports. Other parts of the dossier include recent news, intellectual property information, legal information, and references. Use LexisNexis Corporate Affiliations to find the related entities of a firm, as shown in Exhibit 4-14. An alternative to Lexis

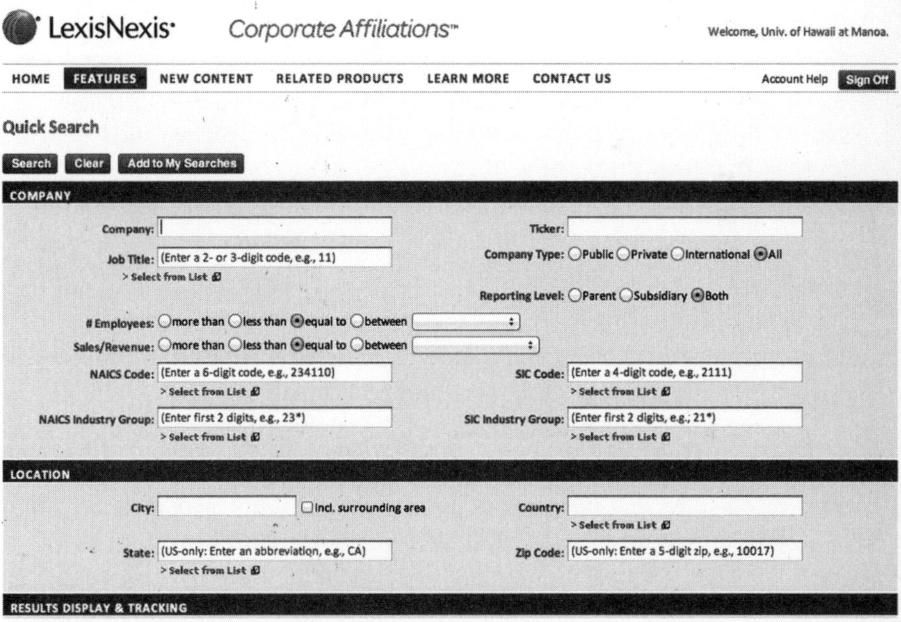

Exhibit 4-14 LexisNexis Corporate Affiliations

Corporate Affiliations is a guidebook titled "How to Find Information about Divisions, Subsidiaries, and Products."

LexisNexis provides access to disclosure information, such as the management discussion and analysis, president's letter to shareholders, and footnotes to the financial statements. The database also provides access to defunct companies.

Standard & Poor's NetAdvantage

Standard and Poor's (S&P) is a ratings service, best known for credit ratings of whether a bond will be paid according to contractual terms. The company has also created notable S&P indices for stock, bonds, commodities, and thematic investing such as green investing. Famous indices include the S&P 500, as well as an index measuring U.S. home prices.

Consider using an alternative database, such as S&P NetAdvantage, to research a company. The opening screen of S&P NetAdvantage on the bottom right provides a handful of guides to using the database. Most of the screen features separate news on the market, bonds, the economy, and industries. The right side of the opening screen has quick links to industry surveys, investment publications, investment advisory reports, and S&P indices, as shown in Exhibit 4-15. Investment publications include bond reports, fund reports, security dealers, and others shown in the drop-down box.

S&P NetAdvantage's opening page also provides direct access to its most popular content, which includes recently updated industry surveys and screeners for the following: advance stock; register of private companies; register of corporations, executives, and directors; mutual fund and corporate bond. Also included are links to Compustat and S&P indices: S&P 500, S&P Midcap 400, and S&P Smallcap 600.

In comparing companies, consider using the S&P 500, which represents stocks selected by S&P as leading companies in various industries and is often used as a benchmark for judging money managers. From the S&P overview of the S&P 500, one is provided with various choices on the left side of the screen, such as viewing S&P 500 vital statistics.

Note that S&P NetAdvantage primarily provides information on public companies, market news, investment analyst reports, industry surveys, and more, as shown in its opening screen. The database includes a

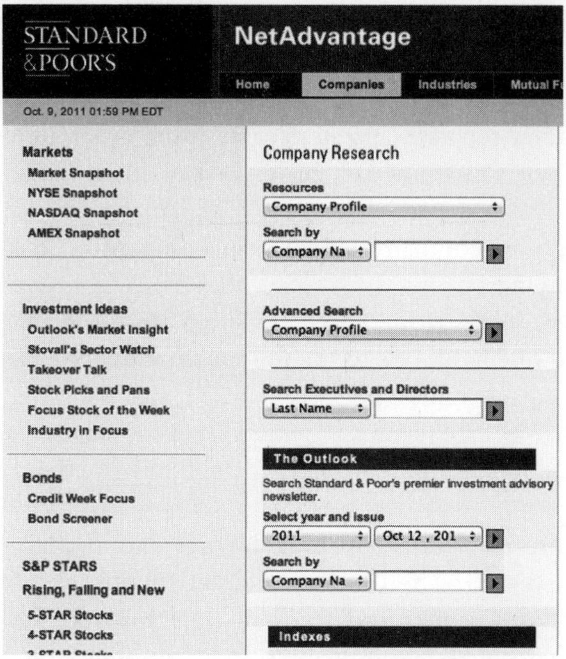

Exhibit 4-15 NetAdvantage

dozen financial and investment publications providing insight for company research and analysis, such as the Bond Guide, Mutual Fund Report, Dividend Record, and S&P's Corporation Records. Use the tabs near the top of the screen in S&P NetAdvantage to go to the type of investment at issue, such as company research.

Take advantage of powerful search functions in S&P NetAdvantage that assist in more fully using the database. Search across multiple databases simultaneously to identify companies that meet specific criteria for analysis. Select from hundreds of database reports and charts. Make comparisons within the industry by choosing from various comparative reports. Find statistics for companies in the portfolio.

Create public information books in S&P NetAdvantage to customize the content desired in a report. Although S&P NetAdvantage is relatively easy to use, view the online help to learn more about reporting, charting for comparisons to major stock indices, and other specialized activities.

Example.   Acquire information on Amazon.

A five-paragraph business summary and similar-length company fact sheet appear. The fact sheet includes the name of the S&P analyst. The news separates press releases from other news about the company. The valuation data provides key stock statistics and per-share data by fiscal year. The "How to Analyze" choice provides insight based on company value, peer comparison, risk assessment, and company news.

S&P rates stocks from 1 to 5, where 5 is a strong buy and 1 is a strong sell. If one has access to the full subscription, one can analyze the stock by company values, peer comparison, risk assessment, and company news. Corporate records provide a list of subsidiaries, general information, bond description, and stock date. Similarly, the database ranks equity funds.

S&P editorial features include market commentary written for individual investors. The Outlook Market Insight offers commentary on prospects for stocks and fixed-income investments. The commentary relies on S&P top analysts and economists on international macroeconomic developments, government actions, interest rates, and inflation.

S&P NetAdvantage offers two directories. The Securities Dealers of North America provides information on over 15,000 offices of brokerage and investment banking firms. The S&P Register allows users to search a business information database of 90,000 public and private companies, with over 70,000 biographies of top company officials.

Other Databases

Westlaw is a massive legal database, similar to LexisNexis. Westlaw works with the courts to correct and clarify court opinions, using attorney editors to enhance the value of the legal analysis. Using these databases enables accountants to search the law in securities and bankruptcy, besides taxation.

Westlaw markets itself as a leading provider of information solutions for professionals in the legal, risk management, corporate, government, law enforcement, accounting, and academic communities. It provides

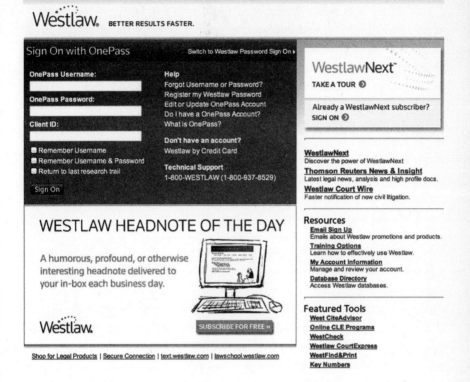

Exhibit 4-16 Westlaw
SOURCE: Reprinted from Westlaw with permission of Thomson Reuters.

some business and financial information in the database. Westlaw's website provides access to WestlawNext, as shown in exhibit 4-16.

Similar to LexisNexis, Westlaw provides various specialized centers, such as the Corporate Finance Center. This is advertised to help "mitigate risk by considering all necessary details, conduct due diligence on markets and parties, negotiate the best terms for your agreements, draft agreements and compliance documents, and monitor covenant compliance on an ongoing basis."

Westlaw has Securities Centers U.S., Canada, and UK; Private Equity Center; and M&A Center. The Securities Centers provide research sources, guidance for disclosure, results from multiple sources of securities filings, and more. The Private Equity Center provides an ability to search through private equity deals. The M&A Center includes about 300,000 global public and private deals.

Westlaw also has a Restructuring Center for business law professionals who build agreements outside of bankruptcy. It advertises itself as having "targeted content and functionality to help you spot issues, perform business due diligence, find precedent agreements, and draft the documents needed to build a solid restructuring deal.

Bloomberg is the premier financial database, providing extensive coverage of global financial markets by delivering data, news, and analysis. The system is a massive data stream delivered in real time. It accesses about five million bonds, equities, commodities, currencies, and funds. It provides news and analytics for about 130 countries and 250 exchanges. Market coverage is broad to include derivatives.

The Bloomberg system is used predominantly by investment professionals. However, there is also Bloomberg for Corporate Treasury, Corporate Finance, and Investment Relations. Bloomberg for Corporate Treasury is geared for corporate treasurers to optimize cash management, to help manage interest rate risk, and to handle foreign exchange risk. Bloomberg for Corporate Finance is geared to chief financial officers who need to optimize debt issuances, measure credit risks, and monitor markets. Bloomberg for Investor Relations is designed to help manage news flow and social media, target investors, and track industry events.

The Bloomberg system works with mnemonic shortcuts, such as typing "PRTU" for portfolios created and "MA" for mergers and acquisitions. Yellow keys on the dedicated Bloomberg terminal define the markets. These yellow keys are as follows:

<GOVT> securities issued by national governments and governmental agencies
<CORP> corporate bonds
<MTGE> mortgages and collateralized mortgage obligations
<M-MKT> money market information
<MUNI> municipal and state bonds
<PFD> preferred stock of public companies
<EQUITY> historical price record for common stock and options
<CMDTY> commodities, futures, and options
<INDEX> interest rates and economic indicators

Green keys are action keys, such as <GO> to activate a function, <NEWS> to gather news, and <PRINT>.

A company search in Bloomberg can pull up litigation highlights, as well as the usual stock performance, financials, and management profiles. Additional information includes corporate holdings, actions, and subsidiaries. The database provides news and information about thousands of companies, both public and private.

In 2012, Bloomberg announced a makeover for its financial news terminal service to make it easier for the user. The revision includes a simpler search engine, consistent user interface, and more logical workflow. Bloomberg and Thomson Reuters each hold about 30 percent of the market for financial news and analysis.

Compustat is another data set reporting annual financials since 1950 and quarterly results since 1962. Compustat prides itself on its data standardization.

Standardization is the process of evaluating and adjusting, using financial models and data collection rules that vary between databases. The degree of standardization by data providers can have a significant impact on making accurate comparisons between companies and assessing the financial health of a company. Differences in the data sets' quality exist based on the degree of standardization in the reported numbers.

For training purposes, consider using Business Insights: Global. One can pull up information on a company, such as revenues and sales per employee, as shown in Exhibit 4-17. Comparisons are also commonly used for trend analysis, which analyzes the information over time. The database also offers business cases and translates the information into several languages. The reader can listen to an audio recording of the case, as shown in Exhibit 4-18.

Corporate group structures, industry information, and market intelligence are especially noteworthy in Hoover's Online. Histories for private and public companies are also available. Hoover's Online attempts to provide objective information on companies by not relying on issuances from a company's corporate staff. Hoover's is a subsidiary of Dun & Bradstreet.

Hoover's website provides a weaker free sample version that doubles as a sales tool for individual purchases of Hoover's Reports. Key features

BUSINESS INSIGHTS: GLOBAL

Research. Analyze. Interpret. Understand.

countries, companies, industries, topics, etc..   Search

Advanced Se

| Home | Compare Countries | Compare Companies | Compare Industries | Case Studies | Saved Items (0) | Search History | Gloss |

Compare Companies

Shar

Chart | Table | Related Articles   Search Metrics: Sales Per Employee over Time ▼ Add/Remove

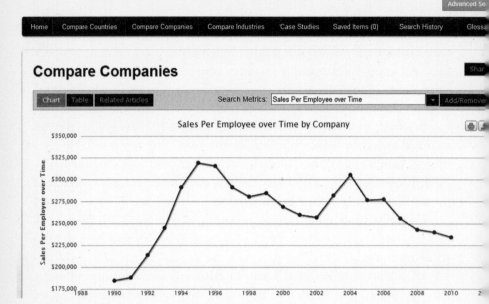

Exhibit 4-17 Business Insights: Global

SOURCE: From Gale. *Business and Company Resource Center.* © Gale, a part of Cengage Learning, Inc. Reproduced by permission. www.cengage.com/permissions.

BUSINESS INSIGHTS: GLOBAL

Research. Analyze. Interpret. Understand.

countries, companies, industries, topics, etc..   Searc

Advanced S

| Home | Compare Countries | Compare Companies | Compare Industries | Case Studies | Saved Items (0) | Search History | Glos |

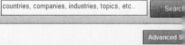

Case Studies

Displaying 1 - 50 of 969   << first < prev **1** 2 3 4 5 6 7 8 9 10 next > last >>   Sort By: Publication Date ▼

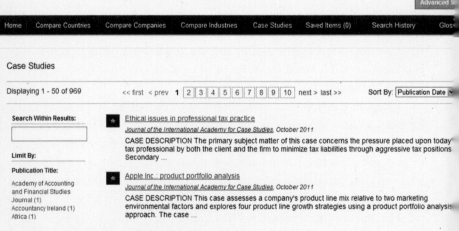

Search Within Results:

Limit By:

Publication Title:
Academy of Accounting
and Financial Studies
Journal (1)
Accountancy Ireland (1)
Africa (1)

⭐ Ethical issues in professional tax practice
Journal of the International Academy for Case Studies, October 2011
CASE DESCRIPTION The primary subject matter of this case concerns the pressure placed upon today' tax professional by both the client and the firm to minimize tax liabilities through aggressive tax positions Secondary ...

⭐ Apple Inc.: product portfolio analysis
Journal of the International Academy for Case Studies, October 2011
CASE DESCRIPTION This case assesses a company's product line mix relative to two marketing environmental factors and explores four product line growth strategies using a product portfolio analysis approach. The case ...

Exhibit 4-18 Business Insights: Global

SOURCE: From Gale. *Business and Company Resource Center.* © Gale, a part of Cengage Learning, Inc. Reproduced by permission. www.cengage.com/permissions.

include the family tree of entities, "first research," which provides analyst preparation of questions such as how seasonal is a company's business, and triggers to send an alert in an email.

Morningstar Investment Research Center provides information on public companies, mutual funds, and exchange-traded funds (ETFs). Other tabs of information are "Markets" and "Articles/Videos." The "Markets" page enables one to read how particular indices, sectors, and style indices are performing. The ETF analyst for exchange-traded funds tracks performance of stock and bond indices.

"Portfolio" in Morningstar provides an X-ray on how the securities are working together. The comprehensive database helps one to analyze how to make an investment decision. The analyst reports in the database are particularly helpful.

Example.   One wishes to invest in a mutual fund but wants some guidance for selecting the appropriate fund.

In Morningstar, click on the tab for "Funds" and out pops a screener. One can select from the almost 30 different screeners or use the Morningstar Custom Built screen. The particular portfolio screen appears (portfolio anchor) in a drop-down box for other choices, as well as a short description of the screen. One can then click to view the results of the screen and see the name of the funds, date of each analyst report if one exists, Morningstar rating, category, year-to-date return, and total assets.

Thomson One Investor Relations is a database offered by Thomson Reuters. The database advertises itself as helping to understand the key factors impacting the price of a stock, anticipation of investor behavior, communication with internal and external communities, and measuring the impact of an investment management program.

Researching Corporate News

While databases are most helpful in providing numerical or quantitative data, qualitative data is often needed, such as an expert's opinion or forecasts for future industry trends. This type of qualitative information is likely to arise in news reports and industry articles. Thus it's worth considering using an article database.

Exhibit 4-19 ABI/Inform

Note that several article index databases exist to help find corporate news or other relevant analysis on a topic. Some article index databases have also expanded to provide company information (see Exhibit 4-19). Also, other types of databases, such as LexisNexis, can outperform article index databases in specialized areas.

Access leading business publications, such as the *Wall Street Journal* and the *Financial Times* using the article index database ABI/Inform Global. This database indexes various international professional publications, academic journals, and trade magazines, with full-text access to about 3,000 of them. See Exhibit 4-20 for the advanced search screen. To search for articles on a particular company, use the advanced search screen, then select "Company/Org" from the drop-down menu.

Business Source Premier is another article index database. It is notable in providing full-text access to many scholarly business journals. The database is part of the EBSCO Host database. One can search from three fields, such as title, company entity, or subject. One can also elect to

ProQuest

Basic	Advanced	Topics	Browse	Publications	📁 My Research
					0 marked items

Databases selected: ABI/INFORM Global

Advanced Search

Tools: Search Tips   Browse Topics

	Citation and abstract

AND ⬍		Citation and abstract

AND ⬍		✓ Citation and abstract

Add a row | Remove a row

	Citation and document text
	Abstract
	Author
Database:	Multiple databases...	Classification code
		Company/Org
Date range:	All dates ⬍	Document feature
		Document ID
Limit results to:	☐ Full text documents only 📄	Document language
	☐ Scholarly journals, including peer-re	Document text
		Document title
		Document type
		Image caption
More Search Options		Location
		NAICS code
		Person
		Product name
		Publication title
		Section
		Subject

Exhibit 4-20 ABI/Inform Advanced Search Screen

limit results in many ways, such as to those offering full text, scholarly journals, or by particular publication. Other ways to limit the results to a manageable number include the company name, industry code, and time period. Exhibit 4-21 provides a look at the database's opening screen.

Factiva provides financial press news, such as the *Financial Times* and the *Wall Street Journal*. It has extensive foreign-language newspapers. Factiva has an archival collection spanning over 50 years. It includes more than 31,000 leading news and business sources. A quick company overview is acquired through its Company and Industry subdatabase. Information on pricing of stocks, mutual funds, bonds, and indices is provided in the Historical Market Data Center.

For international business research, start with the web directory GlobalEDGE's reference desk tab to the Global Resource Directory, as

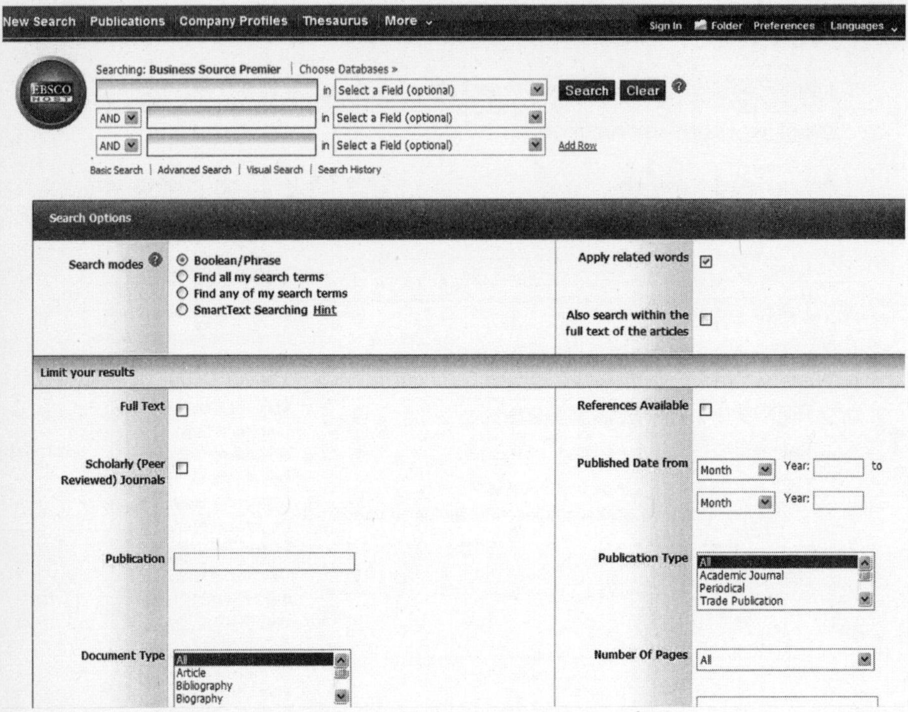

Exhibit 4-21 Business Source Premier
SOURCE: Copyright © EBSCO Publishing, Inc. All rights reserved.

shown in Exhibit 4-22. The directory divides its content in the major international business sources to research, current topics, trade issues, and reference. Research sources include those for multicountry, statistical data sources, rankings, organizations, and publications.

Statistical data sources recommend four websites, such as the CIA's World Factbook (see Exhibit 4-23), the United Nations Statistics Division's statistical database, the World Bank, and enterprise surveys. There are many more websites listed in the Global Resource Directory, each with a short description of its database. Examples of current topics of interest to accountants include outsourcing and corporate governance.

Various helpful directories for international business exist. For example, the Directory of Foreign Firms Operating in the United States lists over 2,000 foreign firms in about 70 countries and over 4,000 U.S. businesses owned by a foreign firm.

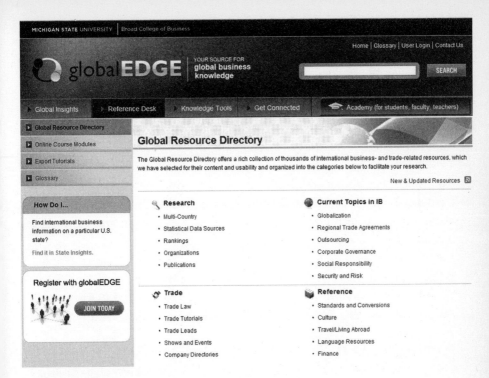

Exhibit 4-22 GlobalEDGE

Exhibit 4-23 CIA World Factbook

Research Tools

Research tools include the AICPA's hardbound reference books, such as *Accounting Trends and Techniques, Financial Report Surveys,* and the *AICPA Audit and Accounting Manual.* Other tools include government and industry databases and websites.

Showing current practice on a particular accounting issue is *Accounting Trends and Techniques.* It also illustrates how companies of various sizes in a wide range of industries have complied with professional standards for financial reporting purposes. This information arose from an annual survey of accounting practices. Reporting practices of selected companies are presented, along with significant trends in reporting practices. Although this AICPA treatise was more important under old U.S. GAAP, when accounting practices occupied part of the GAAP hierarchy, *Accounting Trends and Techniques* still provides value in the form of nonauthoritative examples.

Note that the Financial Reporting Surveys by the AICPA provide a continuing series of surveys that supplement the overview that *Accounting Trends and Techniques* provides. The surveys show in detail how companies in a wide range of industries disclose specific accounting and reporting questions in their financial reports.

Utilize the *AICPA Audit and Accounting Manual* for guidance and extensive examples on conducting an audit. The manual explains and illustrates the procedures for an audit engagement. Auditing topics in the manual include engagement planning, audit approach, and internal control structure. Administrative guidance includes supervision, correspondence, working papers, and quality control aids. Accountants' reports are covered, as well as compilations and reviews. The staff of the AICPA has authored the manual and provided reference to the AICPA's pronouncements.

Use the AICPA's website to help acquire relevant materials. Also, the AICPA has the AICPA Online Professional Library Database providing AICPA materials. These include AICPA professional standards applicable to nonpublic companies, Technical Practice Alerts, AICPA Audit and Accounting Guides, Accounting Trends and Techniques, Audit Risk Alerts, and PCAOB standards. Subscription to the database is available through the AICPA Store: www.CPA2BIZ.com.

One research tool on the Internet is business metasites that have links to a vast array of online business resources. One such business metasite is CEO Express, which contains links to several business magazines, well-regarded news sources such as the *Christian Science Monitor* and the *San Jose Mercury News* for Silicon Valley coverage, and international news sources such as the *London Times* and *Herald Tribune*. Links to business research includes the financial markets, the Securities and Exchange Commission, and online investor services.

Recognize that almost every industry has at least one journal covering news in that industry. Some of these are published by the trade association serving the industry. To locate trade and industry periodicals, go to the University of Florida's online list of industry journals. Also consider trade associations that exist for most industries. Trade association materials are not always released to nonmembers, but usually some information is available on the association's website, such as statistical data about the industry. To find relevant trade associations, use a comprehensive trade directory.

Recognize that U.S. government agencies and well-respected international organizations generally provide reliable information. Take advantage of reports written by such U.S. government agencies as the Securities and Exchange Commission, Department of State, Central Intelligence Agency, Export-Import Bank, and International Trade Administration. Leading international organizations include the World Bank, the International Monetary Fund (IMF), and the Organisation for Economic Co-operation and Development (OECD).

Use statistical data for international business research. The U.S. government, as the world's largest publisher, has such notable statistical publications as the *Federal Reserve Bulletin*, various types of census reference books, and the *Survey of Current Business*. Governments compile an immense amount of statistical data. One online entry point for data gathered by government agency is Fedstats.

Find suppliers or clients through global databases, such as Kompass, a business-to-business database created in Switzerland, covering over 70 countries, two million companies, 860,000 trade names, 23 million product references, and 3.6 million executives' names. Caution: Limitations often apply to foreign databases, especially when they are not geared for an English-language audience.

Valuable books still exist for many business topics, such as for doing business in various countries. Visit a library, its business librarian, and reference books, especially for international business research.

Research Strategies

Recall the four-step process in information collection. The first step is to define the information needed. The second step is to determine the sources to search, the databases, and the parts within the database. The third step is using search techniques and tools. The fourth step is viewing the results and managing the information.

Step one, defining the information needed, depends on the particular task. Evaluate databases in part based on their content. Content depends in part on the reliability of the publisher, the type of information included, the range of years covered in the database, and the particular strengths and weaknesses of the database.

Also evaluate databases by considering database navigation, access, technical support, and training. Navigation examines whether the links are clear and the depth of the information links. Access includes such concerns as whether different fields (i.e., author, publication, date) are separately searchable, as well as the number of simultaneous-users restrictions. Training considers whether online tutorials exist, each page has a link to a help file, and whether live tutorials are possible, as well as their cost.

Accountants may need to assess databases to find specialized news sources monitoring important topics for the industry or the client. Often one must break down broad primary questions into more specific tasks to acquire the data needed to make conclusions. Consider how you plan to use the information before entering an extensive search. Retain a focus on your goals while conducting the research.

Step two, determining the sources, databases, and parts of a database to search, is not always easy. Consider the user-friendliness of the database. Retrieving relevant documents from a vast library is challenging. Generally, use commercial databases, which benefit from investments in the database.

Many databases are now divided into alternative products, depending on the market audience served. Legal databases having tax information increasingly provide business or accounting information. Tax information sources from databases are presented in Chapter 5.

Step three, using search techniques and tools, can include segment searching, connecting terms, memory location, research history, and more. Word choice will also affect the results. Experiment with synonyms, generic terms, or brand names. Double-check spellings of the words. Quotation marks often help to define a phrase.

While searching use a glossary or dictionary, a common search tool in many databases to understand various terms and abbreviations commonly used in the database. The glossary sometimes provides insight into common phrases, such as "due diligence." Using the right terminology in accounting is particularly important.

Step four, viewing the results and managing the information, presents different choices. In viewing the results of the search, results may be available in full-text, annotated, or citation formats. Another choice is citation style for sources, which generally varies from the sciences, social sciences, and humanities. Note that the source is not necessarily the website or the database where the information was located but the entity that compiled the primary data.

Generally the most accurate sources are government data, commercial-resource company data, and studies by universities. Exercise caution when using data from individual companies, politically or economically motivated organizations, or those with small sample sizes. Organize your findings as you conduct the research.

Appendix 3 shows a list of websites for sources mentioned in this chapter.

Summary

Various databases and research tools exist that are useful for accountants. For governmental accounting one needs to use the FASAB Handbook for federal accounting and GARS for state and local accounting. Competing databases exist for providing accounting and auditing standards: RIA Checkpoint and CCH's Accounting Research Manager. One can research industries and companies by using industry codes, various sources, and databases. Such databases include

Mergent Online, LexisNexis, and S&P NetAdvantage. Industry or corporate news can be acquired through a variety of sources, including some specialized databases.

Appendix 1: Checklist for Industry Research

- [ ] Industry Codes
  - [ ] NAICS
  - [ ] SIC
  - [ ] Others
- [ ] Industry Survey
  - [ ] Value Line
  - [ ] Others
- [ ] Trade Organizations
- [ ] Products
  - [ ] Major Products in the Industry
  - [ ] Consumers of the Products
- [ ] Financial Review
  - [ ] Financial Health of the Industry
  - [ ] Patent Examinations
- [ ] Issues in the Industry
  - [ ] Legal
  - [ ] Regulatory Issues Affecting the Industry
- [ ] People in the Industry
  - [ ] Executives
  - [ ] Others
- [ ] Competition in the Industry
  - [ ] Types of Competition
  - [ ] International Competition
- [ ] Specialized Areas Affecting the Industry
  - [ ] History
  - [ ] Geography
  - [ ] Weather
- [ ] Government's Impact in the Industry

Appendix 2: Checklist for Company Research

- ☐ Name of Company
- ☐ Official Legal Name
- ☐ Contact Information
- ☐ Mailing Address
- ☐ Telephone Number
- ☐ Fax Number
- ☐ Email Address
- ☐ Web Address
- ☐ Background on the Company
- ☐ Major Products or Services
- ☐ Industry Codes
- ☐ Analyst Reports on the Company
- ☐ Major Competitors
- ☐ Review of Financial Information
- ☐ 10-K Financial Statements
- ☐ Ratio Analysis
  - Profitability
  - Assets
  - Liquidity
  - Benchmarking Based On
  - Type of Business
  - Size of Business
  - Management Discussion and Analysis
- ☐ Recent Press Releases
- ☐ News Articles
- ☐ Related Entities
- ☐ Major Subsidiaries
- ☐ Business Concerns
- ☐ Risks
- ☐ Litigation
- ☐ People
- ☐ Board Members
- ☐ Major Executives
- ☐ Other

Appendix 3: Websites

Topic	Website
ABI/Inform Global (article index)	www.proquest.com/en-US/catalogs/databases/detail/abi_inform.shtml
Accounting Research Manager	www.accountingresearchmanager.com
AICPA (research tools)	www.aicpa.org
AICPA Online (database)	www.aicpastore.com
AICPA Store	www.CPA2Biz.com
Bloomberg	www.bloomberg.com
Business and Company Resource Center	www.gale.cengage.com/BusinessRC
Business Source Premier (database)	search.ebscohost.com
Canadian Company Capabilities	www.ic.qc.ca
CEO Express	www.CEOExpress.com
Credit Risk Monitor	www.crmz.com
EBSCO Host (article index database)	search.ebscohost.com
Factiva (financial press database)	www.factiva.com
FASAB (Federal Accounting Standards Advisory Board)	www.fasab.gov
Fedstats	www.fedstats.gov
Federal Reserve Bulletin	www.federalreserve.gov/pubs/bulletin
Fitch Ratings	www.fitchratings.com
Forbes	www.forbes.com
Foundation Center (not-for-profit)	www.foundationcenter.org
GASB (Government Accounting Standards Board)	www.gasb.org
GlobalEDGE (international business website)	www.globaledge.msu.edu/
Government documents	www.fdsys.gov
Hoover's (financial database)	www.hoovers.com
International Monetary Fund	www.imf.org
International Trade Administration	www.trade.gov
IPL2 (associations on the net)	www.ipl2.org
Kompass (foreign business database)	www.compass-usa.com
LexisNexis (legal database)	www.lexis.com
Mergent Online (financial database)	www.mergentonline.com
Morningstar Investment Research Center	www.morningstar.com
NAICS (industry code)	www.census.gov/naics
PCAOB (auditing standard setter)	www.pcaobus.org

S&P NetAdvantage	www.netadvantage.standardandpoors.com
SEDAR	www.SEDAR.com
ThomasNet	www.thomasnet.com
Thomson Reuters Checkpoint (database)	checkpoint.riag.com
Thomason Reuters Investment One	www.thomsonretuers.com
U.S. Census Bureau	www.census.gov/eos/www/naics
U.S. Central Intelligence Agency—World Factbook	www.cia.gov/library/publications/the-world-factbook/index.html
U.S. Department of State	www.state.gov
U.S. Export-Import Bank	www.exim.gov
U.S. International Trade Administration	trade.gov/index.asp
U.S. Securities and Exchange Commission	www.sec.gov
University of Florida list of industry journals	businesslibrary.uflib.ufl.edu/journals
Value Line (investment survey)	www.valueline.com
Virtual Pet (industry research)	www.virtualpet.com/industry/howto/search.htm
Wall Street Journal	www.wsj.com
Westlaw (legal database)	www.westlaw.com
World Bank	www.worldbank.org

Chapter 5

Tax Research for Compliance and Tax Planning

T he goal of tax research is to help clients legally minimize taxes within the client's overall goals and desired risk tolerance. Thus, producing the lowest possible tax liability is not necessarily the best objective for the tax advisor. Some clients may not wish to engage in complicated tax plans. Not all clients want to increase their risk of a tax audit with its potential hassle and expense. Some clients want certainty of tax result more than achieving minor differences in the actual cost of the taxes.

Consider tax research as a review of all relevant tax laws to determine the appropriate tax consequences given the facts of a client's situation. Begin tax research by determining the relevant facts. Tax research for compliance is the same as for tax planning. However, tax planning may involve restructuring a proposed transaction so the facts will meet the requirements of the applicable law. Remember that some tax disputes involve questions of fact instead of law. Also, consider the relevancy of the facts, which depends upon the applicable law.

Tax Research Databases

Tax research databases include both primary and secondary sources. A primary source generally comes from the Internal Revenue Code, Treasury Regulations, Revenue Rulings, Revenue Procedures, and case decisions from the various courts. One tax research database's classification of primary sources is shown in Exhibit 5-1. Others will classify primary sources as those from the government having precedential authority.

Secondary sources are often useful for acquiring a basic understanding of the relevant topics. Such secondary tax sources provide expert tax analysis and often cite to primary source material. One popular secondary source is the *Masters of Tax Guide*, which summarizes the tax law in a single volume. Another excellent source is the Bureau of National Affairs' (BNA) *Tax Management Portfolios*. The more than 450 *Portfolios* are in three categories: U.S. Income Tax; Estates, Gifts, and Trusts; and Foreign Income.

Various tax journals, such as *Tax Notes*, *Tax Adviser* (as shown in Exhibit 5-2), *Journal of Taxation*, and law review articles also provide secondary-source insight into a tax topic. A treatise is often a valuable starting point for tax research. Major tax treatises include Bittker and Lokken's *Federal Taxation of Income, Estates, and Gifts* and McKee, Nelson, and Whitmire's *Federal Taxation of Partnerships and Partners*.

The web has enabled government to make its sources more available. The quantity of information from Congress, the IRS, the courts, and others continues to mount. For example, the IRS website provides unofficial versions of the Treasury Regulations, downloadable tax forms and instructions, daily news updates, and more, as shown in Exhibit 5-3. Some popular websites for the tax researcher are presented in the Appendix. Yet a tax database has the advantage of investments in maintaining up-to-date information, better retrieval systems, and other tools to help the researcher.

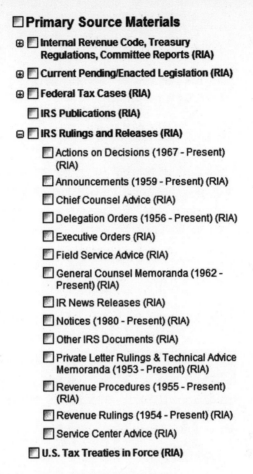

■ **Primary Source Materials**

⊞ ☐ **Internal Revenue Code, Treasury Regulations, Committee Reports (RIA)**

⊞ ☐ **Current Pending/Enacted Legislation (RIA)**

⊞ ☐ **Federal Tax Cases (RIA)**

☐ **IRS Publications (RIA)**

⊟ ☐ **IRS Rulings and Releases (RIA)**

☐ Actions on Decisions (1967 - Present) (RIA)

☐ Announcements (1959 - Present) (RIA)

☐ Chief Counsel Advice (RIA)

☐ Delegation Orders (1956 - Present) (RIA)

☐ Executive Orders (RIA)

☐ Field Service Advice (RIA)

☐ General Counsel Memoranda (1962 - Present) (RIA)

☐ IR News Releases (RIA)

☐ Notices (1980 - Present) (RIA)

☐ Other IRS Documents (RIA)

☐ Private Letter Rulings & Technical Advice Memoranda (1953 - Present) (RIA)

☐ Revenue Procedures (1955 - Present) (RIA)

☐ Revenue Rulings (1954 - Present) (RIA)

☐ Service Center Advice (RIA)

☐ **U.S. Tax Treaties in Force (RIA)**

Exhibit 5-1 Primary Source Materials on Checkpoint

Understand that several publishers offer databases that are useful for tax research. Some researchers use specialized tax research databases, especially those provided by Commerce Clearing House (CCH), which is a division of Wolters Kluwer, and the Research Institute of America (RIA), which is a division of Thomson Reuters. Other researchers use online legal databases, such as LexisNexis. For an important tax issue, check more than one database. Use tax

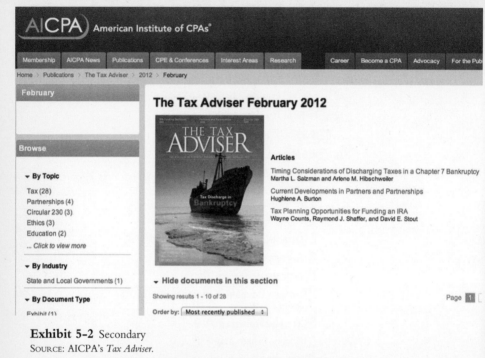

Exhibit 5-2 Secondary
Source: AICPA's *Tax Adviser*.

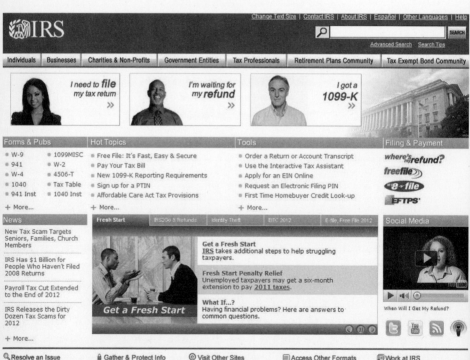

Exhibit 5-3 IRS Website

research databases through a publisher's website, or use a DVD of the database to ensure access when the Internet is not available. A lengthy 2008 comparison of the strengths and weaknesses of these two tax databases and three others exists.[1]

Note that tax databases include not only primary tax authorities, but also a wealth of helpful secondary sources, such as tax services, citators, news updates, and journal articles. They also have sophisticated searching and linking of documents. CCH's tax database IntelliConnect includes CCH's tax services, such as *Standard Federal Income Tax Reporter*, an annotated tax service organized around the Code. An annotated tax service especially has great tools for indexing and finding primary sources, especially tax cases. Another CCH tax service is *Tax Research Consultant*, a topical tax service similar to an encyclopedia. Note that the *Tax Research Consultant* provides a practical, real-world focus on taxes and issues faced every day.

Thomson Reuters's tax database is called Checkpoint. See Exhibit 5-4 for the opening screen when searching federal income taxes. The database includes RIA's tax services: *Federal Tax Coordinator* (FTC), a topical tax service, and *United States Tax Reporter* (USTR), an annotated tax service organized around the Code. Annotated tax services are organized around the Code with each regulation followed by brief summaries of judicial opinions and IRS Revenue Rulings but interpret part of the Code or Treasury Regulations.

Two other major databases for tax introduced in Chapter 4 are LexisNexis and Westlaw. Both provide extensive primary and secondary sources. LexisNexis provides the text of Wiley and Matthew Bender treatises. Westlaw includes the full text of treatises published by the Thomson-West family (including the Thomson Reuters or RIA tax services, and Warren Gorham & Lamont tax treatises).

Besides considering the price in selecting a tax research database, consider the scope of the database contents and the quality of its retrieval systems. Some tax professionals use full legal databases such as LexisNexis rather than tax-specific databases. To prevent overwhelming the tax researcher, these legal databases will assist with a subset of the library for tax.

Enter a tax database's tax service to view updated Code sections. Note RIA Checkpoint's various tax research libraries or practice

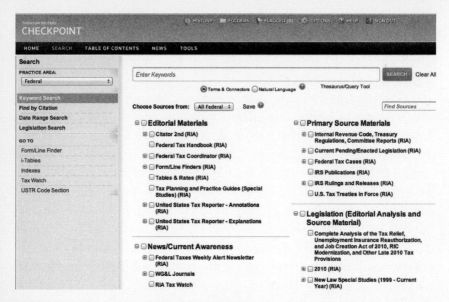

Exhibit 5-4 Checkpoint's Opening Search Screen

SOURCE: Checkpoint® screenshot, published online at http://checkpoint.riag.com. © 2012. Thomson Reuters/RIA. Reprinted with permission. All rights reserved. This information or any portion thereof may not be copied or disseminated in any form or by any means or stored in an electronic database or retrieval system without the express consent of Thomson/RIA.

areas, such as international, federal, state, and local, and estate planning. Various choices for practice areas in tax are provided in a drop-down box on the RIA Checkpoint search screen. After acquiring basic knowledge of a topic, the researcher usually wants to limit the research to the relevant parts of the federal practice area of taxation, such as the Internal Revenue Code and other primary authorities.

Especially for keyword searches, use database search tools. A thesaurus allows one to see synonyms for the search term. This is particularly helpful for keyword and index searches. A date range for a search allows one to limit the search results to a relevant period of time, so as not to get overwhelmed with irrelevant results.

To enhance the research, use database tools, such as proximity connectors and wildcards. Use proximity connectors to enable searching for two terms that are in proximity to each other, but not necessarily next to each other. For instance, placing "w/6" between two terms when searching in CCH IntelliConnect will produce results that contain the two terms within six words of each other. A variety of proximity connectors may exist in a database, such as finding the two terms within the same sentence or paragraph.

Appreciate how wildcard characters enable searching different forms of a word. For instance, adding a wildcard character "!" to "depreciate" ("depreciate!") can yield the results for "depreciate," "depreciating," or "depreciation." Wildcard characters are often represented by an asterisk or an exclamation mark. Some wildcard characters replace only one letter. In CCH IntelliConnect, the wildcard for one letter is represented by a question mark.

Determine the desired display of the search results. CCH's Intelli-Connect default search results mixes the results but displays them by what the CCH software believes is most relevant. RIA Checkpoint by default shows the number of results by source category. The researcher may change the default to the source, which is helpful for researching an answer by weight of authority. CCH refers to a categorized view to see the results by document type, such as grouping the results from the Code.

Tax research databases include the ability to find U.S. tax treaties with a foreign country. Tax treaties address various issues, such as when a visitor is subject to the host country's tax laws. Tax treaties are available on most tax services. For example, CCH reprints tax treaties arranged alphabetically by country, as well as annotations, State Department reports, relevant court decisions interpreting the application of tax treaties, and more. A list of tax treaties is also reprinted in IRS Publication 901, available at the IRS website.

Under these tax treaties, residents of foreign countries are taxed at a reduced rate, or are exempt from U.S. income taxes on certain items of income received from U.S. sources. These tax treaty benefits vary among countries and specific items of income. Treaties are accorded the same weight of authority as the Internal Revenue Code. If any conflict exists between a treaty and the Code, the one later in time prevails. The Internal Revenue Bulletin reprints tax treaties. However, publishers exist that offer greater insight into the tax treaties, such as Matthew Bender's inclusion of Rhoades and Langer's *U.S. International Taxation and Tax Treaties*.

The Internal Revenue Code

Realize that the Code, or the IRC, is the common name for the Internal Revenue Code of 1986 as Amended. The Code compiles most tax statutes passed by Congress. It is located in Title 26 of the United States Code. To cite a specific tax provision, tax researchers use the Code section number followed by specific provisions within that Code section. For example, cite "IRC § 61(a)(1)" as the authority for salary as gross income.

Use the Find by Citation approach in a tax research database as the fastest way to pull up a Code section. On the left side of the screen is the link to using the citation in Checkpoint. The citation approach usually provides a template box to assist the researcher in pulling up the desired Code section or other authority.

Cite a provision within a Code section with as much precision as possible. Drill into the subsections, paragraphs, subparagraphs, and clauses, when possible. Within parentheses following the Code section number, subsections use lowercase letters, paragraphs use numbers, subparagraphs use capital letters, and clauses use lowercase roman numerals.

Only if a Code section existed back under the 1939 codification does the current Code not include a small letter before a paragraph number, such as section 1223(3) for the holding period for stock. Precede the Code section number with "IRC" and either abbreviation for section: "sec." or the symbol "§." For example, IRC § 61(a)(1) states that gross income includes compensation.

Read the general rule of a Code section. This is usually provided in subsection (a). Scan the remaining subsection headings to search for other relevant provisions in the Code section. Tax includes hundreds of "terms of art," such as *gross income*, that have special meanings. Always look for definitions that apply in the section or subsection. Also, over 50 definitions of commonly used terms are contained in IRC § 7701 (see Exhibit 5-5).

Move around within the section reading the headings of the remaining subsections. Sometimes even move into other sections in order to understand the meaning of a phrase used with the Code section. This is especially true if a cross-reference exists to another section. Note little words such as "or" between paragraphs. These words can create big

Sec. 7701. Definitions

TITLE 26, Subtitle F, CHAPTER 79, Sec. 7701.

STATUTE

(a) When used in this title, where not otherwise distinctly expressed or manifestly incompatible with the intent thereof –

(1) Person
The term "person" shall be construed to mean and include an individual, a trust, estate, partnership, association, company or corporation.

(2) Partnership and partner
The term "partnership" includes a syndicate, group, pool, joint venture, or other unincorporated organization, through or by means of which any business, financial operation, or venture is carried on, and which is not, within the meaning of this title, a trust or estate or a corporation; and the term "partner" includes a member in such a syndicate, group, pool, joint venture, or organization.

(3) Corporation
The term "corporation" includes associations, joint-stock companies, and insurance companies.

(4) Domestic
The term "domestic" when applied to a corporation or partnership means created or organized in the United States or under the law of the United States or of any State unless, in the case of a partnership, the Secretary provides otherwise by regulations.

(5) Foreign
The term "foreign" when applied to a corporation or partnership means a corporation or partnership which is not domestic.

(6) Fiduciary
The term "fiduciary" means a guardian, trustee, executor, administrator, receiver, conservator, or any person acting in any fiduciary capacity for any person.

Exhibit 5-5 Example Code Section

differences in the meaning. Perhaps highlight significant words so as to place the reading into proper perspective.

Consider researching committee reports on a topic, especially when a change in the Code is new. Legislative history to a Code section is found in committee reports, which are considered a primary source. Committee reports from the House Ways and Means Committee and the Senate Finance Committee describe proposed changes to the Code. The conference committee report reviews the reconciliation of the House bill with the Senate bill.

Another helpful source is prepared by the staff of the Joint Committee on Taxation. The staff writes a "General Explanation" of new laws, which is more commonly known as the Blue Book. The Joint Committee on Taxation does not mark up legislation. Instead, it conducts studies to assist in the process of drafting legislation.

Committee reports are accessible through a variety of places. Annotated tax services in tax research databases will reprint the most relevant parts of a committee report. The committee report is available in full in the government's federal digital system database. Often subsequent Treasury Regulations are based on the joint committee report. Especially when there are no Treasury Regulations on point, legislative interpretations can help substantiate an interpretation of the Code.

It's often helpful to remain aware of pending legislation. The tax services, such as Checkpoint, make it easy to acquire this information. If one needs to locate the statutory law for prior tax years, most annotated tax services can assist. IntelliConnect does the best job in going back in years the farthest.

Treasury Regulations

The Treasury Department issues Treasury Regulations drafted by the IRS, which is the largest division of the Treasury Department. Search for relevant Treasury Regulations after researching relevant Code sections. Regulations provide general guidance that interpret and clarify the statutory law. Regulations are first published as Treasury Decisions (TDs).

Because regulations sometimes take several years to formulate, occasionally the Treasury Department will issue an advanced notice of proposed rulemaking. New regulations now include a preamble describing the content and purpose of the regulation. Note that while some Code sections have many Treasury Regulations, other sections have none.

The citation to a Treasury Regulation indicates the Code section at issue. It's the number in the citation after the period and before the hyphen. The initial number before the period is the part number that indicates the type of tax at issue. For example, a "1" in front of the regulation means that it is an income tax regulation. Thus, Treas. Reg. § 1.61-1 is an income tax regulation interpreting Code section 61, as shown in Exhibit 5-6. Other popular part numbers are 20 for estate taxes, 25 for gift taxes, and part 301 for procedural rules.

Understand the three major types of Treasury Regulations: final, temporary, and proposed. Most regulations are final. Final regulations are issued only after going through the official process for notice and comment at public hearings. The regulation is then published as a Treasury Decision in the Federal Register and codified into Title 26 of the Code of Federal Regulations.

Prior to finalization, temporary regulations are issued. The citation to a temporary regulation includes a T at the end. Treat temporary regulations as law, unlike proposed regulations. Temporary regulations

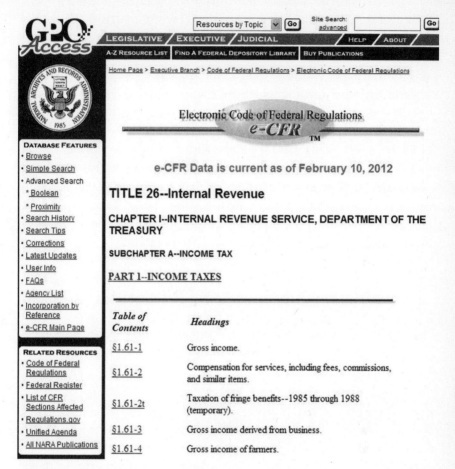

Exhibit 5-6 Example Treasury Regulation

do not require public comment, unlike final regulations. A proposed regulation is not substantial authority. The IRS has sometimes subsequently modified or withdrawn a proposed regulation. The citation to a proposed regulation identifies itself with "Prop." preceding the rest of the citation.

Consider the two types of Treasury Regulations: interpretive and legislative. Interpretive regulations arise under the authority of Code section 7805(a). This regulation expressly provides that the Treasury Department secretary "shall prescribe all needful rules and regulations for the enforcement of this title." Legislative regulations arise when a

Code section directs the secretary of the Treasury to create regulations to carry out the purposes of the section. A taxpayer must comply with both types of final Treasury Regulations, but some consider a legislative regulation stronger authority than an interpretive regulation.

Scan the titles of the regulations that interpret the code section at issue in order to find a relevant regulation. Tax research databases attempt to link the regulations to the related Code section. For example, RIA Checkpoint has a tab for "Regulations" on the top of the display for a Code section. If the title of the regulation appears to have potential application, look over the contents of that regulation. Then carefully read potentially relevant parts of the regulation. Some Treasury Regulations provide clarifying examples on a topic. Others may directly address topics that the relevant Code section did not mention.

Other Administrative Authorities

The IRS issues various administrative authorities besides Treasury Regulations. These include Revenue Rulings, Revenue Procedures, and many nonprecedential authorities.

Revenue Rulings and Revenue Procedures

Know that Revenue Rulings are the IRS's application of the law to a specific set of completed facts. Often Revenue Rulings arise from the IRS National Office's further review of previously issued private letter rulings. In contrast to the general guidance provided in Treasury Regulations, Revenue Rulings provide issues, facts, law, and analysis on applying the law to a particular set of facts. Revenue Rulings are weaker authority than Treasury Regulations, merely representing the IRS's position on an issue. However, Revenue Rulings offer precedential value with the IRS for taxpayers with analogous fact patterns. An example Revenue Ruling is shown in Exhibit 5-7.

Understand that the citation to a Revenue Ruling does not reference the Code section that it addresses. However, for the researcher's convenience, a tax database, such as Checkpoint, will sometimes follow the Revenue Ruling citation with the relevant Code section. The

PART I

Section 1361. – Small Business Corporation

26 CFR: 1.1361(b): Small business corporation defined.
(Also: §§ 401, 501, 1362, 7701, 7871, 305.7871-1.)

Rev. Rul. 2004-50

ISSUE

Is a federally recognized Indian tribal government, as described in § 7701(a)(40)(A) of the Internal Revenue Code, an eligible S corporation shareholder under § 1361?

FACTS

X is a federally recognized Indian tribal government (Indian tribal government) and a shareholder in Corporation, a domestic entity, formed in accordance with the laws of State. Corporation wants to make an election to be an S corporation.

LAW AND ANALYSIS

Section 1361(a) provides that for purposes of this title, the term "S corporation" means, with respect to any taxable year, a small business corporation for which an election under § 1362(a) is in effect for the year.

Section 1361(b)(1) provides that for purposes of this subchapter, the term "small business corporation" means a domestic corporation which is not an ineligible corporation and which does not (A) have more than 75 shareholders, (B) have as a shareholder a person (other than an estate, a trust described in subsection (c)(2), or an organization described in subsection (c)(6)) who is not an individual, (C) have a

Exhibit 5-7 Example Revenue Ruling

researcher should remove the added Code section reference provided by the publisher when citing the Revenue Ruling.

Check the status of a Revenue Ruling by using a citator. For example, the IRS may modify, revoke, or supersede a Revenue Ruling. For convenience, the major tax services provide update links or warnings in assessing the current status of a Revenue Ruling. The Internal Revenue Bulletin (IRB) first publishes revenue rulings. In earlier years, the IRS rearranged the revenue rulings in the Cumulative Bulletin (CB) by Code section number addressed in the ruling.

Revenue Procedures provide procedural information on the tax law, such as inflation adjustments in many threshold numbers, accounting change methods, and procedures for acquiring private letter rulings. They are written by the IRS National Office. Revenue Procedures are published in the same sources as revenue rulings, such as the Cumulative Bulletin and the Internal Revenue Bulletin, as shown in Exhibit 5-8. Thus the citations for revenue procedures cited are the same as for Revenue Rulings.

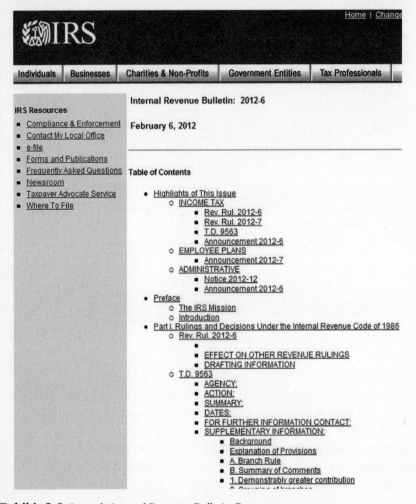

Exhibit 5-8 Example Internal Revenue Bulletin Contents

Nonprecedential Authorities

View other administrative sources by opening up Checkpoint's database for rulings and releases, as previously shown in Exhibit 5-1. The following explains each of these sources, the Internal Revenue Manual, and a few additional sources written within the IRS.

Actions on Decisions (AODs) indicate whether the IRS will follow a significant adverse court opinion in future litigation. Sometimes the

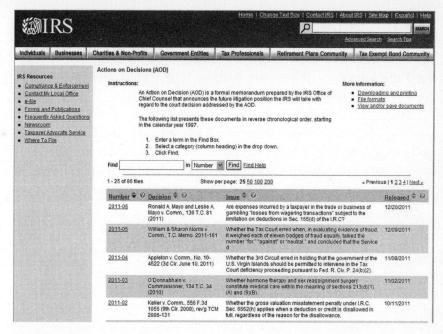

Exhibit 5-9 Finding an AOD

IRS will acquiesce to the result of a decision but not the reasoning. AODs are issued by the National Office to assure IRS consistency for dispute resolution and litigation. Finding an AOD on the IRS's website is illustrated in Exhibit 5-9.

Announcements provide various information to taxpayers, such as the extension of time to file tax returns. Announcements have only short-term value.

Chief Counsel Advice (CCAs) are written advice or instructions interpreting policy from various tax authorities. They are prepared by the Office of Chief Counsel and issued to field or service center employees of the IRS or Office of Chief Counsel.

Delegation Orders (DOs) are orders by the IRS commissioner or chief counsel to delegate to subordinates his or her authority to settle civil or criminal tax cases.

Executive Orders (EOs) establish policy used within the IRS, such as for internal security.

Field Service Advice (FSAs) were taxpayer-specific rulings furnished by the IRS's national office in response to requests made by IRS employees, without the taxpayer's knowledge. FSAs helped determine litigation hazards for enforcement. The IRS stopped writing FSAs in 2004.

General Counsel Memoranda (GCMs) provided the reasons behind the adoption of revenue rulings. They were prepared by the IRS's Office of the Chief Counsel. The IRS stopped writing GCMs in 2002.

The Internal Revenue Manual (IRM) lists the procedures, instructions, and guidelines for the operation and administration of the IRS, such as the audit steps for a revenue agent to take. The IRM is accessible on the IRS's website. See Exhibit 5-10 for its table of contents.

Part 1	Organization, Finance and Management
Part 2	Information Technology
Part 3	Submission Processing
Part 4	Examining Process
Part 5	Collecting Process
Part 6	Human Resources Management
Part 7	Rulings and Agreements
Part 8	Appeals
Part 9	Criminal Investigation
Part 10	Security, Privacy and Assurance
Part 11	Communications and Liaison
Part 13	Taxpayer Advocate Service
Part 20	Penalty and Interest
Part 21	Customer Account Services
Part 22	Taxpayer Education and Assistance
Part 25	Special Topics
Part 30	Administrative
Part 31	Guiding Principles
Part 32	Published Guidance and Other Guidance to Taxpayers
Part 33	Legal Advice
Part 34	Litigation in District Court, Bankruptcy Court, Court of Federal Claims, and State Court

Exhibit 5-10 Internal Revenue Manual Table of Contents

Internal Revenue News Releases (IR News) publicize tax matters of current importance to the general public.

Notices are issued to provide quick guidance for tax practitioners before Treasury Regulations become available. Notices are the equivalent in weight of authority to Revenue Rulings and Revenue Procedures.

Private Letter Rulings (PLRs) are written by the IRS National Office in response to requests by taxpayers concerning the tax consequences of specific proposed transactions.

Service Center Advice (SCAs) address tax administration concerns. They are issued to field or service center employees of the IRS or Office of Chief Counsel.

Technical Advice Memoranda (TAMs) cover completed transactions in response to requests of an IRS district director or chief appeals officer. They are written by the IRS National Office. TAMs only address issues covered by the previously published authorities.

Other documents of interest on the IRS's website include IRS forms and publications. Various documents are located under the Freedom of Information link from the IRS's home page. On this page follow the link to the Electronic Reading Room, found in the right column. These documents are categorized are "Published Tax Guidance," "Nonprecedential Rulings & Advice," "Admin Manuals & Instructions," "Program Plans & Reports," and "Training & Reference Materials." Exhibit 5-11 shows the Electronic Reading Room on the IRS's website.

Nonprecedential rulings include an "information letter." This document provides general statements of well-defined law without applying them to a specific set of facts. Information letters are furnished by the IRS National Office in response to requests for general information by taxpayers or by congressional offices. Another example is Large Business and International (LB&I) Directives, which provide administrative guidance to LB&I examiners to ensure consistent tax administration.

Note that in public accounting practice the usual tax research search will not utilize these lesser administrative sources, other than revenue rulings and revenue procedures. If, however, the accountants' work is scrutinized by a law firm, an exhaustive review of all authorities is likely, even an examination of the nonprecedential authorities written within the IRS.

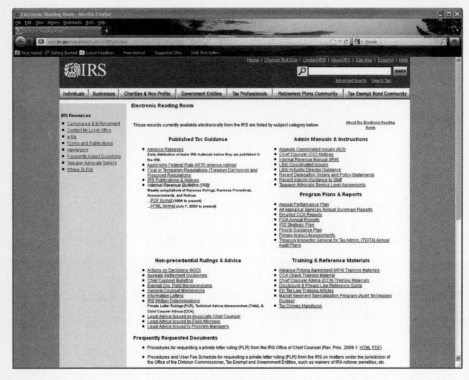

Exhibit 5-11 The IRS's Electronic Reading Room

Judicial Sources

Consider judicial decisions as law interpreting the meaning of the Code or Treasury Regulation in a particular case. Judicial law is created by consistently treating similar cases in the same fashion under the applicable statute and regulations. Tax publishers RIA and CCH provide useful court reporters that include all federal court decisions concerning taxation, except for those from the Tax Court. Thus, included in the court reporters are tax cases from the Supreme Court, courts of appeals, U.S. district courts, and the U.S. Court of Federal Claims.

Use either the RIA court reporter called *American Federal Tax Reports* (AFTR, AFTR2d, AFTR3d) or the CCH product entitled *United States Tax Cases* (USTC). AFTR and USTC are found in the publisher's tax research database: Checkpoint or IntelliConnect. Accountants usually cite non–Tax Court cases using the unofficial sources of either

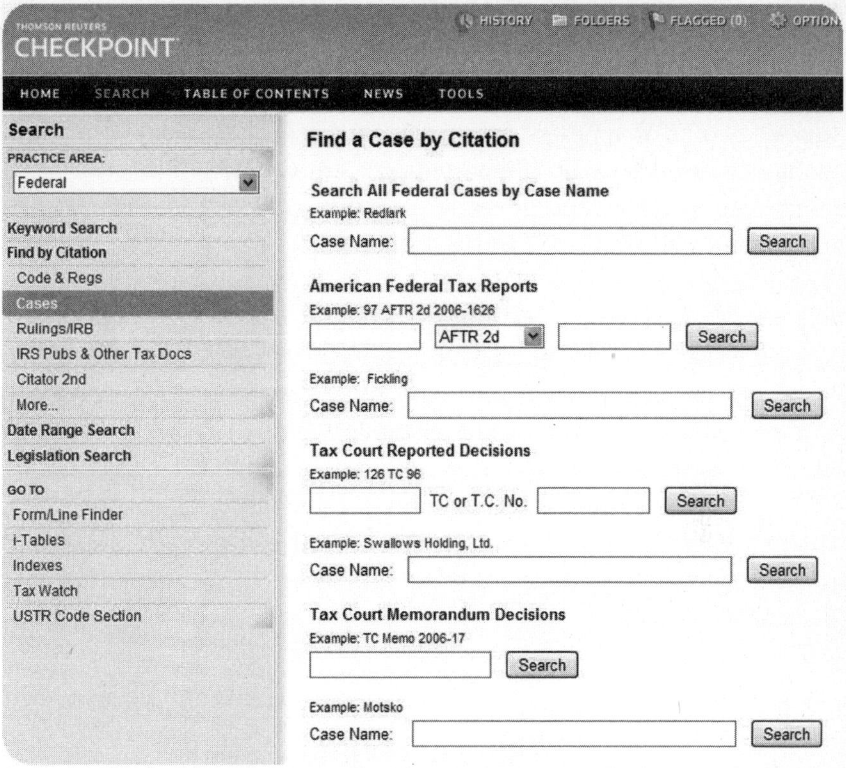

Exhibit 5-12 Checkpoint's Find a Case by Citation

AFTR or USTC. An example of the template for finding a case by citation is provided in Exhibit 5-12.

Examine prior judicial decisions to determine the meaning of a given phrase in the Code. To conduct the research on case law effectively, the tax researcher needs both a working knowledge of judicial concepts and the hierarchy of the various federal courts. Knowledge of the judicial system is necessary to appraise the authoritative weight and precedent of decisions rendered by the various federal courts.

Explain to clients that the U.S. Supreme Court, as the highest court, normally considers less than 10 tax cases each year. While about half of the tax cases heard involve constitutional issues from state courts, a few other tax cases are usually those in which courts of appeal have reached different conclusions on the same issue. Find a U.S. Supreme Court decision in U.S. Supreme Court Reports (U.S.), published by the

U.S. Government Printing Office. Alternatively, find the case in unofficial court reporters, such as AFTR and USTC.

Either the IRS or the taxpayer can request that the Supreme Court review a court of appeals decision. However, the Supreme Court must grant a "writ of certiorari" (reported as "Cert. Granted") for a case to be considered by the Court. For most cases the Supreme Court denies certiorari (reported as "Cert. Denied"), so as not to even consider the case. The decision of the court of appeals will stand when the Supreme Court will not review a case.

Understand that in the U.S. courts of appeals, either the IRS or the taxpayers may appeal decisions of the lower courts. The appeal is made to the circuit in which the taxpayer resides. A map of the circuit courts of appeal is provided on the web as shown in Exhibit 5-13. There are 12 courts of appeals for district courts (11 regional ones, plus the D.C. Circuit). The Court of Appeals for the Federal Circuit will hear appeals on tax issues only if they arise from decisions of the U.S. Court of Federal Claims.

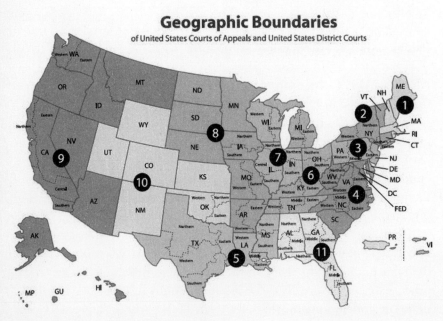

Geographic Boundaries
of United States Courts of Appeals and United States District Courts

Exhibit 5-13 U.S. Circuit Courts of Appeals

Officially, court of appeals decisions are printed in the *Federal Reporter* (F., F.2d, or F.3d). Normally, a review by a court of appeals consists of a panel of three judges and is limited to the application of law, not the redetermination of facts. Courts of appeals are obligated to follow the decisions of the Supreme Court but not those from other circuit courts of appeal.

Seek authorities that are precedent, the principle that governs the use of prior decisions as law. The courts use precedents to build stability and order into the judicial system. Decisions concerning similar prior cases are used as guides when deciding new cases. The process of finding analogous cases from the past and convincing others of the precedential value of those cases is the essence of tax research using judicial authorities.

Determine whether a case is precedent by the hierarchy of the courts. A Supreme Court decision on an issue is precedent for all courts, as long as the statute remains unchanged. A taxpayer sometimes tries to argue a narrow application of the Supreme Court's holding or interpretation of the law so as to distinguish the unfavorable precedent. Court of appeals decisions provide precedent for all cases in their respective circuits. The decisions of other circuit courts of appeals are not precedent, but possibly influential.

In reading a case, understand that the case headnotes provide a brief summary of the issues. Headnotes are helpful in initially determining whether a case is relevant. They also provide insight as to the following material in the case. They are written either by the court reporter or the editors of a major legal publisher.

Original Jurisdiction Courts

Original jurisdiction courts include the Tax Court, the Court of Federal Claims, and U.S. district courts. These are the courts where the taxpayer may appeal an IRS audit or IRS administrative decision on an audit.

Encourage clients to use the Tax Court to litigate an IRS audit adjustment in order to avoid prepaying the amount of taxes in dispute. Besides not having jury trials, the Tax Court has unique rules to expedite the court's process, such as requiring the taxpayer and the IRS to

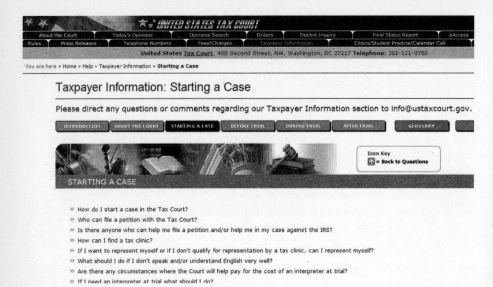

Exhibit 5-14 The Tax Court's Process

work together to establish the facts. Although the Tax Court is located in Washington, D.C., judicial hearings are held in several major cities for brief times during the year.

Expect a Tax Court case to involve only a single judge, who submits an opinion to the chief judge. On rare occasions, an "en banc" decision occurs, which involves a review by all 19 of the Tax Court judges for an important, novel, or unusual tax issue. The Tax Court's website reprints its recent decisions, as well as providing the Tax Court's rules of practice and other valuable information, as shown in Exhibit 5-14.

Differentiate two types of Tax Court cases: regular and memorandum. A regular decision (published in the *United States Tax Court Reports*, or TC) is when the Tax Court's chief judge decides that a case is announcing a new principle in the law. A memorandum decision (published in the *Tax Court Memorandum Decisions*, or TCM or TC Memo) is made if the Tax Court is just applying already announced principles to a different set of facts. Prior to 1943, the United States Board of Tax Appeals (BTA) was the Tax Court's predecessor.

Understand that the IRS will issue either an acquiescence or non-acquiescence for most Tax Court regular decisions that the IRS has lost. Acquiescence means the IRS plans to follow the decision of the

Tax Court when future cases arise with similar facts and circumstances. A nonacquiescence indicates that the IRS will not follow the Tax Court's decision when handling similar cases. This IRS issuance does not apply to either memorandum decisions or decisions by any other courts. Published in the IRB and CB are the announcements of either acquiescence (Acq.) or nonacquiescence (Nonacq.).

Consider using the Small Claims division of the Tax Court for tax disputes of $50,000 or less. The advantage to the taxpayer is a less costly procedure for the Small Claims division's expedited process. The disadvantage of selecting the Small Claims division of the Tax Court is that no appeals are allowed. The government does not publish the Small Claims division decisions because such decisions do not have precedential value. However, commercial databases may include some of these opinions.

The Tax Court follows precedent set by the appellate court of the circuit in which the taxpayer resides. Thus consistency in the application of law is maintained within a jurisdiction, even though an inconsistency may exist in the law's application to taxpayers residing in other circuits.

If precedence in Tax Court is unfavorable, sue for a refund in either the U.S. Court of Federal Claims or one of the almost 100 U.S. district courts. Since tax cases represent about 25 percent of the workload in the U.S. Court of Federal Claims, file a refund claim in this court if an intricate understanding of the tax law is needed by the judge. This court was previously called the U.S. Claims Court and the U.S. Court of Claims. See Exhibit 5-15 for the website of the Court of Federal Claims.

If an emotional appeal is part of the trial strategy, sue for a refund in U.S. district court in order to get a jury trial. U.S. district court cases are officially published in the *Federal Supplement* (F. Supp. or F. Supp. 2d).

Steps in Conducting Tax Research

Conduct tax research by the following five steps:

1. Investigate the facts and identify the issues.
2. Collect the appropriate authorities.
3. Analyze the research.
4. Develop the reasoning and conclusion.
5. Communicate the results.

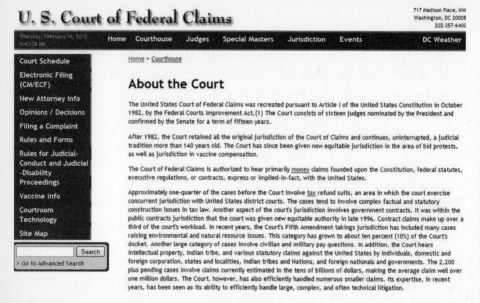

Exhibit 5-15 U.S. Court of Federal Claims Website

Step 1: Investigate the Facts and Identify the Issues

Document the relevant facts of a case. Ask the taxpayer for additional information, as needed. Sometimes the client may fail to provide all the necessary information. Clarify the factual situation in order to conduct efficient tax research. Exercise due professional care in acquiring the facts and identifying the relevant legal issues, regardless of the amount of money at issue. Understand that most cases with the IRS are settled without the necessity of a trial.

Usually, the facts are stated in chronological order. Provide a date for each event. Where facts are documented, provide references where possible. Use the research on the law to help determine the relevance of the facts. It's best to restate the relevant facts for the client to see, in order to check for their accuracy and completeness.

Use an iterative process for identifying the precise legal issue, refining the issue as one develops more sophisticated knowledge of the relevant law. Incorporate in the issue both the critical facts and the precise location within a Code section for the focus of the research. The location of the issue helps show laser-like precision as to the real legal issue. Write each issue in a separate sentence. Then rearrange the issues in logical order.

Note that tax problems may appear deceptively simple to taxpayers. The taxpayer is often interested only in the final outcome and tax planning advice. Such client-focused information belongs in a letter to the client, along with any tax planning advice.

Step 2: Collect the Appropriate Authorities

Use secondary authority to help the initial research. Secondary sources also include:

- Tax service explanations, such as in RIA's *Federal Tax Coordinator*
- Treatises and textbooks
- Tax newsletters and websites

Search techniques needed to collect the appropriate tax authorities can include the keyword, table of contents, index, and citation approaches. Consider using a keyword search to find relevant cases interpreting the Code or regulations. A keyword search is especially popular with those having a "goggle mentality." However, a keyword search is not always the most effective way to search for legal authority resolving a tax issue. One problem is that the search engines for different databases do not always search the entire database. A second problem is that a keyword search is likely to overload the researcher with many documents that are not on point. Use filters when viewing search results so as to narrow the results by document type and probable relevance.

Examine a table of contents in depth to find some relevant law. Drilling down in the table of contents enables one to browse the selected content. Instructions for the CCH IntelliConnect table of contents approach, also known as browsing, are illustrated in Exhibit 5-16.

The drill-down search approach in a tax database enables one to proceed from the relevant Code section. After drilling down to the relevant Code section, enter the tax services to find relevant annotations of cases that interpret that Code section. Annotations provide a one- or two-sentence explanation of the case. For example, when one finds the relevant Code section and provision within it, most online tax services will provide hyperlinks to the authorities discussed. If the case appears potentially relevant, the researcher should then read the entire case to

Browsing

 ?

Every library, publication, database and tool in your subscription, within your selected Practice Areas, is available on the Browse tree.   The Browse tree enables you to navigate through successive levels of content hierarchy.   It is automatically open on the Home page when you login in.   There is also a link on the tool bar to access the Browse tab.

To Browse through your subscription content:
1. Click a **+** to expand item(s) and "drill down" to documents.
2. When you click a **document**, it will display on the right.

 ?

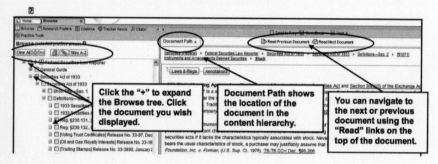

Exhibit 5-16 IntelliConnect's Table of Contents Approach

ensure its relevance, extract sufficient information to understand the case, and write a general paragraph on that case.

Note that the index approach is similar to viewing an index in the back of the book. Indices exist for the Code, tax services, and selected other sources. Access to the indices in Checkpoint is near the bottom left side of the opening research screen. Starting with the index approach can help researchers identify the appropriate terminology for then using a keyword search.

Collect the authorities quickly by using the citations approach. Follow the template style for entering a case, as shown in Exhibit 5-12. Whether one uses hardbound books or online tax databases to find the case is irrelevant; the citation format is the same. Case citations generally use the following format: case name, volume number, court reporter series, initial page number where the case begins. In parentheses at the end of the citation is the court, if not evident from the court reporter, and the year of the court's decision.

Usually the most difficult part of the search into legal authorities is to find relevant judicial cases. While not every Code section and regulation has judicial cases interpreting their language, most Code sections have cases that have applied the statutory and administrative law to a particular set of facts.

Cite Supreme Court decisions, which are published by the U.S. Government Printing Office with *U.S. Supreme Court Reports* (U.S.). They are also unofficially published by such reporters as AFTR and USTC. A parallel citation may exist to show multiple locations for finding the same case. A citation to a case need not include any nonofficial sources for accessing the case; however, it's often helpful to include such information.

Remember that court of appeals decisions are officially published in the *Federal Reporter* (F., F.2d, or F.3d), and the tax decisions are unofficially reprinted in RIA's AFTR series and CCH's USTC. The first name in a case citation indicates the party appealing the prior court's decision. The following citation refers to a 2007 decision by the Seventh Circuit Court of Appeals: *United States v. BDO Seidman*, 492 F.3d 806 (7th Cir. 2007).

Note that U.S. district court decisions are officially published in the *Federal Supplement* (F. Supp. or F. Supp. 2d). Finding the decisions of the U.S. Court of Federal Claims and its predecessor courts is more complicated. Decisions rendered between 1929 and 1932 and after 1959 appear in the *Federal Reporter—2d or 3d Series* (F.2d or F.3d), while those issued between 1932 and 1960 are in the *Federal Supplement* (F. Supp.). Many times a parallel citation is used to show multiple places where the case is found. While publishers place their own references first, the researcher should place the official citation first.

Distinguish Tax Court case citations for regular and memorandum decisions, because they are in different reporters. Tax Court regular decisions are published by the government in *United States Tax Court Reports* (TC). The Tax Court's recent decisions are also available on its website. Tax Court memorandum decisions are published by RIA and CCH reporters called *Tax Court Memorandum Decisions* (RIA TC Memo or TCM). The citation to RIA TC Memo varies from the usual case citation by not having a volume number and page number. Instead, a paragraph reference is sometimes used, followed by the number that consists of the year of the decision, then hyphen, then number of the decision, such as *Franke v. Commissioner*, RIA TC Memo 2011-10.

To find a citator listing using the Citator:

1. Click the **Citator** on the tool bar.
2. Click the '+' to expand a library in left navigation pane.
3. Click the title of a template in the left navigation pane so correct template appears in the right pane.
4. Scroll down the template to find the specific document type you wish to retrieve.
5. Enter the needed information for the citation. If you know the case name, you can type it in the appropriate field at the top

6. Click **Go**. The system displays a Citator listing for all documents associated with the citation you entered on the template (in a new results tab). Click the one you want

Exhibit 5-17 IntelliConnect's Citator

Write proper citations to enable others to collect the authorities quickly. Whether one uses an online tax database or a hardbound tax service to find the case is irrelevant; the citation is the same. When one uses a tax research database, note that the database's style of case citation may differ slightly from the official style that the tax researcher should use. Tax publishers will skew the citation to emphasize their own sources and add information they believe is helpful.

Use a citator to check whether a case continues to have validity. A case that is referenced is referred to as a cited case. A citator indexes cited cases. A citator first presents the judicial history of a case. It also traces subsequent judicial references to the case. Favorable references of a court's reasoning strongly influence other courts. Instructions in using CCH's citator are provided in Exhibit 5-17.

Warning: A citator does not provide insight into whether a case remains valid after changes in the Code. The researcher must use professional judgment in making that decision.

In using the citator, the researcher enters the citation for the case to evaluate. Note that a drop-down template box may provide the different reporters. Also, remember that some citations also examine the subsequent status of revenue rulings. A ruling may have been modified, superceded, revoked, or made obsolete by new tax law developments.

In Checkpoint, the citator is placed in the menu under find by citation. While the CCH's citator merely directs the researcher to a citing case's first page, the RIA's citator gives a pinpoint citation within a case.

Step 3: Analyze the Research

Acquire a basic knowledge of primary tax authorities to place the research in context. Such knowledge should include both understanding the nature of the sources and where to locate them. By understanding the legal hierarchy of tax authorities, the researcher can assess their relative weight. For cases, the strength of authorities varies depending on the court, the client's set of facts, and the age of the decision as a proxy for a greater likelihood that the law may have changed.

Check the analysis of one's tax research, because the analysis is often the most difficult part of tax research. General guidelines for analysis are listed below:

1. The Code is the strongest authority. However, the Code does not always answer many questions arising from a given factual situation.
2. Treasury Regulations are the next strongest authority.
3. Court decisions interpret the Code and regulations. A court can overturn a Code section only if it is unconstitutional. A court will overturn a Treasury Regulation only if the regulation is totally unreasonable.
4. Supreme Court cases apply to all taxpayers. Circuit court of appeals decisions apply only to taxpayers residing in that circuit. However, circuit court cases are often influential elsewhere.
5. IRS Revenue Rulings and Revenue Procedures are binding only on IRS revenue agents, not on the courts. Thus, Revenue Rulings as weight of authority exists only if the taxpayer is arguing before the IRS.[2]

Steps 4 and 5: Develop the Reasoning and Conclusion, and Communicate the Results

Use professional tax judgment to come to a solution on a tax issue. This judgment is especially shown in the application of tax authorities. Always consider the weight of authority so as to start with the strongest, most logical source, such as a Code section or subsection. For cases, try to use the strongest cases possible.

The strength of authority of a case depends on the level of the court, whether the judge's remark was the holding of the case or merely influential passing remarks (dicta), and the similarity of the facts. The reasoning includes a discussion of how each potentially relevant legal authority is applied to the set of facts or is distinguishable from them. Thus the best application integrates the facts with each legal authority discussed.

Document the relevant law. Begin by discussing a relevant Code section. Follow it by any regulation interpreting the relevant Code section language. For court decisions, devote a paragraph for each one to summarize the facts, the court's holding, and its reasoning. Apply each source discussed in the reasoning before reaching a conclusion. Provide the proper citation to the referenced sources. In certain situations, no clear solution is apparent due to unresolved issues of law or perhaps incomplete facts from the client.

Documentation of the research process is especially important if the client is audited on this tax issue. When the tax return is completed under audit, prepare for the possibility that the person who completed the tax return roughly two years ago may have left the employer. Thus carefully document the research to avoid both potential IRS penalties and possible litigation from an unhappy client. An example tax research memo is provided in the next section.

Note in the example memo that the issue identifies where in the Code the legal issue arises. The conclusion then answers the legal issue. Although some firms will combine discussion of the law and the application into just a section on reasoning, too often the application then gets shortchanged. It's best to lead the reader as to how each piece of law applies. Support each research conclusion with reasoning showing a detailed, logical analysis of the law and application.

For tax planning, determine how to structure the facts and possible legal alternatives for the client's problem. The research memo changes a little, so the professional should present the likely consequences for each alternative. Let the client, in discussion with the tax professional, select the best alternative plan of action given the facts. Review the quality of all communications with the client or with the IRS. Sign and date any written communications.

The client letter generally provides little, if any, technical jargon. Understand that a client who is unable to judge the quality of the research may evaluate the quality of clear communication as a proxy for the likely quality of the tax research.

Example Tax Research Memo

The following is an example of a tax research memo regarding a fictitious company. The style of the memo is common, with subheadings for the facts, issue, conclusion, discussion of the law, and application. Sometimes the discussion of the law and application are together in a section labeled reasoning.

Facts

Jane Miyataki started Jane Edibles, Inc. (JEI) in 2011, as an S corporation. In forming the business, Jane borrowed $50,000 to purchase 100 percent of JEI's voting stocking. The company has 19 other investors who own 900 shares of the S corporation's nonvoting stock.

In 20X6, Jane discovered that Sue, one of the company's investors, made a gift of 50 shares of JEI stock to an irrevocable trust on April 22, 2012. The trust will dissolve upon Sue's death, and the remaining income and corpus will be distributed to her five children and Aloha United Way. The trust is not a grantor trust as specified in § 671.

Issue

Whether the transfer of S corporation stock into a non-grantor trust is an inadvertent termination of an S corporation status qualifying for relief under § 1362(f)?

Conclusion

If a taxpayer reports, corrects, and makes the required adjustments resulting from the termination in a timely manner, the IRS will waive the terminating event, allowing the corporation to retain its election.

Discussion of the Law

An S corporation is a small business corporation required by § 1361(a)(1). To qualify as a small business corporation, its shareholders must be an individual or an allowable estate, trust, or organization, § 1361(b)(1).

A trust may be a shareholder of an S corporation if it is owned by an individual as required by § 1361(c)(2)(A)(i). A trust is deemed to be owned by an individual if it falls within the requirements of § 671.

A business's S corporation status is terminated when it no longer is a small business corporation, §1362(d)(2). If a termination is a result of a specific event that caused the corporation not to meet the small business requirements, the S corporation is terminated as of the day the event occurs, Reg. § 1.1362–2(b)(2).

When there is a termination, for tax purposes, a corporation will be treated as an S corporation to the day of termination, and will be treated as a C corporation for the remainder of the year. As such, the activities of the company will be prorated between the time it was an S corporation and a C corporation under § 1362(e).

If the IRS determines that a company terminated its S corporation status inadvertently, the company is granted relief and is treated as an S corporation, § 1362(f). A termination is inadvertent if the terminating event was not within the corporation's control, nor part of a plan to terminate the election, or was done without the knowledge of the corporation under Reg. § 1.1362–4(b). To receive relief, the company must also report to the IRS within a reasonable period of discovering the termination and agree to adjustments that the IRS may require, Reg. § 1.1362–4(a).

In Rev. Ruling 86-110, 1986-2 C.B. 150, a majority share-holder of an electing small business corporation transferred shares of the S corporation to two irrevocable trusts. The trusts were not eligible shareholders under the trust requirements of § 1361, since the trusts were not owned by an individual under § 671. As a result, the transfer terminated the S corporation election. In making the transfer, the majority shareholder did not intend to terminate the election, and would not have trans-ferred the stock knowing there would have been a termination.

The majority shareholder reported the inadvertent termina-tion within a reasonable amount of time, and corrected the problem so that the corporation could once again meet the requirements of a small business corporation. The other share-holders also agreed to make any prior period adjustments speci-fied by the IRS. Since the corporation reported, corrected, and adjusted for the inadvertent termination, the IRS waived the termination and allowed the company to continue being treated as an S corporation.

Application of the Law to the Facts

Since Sue's trust is not a grantor trust under § 671, she is not a deemed owner of her trust required by § 1361(c)(2)(A)(i). As a result, the trust is an ineligible shareholder under § 1 361(b)(1)(B) causing JEI to no longer qualify as a small business corporation under § 1631(a)(1). Because JEI fails to meet small business corporation requirements, the S corpora-tion status is terminated as of April 22, 2012, defined in Reg. § 1.1362-2(b)(2) and § 1362(d)(2). With the termina-tion, JEI will be both an S and C corporation for 2012 and will be required to allocate activities of the business between those two periods as required by § 1362(e).

Jane's situation is similar to the revenue ruling in that a shareholder transferred stock to an irrevocable trust(s). The trusts were alike in that they both did not meet the eligibility trust requirements of § 1361 and were not owned as defined by § 671, which caused an automatic termination of its S corpora-tion election. Jane also did not intend to terminate the election like the majority shareholder. If Jane is similarly able to prove that the termination was inadvertent under Reg. § 1.1362–4(b) and make the adjustments under Reg. § 1.1362–4(a), JEI can continue to operate as an S corporation under § 1362(f).

The Tax Research Environment

Explore the IRS's website for tools to help with tax compliance. All forms and publications of the IRS are downloadable from the IRS's website. *IRS Publications* is a series of Internal Revenue Service documents on common tax issues, which provide explanations and associated forms. Exhibit 5-18 shows tools for the tax professional that provide information needed to file clients' tax returns. The IRS website contains many valuable web pages, such as the one on reporting uncertain tax

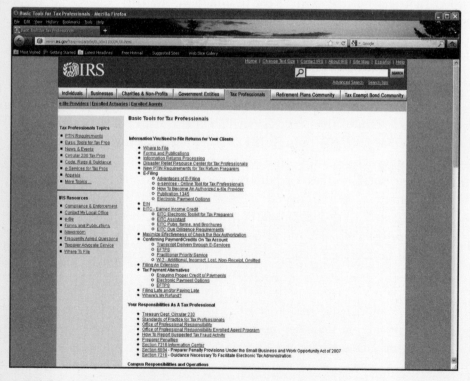

Exhibit 5-18 IRS Tax Tools

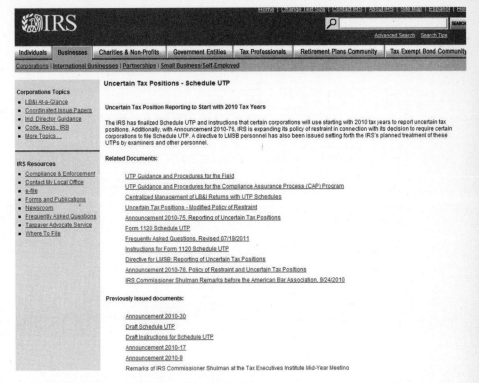

Exhibit 5-19 Reporting Uncertain Tax Positions

positions, as shown in Exhibit 5-19, and the one on taxpayer appellate rights within the IRS, as shown in Exhibit 5-20.

The quality of tax research initially performed and documented should prepare for handling a tax audit. While all tax returns go through computational checking, some face real scrutiny through an audit. To understand the tax research environment, one must have basic knowledge of the various types of civil tax audits, as well as research if the IRS has a Tax Audit Guide on the industry, as shown in Exhibit 5-21. These guides provide insight into the issues and accounting methods unique to an industry.

Individual Face-to-Face Tax Audits

Only about 1 percent of individuals are selected for audit, but audit probabilities increase with higher incomes. For example, about

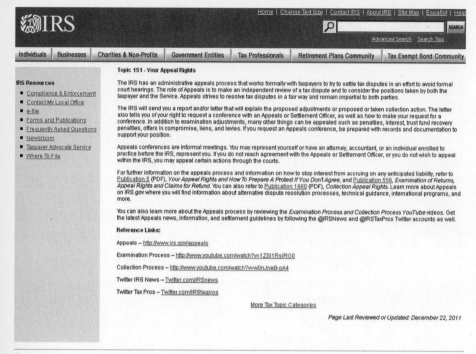

Exhibit 5-20 Taxpayer Appellate Rights

3 percent of individuals with more than $200,000 of taxable income are audited each year.

Often, audit selection is based on having a prior audit with a deficiency, self-employment income (Schedule C), or unusually large deductions. Some factors that increase audit chances include but are not limited to: (1) cash-oriented businesses, (2) the home office deduction, (3) excessive business or itemized deductions for the income level, and (4) the Earned Income Tax Credit. Some of the most frequently audited items for individuals include dependent exemptions, noncash charitable contributions, casualty losses, medical expenses, and travel and entertainment. Other areas of common audit interest may include repairs or capital improvements, bad debts, improper education-related deductions, and tax credits.

When confronted with an individual tax audit the most important strategy is to maintain an adversarial role, yet display professional

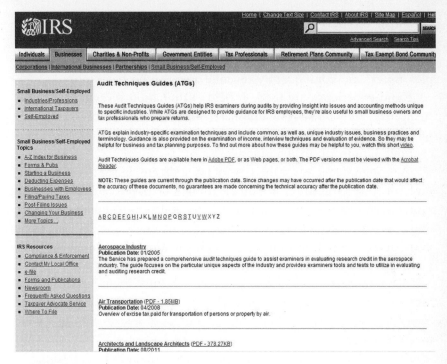

Exhibit 5-21 Tax Audit Guides

courtesy toward the agent. Many practitioners fail to remember that the Taxpayer Bill of Rights guarantees representation before the IRS, a recording of any proceeding, and an IRS explanation of its tax position. This means that taxpayers have a right to know why the IRS is requesting information and how it will use the information. Good representation has the ability to present facts clearly, concisely, and with conviction. Remembering this will help to increase chances for a successful audit.

Small Business Audits

Small business audits are performed by revenue agents on corporations, S corporations, and partnerships with assets under $10 million. The audit population is about 9 million small businesses and 41 million self-employed persons. About 2 percent of individuals with Schedule C business income and expenses are audited each year. Many of these audits are the results of tax shelters, high income, and offshore issues.

Small business audits are generally conducted on the taxpayer's premises, where the taxpayer's books and records are maintained, and are referred to as "field examinations." These audits involve more complex issues, and consequently revenue agents who have more knowledge and experience are used. A field examination is open-ended: An agent may freely pursue any unusual items in the tax returns or taxpayer records. Field examinations have recommended changes about 70 percent of the time for small businesses.

Although strategies for this type of tax audit are similar to those previously discussed, the most important thing a taxpayer can do is acquire professional representation, such as a CPA skilled in handling tax audits. Some special strategies may be needed depending on the size and scope of the audit. It is not uncommon for representation to perform a "preliminary" audit on the tax return before the IRS begins an examination. This will allow preparation for areas of weakness or insufficient information to substantiate the taxpayer's claims. The taxpayer needs to have detailed books and records that clearly indicate sources of information that were used on the tax return. In many instances, IRS agents will allow for substitute records or information that will partially substantiate the claim.

Partnership Tax Audits

Partnership tax audits are unique in having several provisions appearing in the statutory law (IRC §§ 6221 and 6234). Each partner receives notice that the IRS will begin a partnership tax audit. The partnership items are audited at the partnership level rather than the individual level. A partner must treat all items consistently with the partnership return (IRC § 6222). At the end of the audit, the IRS mails a notice of final partnership administrative adjustment to the tax matters partner. An exception to this process involves "small partnerships," those with 10 or fewer partners, which are exempt from this procedure.

The IRS has a *Partnership Audit Technique Guide* (2002). The guide identifies the information document requests (IDRs), such as acquiring a copy of the partnership agreement and all amendments, partnership tax return, loan documents, any side agreements, indemnification agreements, or security agreements. Given the nature of partnership taxation, one of the most commonly scrutinized areas includes outside basis calculations and computation of loan allocations. A partnership audit begins by ascertaining the method of accounting for the balance sheet, securing taxpayers' working papers for Schedule M reconciliation, and analyzing the different accounts.

The most beneficial strategy to employ when preparing for a partnership tax audit is to obtain a copy of the *Partnership Audit Technique Guide*. Inside the guide are likely interview questions, examination techniques, and how tax issues are identified. Another item that warrants attention is the possibility of settling the case before an audit. The "tax matters partner" should consider settling a case, even if on a relatively unfavorable basis, in order to prevent the statute of limitations from remaining open and potential costs increasing.

LB&I Tax Audits

Large Business and International (LB&I) is the largest division of the IRS. It handles all corporations, S corporations, and partnerships with assets of $10 million or more. S corporations and partnerships comprise about 70 percent of the LB&I taxpayers or audit population. Businesses with assets over $10 million have about a 15 percent chance of an audit, while about one-third of businesses with over $1 billion of assets are audited. Individuals having more than $10 million of income also are audited by LB&I in its Global High Wealth Industry Group. Audit selection factors include the taxpayer's current level of compliance, time needed for audit, expected results, and the effect on future tax returns.

LB&I tax audits are performed by revenue agents and specialist revenue agents, within the direction of an LB&I team manager, often as part of a "coordinated industry case." A written audit plan is created with three basic parts: taxpayer information section, case manager's instructions to the audit team members, and audit procedures to use.

Audit selection for LB&I tax audits increases based on computerized matching of information on the tax return with data from third parties, abusive tax avoidance transactions participants, or large corporate returns. Some additional factors influencing audit selection include abnormal deductions, high compliance risks (such as cash operations), and whether a related business or partner has problems. Almost 40 percent of tax returns are selected by using a confidential computer model score, such as for unreported income. The extensive audit planning by the LB&I audit team includes meeting with specialists and legal counsel to discuss potential issues. The team manager reviews prior Revenue Agent Reports, the planning file, existing analysis, SEC reports, and other pertinent data. Preliminary meetings with the taxpayer are often needed to discuss commitments.

Prior to issuing information document requests (IDRs), the audit team will review all IDRs with the taxpayer for completeness and agree to standard response times for the IDRs. Common IDRs include copies of corporate minutes, annual statements, audit reports, and related tax returns. Additional documentation that may be needed to understand the corporation include summary of the corporation's structure, chart of accounts for all entities, year-end trial balances for related entities, and possibly the tax accrual work papers.

The IRS will prepare an audit timeline jointly with the taxpayer, consider third-party contacts early, and acquire advance access to the taxpayer's electronic data for the computer audit specialist's statistical sampling of the taxpayer's records. The IRS shares subsequent risk analysis results with the taxpayer and narrows the focus to the most significant issues after preliminary information is received. It is customary that the IRS will not substitute additional audit issues when issues are dropped or narrowed.

Field examinations in LB&I now use "issue focus" with an audit team approach. This audit team is comprised of revenue agents and various experts. The Issue Focus Program centralizes command and control of "high risk" compliance issues. LB&I's Issue Focus has a concentrated audit focus on high-risk tax issues. Coordinated management of top issues promotes consistency in resolving across industries, to provide the field with clear guidance on addressing major compliance issues.

The issues are prioritized by three tiers based on prevalence across industry lines and the level of compliance risk. Each issue is developed by an "issue management team" but owned by one "issue owner executive." Tier I issues represent "High Strategic Importance" and involve a large number of taxpayers, significant dollar risk, substantial compliance risk, or high visibility, where there are well-established legal positions. IRS guidance is nondiscretionary—field personnel

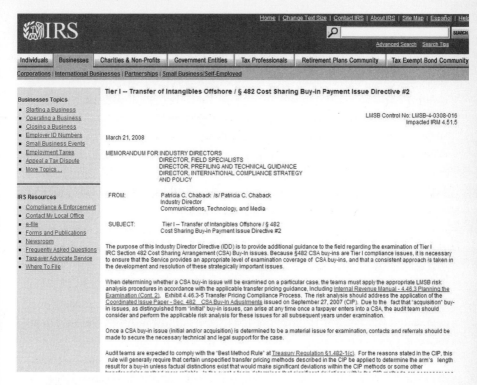

Exhibit 5-22 Issue Focus Example

must follow it in all cases. These are shown in Exhibit 5-22. Tier II issues represent "Significant Compliance Risk." They include emerging issues or those needing further clarification and guidance. IRS guidance provides field personnel with discretion based on the taxpayer's facts and circumstances. Tier III issues represent important industry-related issues that LB&I teams should consider when conducting their risk analyses. Perhaps they will use Audit Technique Manuals or "coordinated issue papers" by LB&I, which are not official IRS pronouncements on the issues.

Audit strategies for the taxpayer include meeting the expectations of LB&I to provide routine start-of-audit information, providing financial information in electronic format to reduce the number of information document requests, and advising of scheduling conflicts that could result in delays. It is essential that the taxpayer advise the LB&I audit team if the taxpayer can't meet deadlines.

One alternative audit to the traditional audit is the Compliance Assurance Program (CAP). CAP enhances compliance with tax laws through real-time monitoring, review, and issue resolution. CAP provides tax certainty sooner and reduces taxpayer burden. Audits begin about 19 months after filing the return and average about 14 months. LB&I audit teams interact directly with taxpayers to understand their business operations, review significant business transactions, conduct risk assessment to evaluate tax compliance and tax reserves, identify issues for resolution, and provide compliance guidance. If under CAP, agreement is not reached on the issues, the taxpayer can still use IRS dispute resolution procedures, such as "Fast Track Settlement."

A second audit alternative to LB&I tax audits are Pre-Filing Agreements. Pre-Filing Agreements provide taxpayers with opportunity to request that revenue agents examine and resolve potential issues before the tax returns are filed. Issues are often factual ones involving well-established law. For example, a Tip Rate Determination Agreement negotiated the rate for tip income for the restaurant industry in a specific vacation destination.

A third alternative to the traditional audit is Limited Issue Focused Examinations (LIFE). LIFE requires a commitment by both the IRS and the taxpayer with a MOU (Memorandum of Understanding) governing key parts of the audit. Agreement must exist on dates, issues, and frank discussions. If the taxpayer adheres to the MOU and the audit results are within the materiality threshold, the IRS will not expand into other issues.

Transfer Pricing and International Tax Audits

Transfer pricing audits are performed by LBI audit teams. Influencing audit selection are the presence of high-value intangibles, such as patents; cost sharing agreements, such as payments of management fees; allocations of expenses based solely on revenues; and restructuring of the multinational's corporate group or international operations, especially to a tax haven.

Strategies in a transfer pricing audit are to follow the regulations and conduct transfer pricing studies with extensive formal contemporaneous documentation including details of controlled transactions and functional and risk analyses. Taxpayers should always maintain justification of the transfer pricing method used and copies of intercompany agreements. Transfer pricing audits are one of the few tax audits where the expense of potentially litigating the results of the audit is sometimes advisable, because of the high assessments that sometimes arise.

An alternative to a transfer pricing audit is an advance pricing agreement (APA). An APA is a voluntary, binding contract between a government and a company, made after extensive prefiling discussions. It determines the appropriate transfer pricing method, comparables, adjustments, and critical assumptions for the APA's future duration. Advantages of APAs are to short-circuit a difficult transfer pricing audit, to obtain future tax certainty, and to handle high-risk transfer pricing issues. To eliminate the risk of double taxation by two countries, taxpayers use the IRS to negotiate a bilateral APA, an agreement with another government's tax agency ("competent authority"). Taxpayers avoid adjustments or penalties from a transfer pricing audit if the taxpayer complies with the APA. A major advantage of an APA is the prevention of protracted litigation costs that are common in transfer pricing disputes. Exhibit 5-23 shows how the IRS provides more information on APAs.

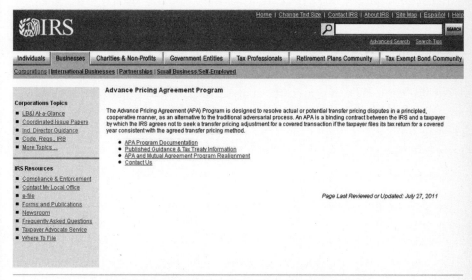

Exhibit 5-23 Advance Pricing Agreement

International tax audits, besides the transfer pricing issue, have several complex issues that revenue agents refer to international specialists. Some of the issues include a situation when the foreign tax credit is more than $25,000, when tax shelters exist, when tax treaties are involved, or when international mergers have occurred.

Tax research from the perspective of other countries is increasingly possible. International tax portals exist that look at the tax law and agencies in other countries. See, for example, the international tax sites at taxsites.com.

Audits of Specialized Industries

Audits of many specialized industries by their nature are complex and technical. Therefore, the IRS has created special audit procedures for over 40 specialized industries. These differences were originally developed through the Market Segment Specialization Program as coordinated issue papers. A prime example is the petroleum industry. Originally, a coordinated issue paper was created for the industry; special audit procedures now exist. Most of the coordinated issue papers are industry-specific. However, some papers cross all industry lines, such as those for Dollar Value LIFO.

The newer guides are referred to as Tax Audit Guides or Audit Technique Guides. They provide the audit procedures to assure a quality audit for a taxpayer in that specialty industry. LB&I has several major industry groupings, such as a group on financial services and health care. By using industry analysis for the audit plan, the IRS has a stronger business risk approach to auditing. Industry specialists play a major role in the audit of specialized industries.

A strategy for avoiding these types of audits would be to review the Audit Technique Guides. Study of this material will allow the taxpayer to more fully understand areas of the tax law that are subject to higher scrutiny and verify that current application of tax law is consistent with agreed-upon policies. In general, taxpayers should perform "self-analysis" of tax papers to determine areas that might be questionable or seem inconsistent. The intent is not to manipulate numbers, but to identify certain areas that might draw attention from the IRS, and also recognize potential errors on the return.

Pension Plan Audits

Pension plan audits are performed by an "employee plan" audit team. Audit team members include a team coordinator who is a pension plan expert, a computer audit specialist, an actuary, an attorney, and an employment tax specialist. Currently, the IRS audits less than 1 percent of roughly 700,000 large pension plans. However, audited pension plans hold 60 percent of total plan participants and 70 percent of total pension plan assets.

Selection for pension plan audits places priority on noncompliant taxpayers, rather than analytically reviewed mistakes. Audit selection may also arise from the number of participants in the plan(s), gross assets in the plan(s), contributions to the plan(s), and the number of plans of the controlled group. Other factors may include number of related entities, potential national impact, effect on plan participants, referral information, and field input.

To construct an audit plan for pension plan audits, the IRS reviews IRS Form 5500z, the employer's compliance history, and regulatory documents such as SEC and Department of Labor information. The employer is notified to provide plan documents, payroll information, and electronic records. The opening conference of a pension plan audit is between the audit team members, the employer, and its representative. Here they discuss the items for review, the audit's anticipated length, and Information Document Requests. Major pension plan audit issues are provided on the IRS's website. For example, the IRS examines termination or partial termination—potential vesting/distribution issues. A major issue examined by the IRS is the possibility that the acquiring employer might fail to offer all optional benefits on distributions of transferred assets from merged plans in an acquisition.

The most important strategy for handling a pension plan audit is to work with the audit team to resolve the issues on a timely basis. During the audit when the audit team identifies an issue, the employer is notified to acquire the employer's statement of relevant facts and its position with respect to each identified issue. Prepare for the audit by having readily available pension plan documents, amendments, requested records efficiently organized, and determination letters/opinion letters. The taxpayer or representative should expect to explain pension plan terms, the operation of the plan (test results), and administrative processes, including internal controls. It is critical to use an annual self-audit of the pension plan to minimize potential problems with the IRS and to identify plan errors resolved through self-corrections, as well as unresolved errors. If there is a pension plan failure, it is important to note that most pension plan failures are resolved using the Self-Correction Program or the Audit Closing Agreement Program.

Employment Tax Audits

Taxes examined in employment tax audits include income tax withholding, FICA (Social Security and Medicare taxes), and the Federal Unemployment Insurance Tax. Historically, the audit rate for employment taxes has been substantially less than 1 percent of the tax returns. Although all businesses are subject to audit, businesses that claim a high rate of independent contractors are much more likely to get audited than those that don't. Typically, the audit is triggered by complaints of an individual's claim for unemployment benefits, but the business never reported the individual as an employee. Audit chances increase if the tax returns are regularly filed late, the taxpayer failed to report the wages of all employees (i.e., part-time or seasonal workers), or noncash compensation exists.

As part of the IRS's National Research Program (NRP), over three years about 6,000 employers were selected for an intensive employment tax audit. The purpose of the intensive NRP audit is research to design profiles for use in future tax audits. The most commonly addressed issue in an audit is worker classification in which an independent contractor may qualify as an employee. However, in many cases the IRS cannot reclassify workers retroactively under IRC § 530. Other issues for an employment tax audit include fringe benefits, officer compensation, and tip reporting income.

A major strategy in an employment tax audit is to prepare an analysis before responding to the IRS. Review all relevant documents, obtain legal counsel early, and negotiate for a focus on a test year.

In order to avoid a long-drawn-out and costly audit, the taxpayer should concede tax items that are wrong or weak. The taxpayer needs to understand that the IRS has agreements to share information with state tax agencies.

Estate Tax Audits

Estate tax audits are performed by estate tax examiners. The examiners have a legal education background that aids in the analysis of the property rights. The IRS audits about 20 percent of estates with gross estate exceeding $5 million.

Selection for an estate tax audit is more likely if one has substantial real estate holdings. The IRS will scrutinize the taxpayer's method of valuing the property. With estate tax returns that contain closely held stock, controversies will arise on its valuation. Any life insurance on the decedent that was not included in the gross estate increases probabilities for audit. Other key issues that signal a potential audit would include but are not limited to: jointly held property if owned by someone other than the decedent's spouse, transfers within three years of death, and the use of alternate valuation.

Strategy for handling an estate tax audit begins long before the actual notice is received by the taxpayer. When establishing and filing an estate tax, careful documentation of each item of the estate is important as well as complying with the detailed estate tax regulations. A specific area where critical and detailed documentation is necessary is a discount in stock valuation.

Exempt Organizations Examinations

For large entities (more than $100 million in revenue), the IRS uses a Team Examination Program to audit tax-exempt organizations. While the audit population is about 1.8 million tax-exempt organizations, the IRS audits less than 1 percent of the tax-exempt organizations. However, in recent years audits of exempt organizations have increased. While a controversial area within this category is the audits of churches, many taxpayers are hiding under the guise of churches and establishing exempt organizations that are strictly for tax avoidance.

The exempt organization examinations are generally compliance audits handled through correspondence. Common are follow-up letters to the taxpayer's Form 990 information, compliance checks for targeted compliance initiatives, limited-scope examinations, and market segment studies.

Compliance checks review tax returns and information returns. They verify timely filing of returns and deposits of taxes. Compliance checks often are used for large government entities. They also review internal controls and evaluate procedures, such as tracking payments to vendors. A compliance check differs from a tax audit because a compliance check does not inspect the taxpayer's books and records and does not determine tax liability.

Exempt organization audits start with an information document request, such as the articles of incorporation, bylaws, resolutions of the board, and minutes of the board. Business documents sought could also include contracts and donor lists. It is not uncommon for the IRS to also review websites and tax records. The IRS may ask for a copy of the application for recognition for tax exemption, reconciliation work papers, employment tax returns, and returns of affiliated organizations. Accounting records sought may include financial statements, payroll and pension plan records, and transactions between the organization and directors of the organization.

Audits of exempt organizations have increased in recent years. Issues of concern have included employment tax compliance, university-related unrelated business income, political activity compliance, and executive compensation (loans to officers). Organizations of special concern include gambling organizations, community foundations, credit counseling organizations, and tax-exempt hospitals.

One of the most important strategies to employ would be to have a tax advisor with a power of attorney. The tax advisor can help assess the potential scope and length of an audit and identify key areas of the revenue agent's interest. Major issues may include unrelated business income tax or political activity. It is more efficient to give the IRS one contact person for any documents or information. In order to prevent IRS "fishing expeditions," it is important to request specificity of documents for review. Some simple tips for an efficient audit would include reviewing all documents that will have copies sent to the IRS, placing documents in good order, not producing documents without explanation, and not editorializing unless absolutely necessary.

Regulation of Tax Professionals

Tax professionals are regulated by professional standards and penalties for wrongdoing. Professional standards affecting tax practice include the registration requirement for tax return preparers, the AICPA Statements on Standards for Tax Services, and Circular 230.

Tax preparers must register annually with the IRS to acquire a Preparer Tax Identification Number. Certified public accountants (CPAs), attorneys, and enrolled agents who are active and in good standing with their licensing agency have no additional requirements. The same is true for supervised preparers and non-1040 preparers. All others must also pass a competency test and take continuing education courses annually.

The AICPA has a Code of Professional Conduct for CPAs. The AICPA Code provides an enforceable comprehensive code of conduct, a guide for AICPA members for complex questions, and assurance to the public. For tax practice, this is supplemented by AICPA Statements on Standards for Tax Services (SSTSs). The AICPA's website has these SSTSs with other materials on taxation. Topics addressed in the SSTSs as of 2012 are as follows:

- Maintain a reasonable belief that client's tax return position has a realistic possibility of success on the merits (SSTS 1).
- Make reasonable effort to obtain information to answer all questions on the tax returns (SSTS 2).
- Rely on client information without verification unless the information appears incorrect, incomplete, or inconsistent. Preparers are not required to examine supporting documents (SSTS 3).
- Use estimates if impractical to obtain exact data and if estimates appear reasonable (SSTS 4).
- Realize that prior year disposition of an issue may not prevent recommending a different treatment of a similar item in a later year (SSTS 5).

- Inform the client upon discovery of an error and recommend appropriate measures for the client to take (SSTS 6).
- Reflect professional competence in the form and content of advice to clients. Use written communication for complex matters, but oral communication is permitted for simple matters (SSTS 7).

Tax return preparers must exercise due diligence in gathering and assembling facts that are potentially relevant to a tax return position. They must also clearly communicate with the client any concerns about potential tax reporting positions. This would include discussions with clients about any potential taxpayer penalty consequences of a tax return position.

Tax return preparer penalties include Code § 6694 penalties on preparers whose tax returns take positions not fully supported by current law. Additionally there are penalties for failing to meet various disclosure requirements. Finally, criminal preparer penalties also exist, such as fraud—willfully aiding the preparation of any tax-related matter that is fraudulent as to any material matter (Code § 7206(2)).

The IRS issued Circular 230 in part to provide strict standards on any written tax advice. A taxpayer may rely on a "covered opinion." A covered opinion includes any written tax advice not otherwise disclaimed in the advice. The disclaimer must prominently state that the advice was not "intended or written by the practitioner to be used, and that it cannot be used by the taxpayer, for the purpose of avoiding penalties that may be imposed on the taxpayer." Thus most accounting firms add such a disclaimer to routine emails.

Summary

Tax research is challenging but exciting. One should use secondary sources such as tax research database services to help find relevant primary authorities. One's inspection of the Code, the Treasury Regulations, cases, and other administrative sources must carefully analyze the primary authorities. One needs to understand the court hierarchy to determine whether a case is precedent or merely influential. Essentially, one follows five steps in the research process: investigate the facts and identify the issues, collect the appropriate authorities, analyze the research, develop the reasoning and conclusion, and communicate the results. The tax research environment is defined by the different types of tax audits and the regulation of the profession.

Notes

1. Katherine Pratt et al., "The Virtual Tax Library: A Comparison of Five Electronic Tax Research Platforms," *Florida Tax Review* 8 (2008): 933.
2. Thomas Weirich, Thomas Pearson, and Natalie Churyk, *Accounting & Auditing Research: Tools & Strategies,* 7th ed. (Hoboken, NJ: John Wiley & Sons, 2010), 145–146.

Appendix: Selected Tax Websites

Primary Sources

U.S. Code	uscode.house.gov
Treasury Regulations	www.gpo.gov/fdsys
Cases	caselaw.findlaw.com
Tax Court decisions	ustaxcourt.gov

Agencies or Committees

Internal Revenue Service	www.irs.gov
House Ways and Means Committee	waysandmeans.house.gov
Joint Committee on Taxation	www.jct.gov
Senate Finance Committee	www.finance.senate.gov

Tax Publishers

BNA	www.bna.com
CCH	www.cchgroup.com
LexisNexis	www.lexisnexis.com
Tax Analysts	taxanalysts.com
Thomson Reuters Checkpoint	checkpoint.riag.com
Westlaw	westlaw.com

Reference Sites

TaxSites Directory	taxsites.com
Tax Almanac	www.taxalmanac.org
Tax Foundation	www.taxfoundation.org

Chapter 6

Assurance/Auditing Research

Introduction

Two major sets of standards that have typically been applied by professionals in the United States include U.S. GAAP, discussed in Chapter 2, and auditing standards, discussed in this chapter. However, because information technology and third-party requests have had a significant impact on the accounting profession and society in general, the public accounting profession has focused on its willingness and ability to design and offer additional "value-added" services, in addition to such traditional services as tax preparation and auditing. Technological changes have encouraged accounting professionals to transform from "number crunchers and certifiers of information" to "decision support specialists and enhancers of information."

Many professionals who keep abreast of the major changes in the profession and technology have adapted their practices and market orientation to these new "value-added" assurance services. Some practitioners are also expanding the area of consulting services offered to clients. As a result, the practitioner/researcher must become aware of these new assurance services and the related authoritative standards and restrictions that apply in offering these services.

Assurance Services

In order to focus on the needs of users of decision-making information and improve the related services that accountants provide, an AICPA Special Committee on Assurance Services conducted research that consisted of assessing customer needs, external factors, information technology, and needed competencies to offer these new "value-added services." These services are referred to as "assurance services" and defined by the AICPA Committee as follows:

Assurance services are independent professional services that improve the quality of information, or its context, for decision makers.

Notice that this definition of assurance services implies that the service itself, not necessarily just the report, will add value to the user. In addition, an independent professional must offer the assurance services in order to improve the quality of the information or its context. Current examples of such assurance services proposed by the AICPA include CPA WebTrust, CPA Prime Plus, and CPA Performance View services. These services relate to the integrity of web-based services, the assurance of elder-care services, and assurance related to performance measurement systems, respectively.

These assurance services are considered three-party contracts—the client, the assurer (that is, the accountant), and the third party to whom the accountant is providing assurance. An example of an assurance service engagement is where Consumers Union tests a product and reports the results or ratings in its publication *Consumer Reports*.

An overview of assurance services versus consulting services is presented in Exhibit 6-1. Specific details are provided in the following sections of this chapter. As depicted, the traditional audit service

		Attestation Services
	Electronic Commerce	
Assurance Services Examples	Risk Assessment	Audits
	Health Care Performance	Review of Interim Financial Statements
	Information Systems Reliability	Agreed-upon Procedures Engagement
	Business Procedure	Reporting on an Entity's Internal Controls

	Litigation Support	Logistic Services
Consulting Services Examples	Computer Instructions	Business Validation
	Market Studies	Bankruptcy Services

Exhibit 6-1 Assurance and Consulting Services
SOURCE: From *Accounting & Auditing Research: Tools & Strategies*, 7th ed. Reprinted with permission of John Wiley & Sons, Inc.

is an attestation function that falls under the broader term of *assurance services*. As a professional conducting research, one must recognize the professional standards for attestation and consulting engagements.

Consulting Services and Standards

Attestation and audit services are considered special types of assurance services. Consulting services do not fall under the umbrella of assurance services. Historically, consulting services offered to clients (two-party contracts) by CPAs were referred to as management consulting services or management advisory services. These services have generally evolved from accounting-related matters in connection with audits or tax engagements. In a consulting engagement, the CPA develops findings and conclusions, which are followed with recommendations for the benefit of the client. This is in contrast to an attest engagement (a three-party contract) whereby the CPA reports on the reliability of a written assertion that is the responsibility of a third party. Examples of consulting engagements include litigation support services, computer installation engagements, and various market studies for clients.

The typical consulting engagement is quite similar to the research process presented in this text. The consulting engagement would normally include

- Determination of the client's objectives.
- Fact finding.
- Definition of the problem.
- Evaluation of the alternatives.
- Formulation of a proposed action.
- Communication of the results.
- Implementation and follow-up.[1]

Professional standards for consulting services include general standards and specific consulting standards. In rendering professional services (including consulting), general standards of the profession are located in the AICPA's Code of Professional Conduct. In addition, the AICPA's Management Consulting Services Executive Committee has issued *Statements on Standards for Consulting Services* (SSCS), which provide standards for the practitioner rendering consulting services. These standards are located in the AICPA's Professional Standards database also discussed later in this chapter.

Auditing Standard-Setting Environment

Auditing is indispensable in a society where credit is extended widely and business failures regularly occur, and where investors wish to study the financial statements of many enterprises. The purpose of the audit report is to add credibility to the financial information. The general environment for auditing is very dynamic and constantly evolving as various factors affect the audit process.

The independent auditor's role serves as a secondary communication function; the audit opinion is expressed on the financial information reported by management. The auditor's primary concern is whether the client's financial statements are presented in accordance with generally accepted accounting principles (GAAP). The auditor must conduct the audit in a manner that conforms to auditing standards and must take actions that are guided by professional ethical standards. In addition, in nonaudit engagements the accountant must use relevant attestation standards and statements for compilation and review services, as well as standards for accountants' services on prospective financial information (that is, forecasts and projections).

Attestation Services and Standards

Society increasingly seeks attestation services (a subset of assurance services) from the accounting profession. In the past, attestation services were normally limited to audit opinions on historical financial statements based on audits that followed generally accepted auditing standards (GAAS).

More recently, professional accountants render opinions on other representations, such as reporting on an entity's internal controls. Accountants were concerned that existing standards or guidelines did not meet the demands of society. As a result, the AICPA developed attestation standards titled *Statements on Standards for Attestation Engagements* (SSAE) and related interpretations to provide a general framework for attest engagements.[2]

The term *attest* means to provide assurance as to the reliability of information. The AICPA has defined an attest engagement as follows:

> An attest engagement is one in which a practitioner is engaged to issue or does issue a written communication that expresses a conclusion about the reliability of a written assertion that is the responsibility of another party.[3]

Whether the attestation service is for the traditional audit of financial statements or reporting on an entity's internal control or prospective financial information, the professional accountant must follow certain guidelines and standards in rendering these attestation services. In conducting an attest engagement, the professional accountant reviews and conducts tests of the accounting records deemed necessary to obtain sufficient evidence to render an opinion. Choosing the accounting records and other information to review and deciding the extent to examine them are strictly matters of professional judgment, as many authoritative pronouncements emphasize.

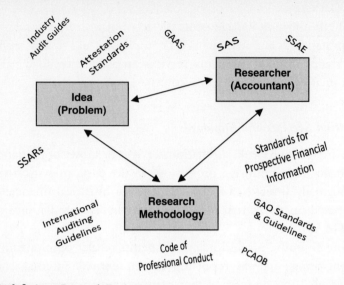

Exhibit 6-2 Attest Research Environment
Source: From *Accounting & Auditing Research: Tools & Strategies*, 7th ed. Reprinted with permission of John Wiley & Sons, Inc.

Exhibit 6-2 presents the main elements of the attestation environment that face accountants in conducting the research for an attest engagement. Exhibit 6-3 presents an overview of attest engagements and relevant guidelines. The following sections of this chapter provide an overview of the standard-setting environment for attestation services, the auditing standard-setting process, authoritative auditing pronouncements, and the role of professional judgment in the research process. The chapter also includes a discussion of how the researcher uses the AICPA's Online Publication database in research, a summary of the attestation standards and compilation and review standards, and an overview of auditing in the public sector and the international dimensions of auditing.

During the last decade, as the range of attestation services has expanded, many CPAs have found it difficult to apply the basic concepts underlying GAAS or the Standards of the Public Company Accounting Oversight Board (PCAOB) to various attestation services. Attestation services have also included the following examples: reporting to the client on which computer system is the cheapest or has the most capabilities, reporting on insurance claims data, reporting on compliance with

Exhibit 6-3 Attest Engagements and Guidelines

Attest Engagement	Guidelines	Issued by
Audit and attest services for nonpublic companies	Generally Accepted Audit Standards (GAAS) Statements on Auditing Standards (SASs)	Auditing Standards Board (ASB)
Accounting and Review Services	Statements on Standards for Accounting and Review (SSARs)	Accounting and Review Services Committee (ARSC)
Accountant's Services on Prospective Financial Information	Statements on Standards for Accountant's Services on Prospective Financial Information	Auditing Standards Board
Other attest services	Statements on Standards for Attestation Engagement	ASB, ARSC, and the Management Consulting Services Executive Committee
Audit and attest services for public companies	Auditing and Related Professional Practice Standards	Public Company Accounting Oversight Board (PCAOB)

SOURCE: From *Accounting & Auditing Research: Tools & Strategies*, 7th ed. Reprinted with permission of John Wiley & Sons, Inc.

regulatory requirements, and reporting on prospective financial statements. (In one instance, Wilson Sporting Goods' request that Wilson's Ultra golf ball outdistanced its competitors was attested to by an accounting firm!)

Consequently, the AICPA has issued Statements on Standards for Attestation Engagements, Statements on Standards for Accounting and Review Services, and Statements on Standards for Accountants' Services on Prospective Financial Information to provide a general framework and set reasonable guidelines for an attest function. The desire is to respond to the changing environment and demands of society.

The broad guidelines for an attest engagement were issued by the AICPA's Auditing Standards Board (ASB) in conjunction with the Accounting and Review Services Committee and the Management Consulting Services Executive Committee. As listed in Exhibit 6-4, these attestation standards do not supersede any existing standards but are considered a natural extension of the 10 generally accepted auditing standards. The design of these attestation standards provides guidance to

General Standards

1. The practitioner must have adequate technical training and proficiency to perform the attestation engagement.
2. The practitioner must have adequate knowledge of the subject matter.
3. The practitioner must have reason to believe that the subject matter is capable of evaluation against criteria that are suitable and available to users.
4. The practitioner must maintain independence in mental attitude in all matters relating to the engagement.
5. The practitioner must exercise due professional care in the planning and performance of the engagement and the preparation of the report.

Standards of Field Work

1. The practitioner must adequately plan the work and must properly supervise any assistants.
2. The practitioner must obtain sufficient evidence to provide a reasonable basis for the conclusion that is expressed in the report.

Standards of Reporting

1. The practitioner must identify the subject matter or the assertion being reported on and state the character of the engagement in the report.
2. The practitioner must state the practitioner's conclusion about the subject matter or the assertion in relation to the criteria against which the subject matter was evaluated.
3. The practitioner must state all of the practitioner's significant reservations about the engagement, the subject matter, and, if applicable, the assertion related thereto in the report.
4. The practitioner must state in the report that the report is intended solely for the information and use of the specified parties under the following circumstances:

   - When the criteria used to evaluate the subject matter are determined by the practitioner to be appropriate only for a limited number of parties who either participated in their establishment or can be presumed to have an adequate understanding of the criteria.

   - When the criteria used to evaluate the subject matter are available only to specified parties.

   - When reporting on subject matter and a written assertion have not been provided by the responsible party.

   - When the report is on an attest engagement to apply agreed-upon procedures to the subject matter.

Exhibit 6-4 Attest Standards

SOURCE: *AICPA Professional Standards*, vol. 1, AT, Section 101.

the professional to enhance both consistency and quality in the performance of attest services.

Auditing Standards

Auditing standards differ from audit procedures, in that auditing standards provide measures of the quality of performance, whereas audit procedures refer to the specific acts or steps to perform in an audit engagement. Auditing standards do not vary; they remain identical for all audits. Audit procedures often change, depending on the nature and type of the entity under audit and the complexity of the audit.

Currently, three major organizations have the responsibility of setting auditing standards for U.S. auditors, which include the AICPA's Auditing Standards Board (ASB), the U.S. Public Company Accounting Oversight Board (PCAOB), and the International Auditing and Assurance Standards Board (IAASB), which issues international standards. Each of these organizations is highlighted in the following sections.

ASB. Accounting firms that audit financial statements of nonpublic entities in the United States are required to comply with the auditing standards promulgated by the ASB. In contrast to generally accepted accounting principles (GAAP), which are not identified with exactness, the AICPA had formally adopted 10 broad requirements for auditors to follow in examining financial statements, classified as general standards, fieldwork standards, and reporting standards. In 2003, the PCAOB adopted these 10 standards with its own developed standards and referred to them as "the standards of the PCAOB." However, in an attempt to improve the clarity of the standards and to converge with the international standards, the ASB has replaced the 10 standards with a comprehensive description titled "the principles underlying an audit conducted in accordance with generally accepted auditing standards." These 10 requirements, referred to as the generally accepted auditing standards (GAAS) as adopted by the PCAOB, are listed in Exhibit 6-5. In addition to the issuance of GAAS, the AICPA publishes a series of Statements on Auditing Standards (SASs).

General Standards

1. The audit is to be performed by a person or persons having adequate technical training and proficiency as an auditor.
2. In all matters relating to the assignment, an independence in mental attitude is to be maintained by the auditor or auditors.
3. Due professional care is to be exercised in the performance of the audit and the preparation of the report.

Standards of Field Work

1. The work is to be adequately planned and assistants, if any, are to be properly supervised.
2. A sufficient understanding of internal control is to be obtained to plan the audit and determine the nature, timing, and extent of tests to be performed.
3. Sufficient appropriate evidential matter is to be obtained through inspection, observation, and confirmations to afford a reasonable basis for an opinion regarding the financial statements under audit.

Standards of Reporting

1. The report shall state whether the financial statements are presented in accordance with generally accepted accounting principles (GAAP).
2. The report shall identify those circumstances in which such principles have not been consistently observed in the current period in relation to the preceding period.
3. Informative disclosures in the financial statements are to be regarded as reasonably adequate unless otherwise stated in the report.
4. The report shall contain an expression of opinion regarding the financial statements, taken as a whole, or an assertion to the effect that an opinion cannot be expressed. When an overall opinion cannot be expressed, the reasons therefore should be stated. In all cases where an auditor's name is associated with financial statements, the report should contain a clear-cut indication of the character of the auditor's work, if any, and the degree of responsibility the auditor is taking.

Exhibit 6-5 Generally Accepted Auditing Standards (PCAOB Adopted)
SOURCE: PCAOB, Auditing Standards.

SASs supplement and interpret the 10 generally accepted auditing standards and now the ASB principles by clarifying the audit procedures or prescribing the auditor's report in both form and content. SASs serve as the primary authoritative support in conducting an audit and are a significant source of authoritative information when conducting auditing research. In 2004, the AICPA's Auditing Standards Board initiated a major project to clarify SASs, Statements on Quality Control, and Statements on Standards for Attest

Engagements not only to make them easier to read, but also to attempt to converge its standards with the International Standards on Auditing (ISAs) promulgated by the IAASB, while also avoiding any conflicts with the PCAOB auditing standards. The clarified SASs were developed using equivalent ISAs as a base and are located in the AICPA's Professional Standards database as explained later in this chapter.

Thus, the codification of ASB auditing standards organizes logically the essence of the auditing standards and follows the structure of the Principles underlying an Audit Performed in Accordance with GAAS. The following shows how the SASs are reorganized by the ASB in their clarity and convergence project. The prefix AU-C is used to refer to the clarity standards codified auditing topic. The designated sections and related titles appear as follows:

- Preface
- 200–299 General Principles and Responsibilities
- 300–499 Risk Assessment and Response to Assessed Risks
- 500–599 Audit Evidence
- 600–699 Using the Work of Others
- 700–799 Audit Conclusions and Reporting
- 800–899 Special Considerations
- 900–999 Special Considerations in the United States

The PCAOB is currently using the codified version of the auditing standards as interim standards. The PCAOB is constantly reviewing and updating audit standards for public companies.

Various forms of GAAS are also recognized by governmental and internal auditors. The Government Accountability Office (GAO), through the Comptroller General of the United States, has issued Governmental Auditing Standards, often referred to as the Yellow Book. The Institute of Internal Auditors has also issued auditing standards, called the Standards for the Professional Practice of Internal Auditing, under which internal auditors operate. The comptroller general has established the U.S. Auditing Standards Coordinating Forum, composed of members from the PCAOB, GAO, and the ASB. The forum meets several times during the year to facilitate coordination and constructive working relationships between the groups. The main focus of discussion is the convergence of auditing standards among the forum members.

PCAOB. The Public Company Accounting Oversight Board (PCAOB or Board) has the legal responsibility under the Sarbanes-Oxley Act to establish GAAS, attestation, ethics, and quality control standards for those accounting firms auditing public companies. This Board has adopted a rule that requires all registered public accounting firms to adhere to the Board's auditing and related practice standards in connection with the preparation or issuance of any audit report for an issuer and in their auditing and related attestation practices. Going forward, the Board's new standards are called Auditing and Related Professional Practice Standards.

Standards for auditors of nonpublic companies are currently within the domain of the AICPA. The reconstituted mission of the AICPA's Auditing Standards Board (ASB) includes the following three main issues:

1. To develop auditing, attestation, and quality control standards for nonissuer engagements, such as privately held commercial entities, not-for-profit organizations, and governmental entities.
2. To contribute to the development and issuance of high-quality national and international auditing and assurance standards.
3. To respond to the needs for practical guidance in implementing professional standards.

The PCAOB initially adopted as interim standards the AICPA's auditing, attestation, and quality control standards, as well as the AICPA's ethics and independence standards. Thus, the PCAOB uses the AICPA standards, as of April 2003, as the authoritative standards for public company audits until superseded or amended by the PCAOB. All the PCAOB Standards can be located at its website: www.pcaobus.org.

IAASB. The International Federation of Accountants (IFAC) has had a broad objective to develop a worldwide accounting profession with harmonized standards. To meet the objective relating to auditing standards, the IFAC initially established the International Auditing Practices

Committee to develop and issue International Standards on Auditing on the form and content of audit reports.

The purpose of the International Standards on Auditing (ISA) is to improve the uniformity of auditing practices throughout the world. In addition, the IAPC issues International Auditing Practice Statements (IAPSs) that provide practical assistance in implementing the International Standards but do not have the authority of the International Standards. In 2002, IFAC created a new International Auditing and Assurance Standards Board (IAASB) that now has the responsibility of developing international auditing standards. More recently, a Public Interest Oversight Board was created to review the IAASB.

The ISAs apply to every independent audit of financial information, regardless of the type or size of the entity under audit. Within each country, however, local regulations govern. To the extent that the ISAs conform to the specific country's regulations, the audit will be considered in accordance with the *Standards*. In the event that the regulations differ, the members of the IAASB will work toward the implementation of the ISAs, if practicable, within the specific country. These standards and other publications of the IAASB are available at www.ifac.org.

Moving forward with auditing standard setting, there exists a movement for standards convergence similar to the convergence to IFRS. The GAO's position on auditing standards convergence is that standard setters should work together to achieve core auditing standards that are universally accepted. Where there is a clear and compelling reason, the individual standard-setting bodies should develop additional standards necessary to meet the needs of their respective constituencies. The nature of any differences from core auditing standards and the basis for the differences should also be communicated. The GAO is working with the International Organization of Supreme Audit Institutions (INTOSAI) to advance government auditing standards in the international arena.

The official position of the ASB on convergence is that it will develop standards (SAS) using the International Standards of Auditing (ISA) as the base standard and modify the base standard only where modifications are deemed necessary to better serve the needs of U.S. users of audited financial statements of nonissuers.

Auditing Standard-Setting Process

Concern has always existed as to who should set auditing standards for the independent auditor. Prior to the establishment of the SEC, Congress debated having audits conducted by governmental auditors; however, the auditing standard-setting process remained in the private sector. SASs were created by the Auditing Standards Board (ASB) as the AICPA's senior technical committee on auditing standards.

Auditing interpretations on the application of SASs are created by the staff of the Auditing Standards Division of the AICPA. The interpretations are not considered as authoritative as SASs. However, auditors must justify any departure from an auditing interpretation issued by the Auditing Standards Division of the AICPA. Other publications of the Auditing Standards Division include a number of Industry Audit Guides (Exhibit 6-6) and

---

Airlines
Analytical Procedures
Assessing and Responding to Audit Risk in a Financial Statement Audit
Audit Sampling
Auditing Derivative Instruments, Hedging Activities, and Investments in Securities
Auditing Revenue in Certain Industries
Brokers and Dealers in Securities
Compilation and Review Engagements
Construction Contractors
Depository and Lending Institutions
Derivative Instruments
Employee Benefit Plans
Entities with Oil and Gas Producing Activities
Federal Government Contractors
Gaming
Government Auditing Standards and Circular A-133 Audits
Health Care Entities
Investment Companies
Life and Health Insurance Entities
Not-for-Profit Organizations
Property and Liability Insurance Companies
Prospective Financial Statements
Reporting on Controls at a Service Organization (SOC 2)
Service Organizations: Applying SSAE No. 16 (SOC 1)
State and Local Governments

Exhibit 6-6 AICPA Audit and Accounting Guides
Source: AICPA Online Professional Library.

Primary Authoritative Support

A. General Application
   1. Generally Accepted Auditing Standards (ASB)
   2. Statements on Auditing Standards (ASB)
   3. Auditing and Related Professional Practice Standards (PCAOB)
   4. Auditing Interpretations
   5. AICPA Code of Conduct
   6. Internal Auditing Guidelines

B. Special Application to Certain Entities
   1. Industry Audit Guides
   2. Statements of Position of the Auditing Standards Division
   3. GAO-Government Auditing Standards

Secondary Authoritative Support

A. Audit Research Monographs
B. AICPA Audit and Accounting Manual
C. Journal articles and textbooks

Exhibit 6-7 Auditing Authoritative Support
SOURCE: Modified from *Accounting & Auditing Research: Tools & Strategies*, 7th ed. Reprinted with permission of John Wiley & Sons, Inc.

Statements of Position. These guidelines are recommendations of various AICPA committees and task forces when applying generally accepted auditing standards to industry-specific audit engagements. The auditor needs to be aware of these interpretative guidelines and should be prepared to explain any departures from such audit guidance.

An overview of the current hierarchy of authoritative auditing support is presented in Exhibit 6-7. The auditor needs to understand each of the sources listed, particularly the PCAOB's auditing standards and the predecessor SASs by the AICPA.

Unlike an audit that expresses whether the financial statements are in conformity with GAAP, the accountant's examination of prospective financial statements provides assurance only as to whether (1) the prospective financial statements conform to the AICPA's guidelines, and (2) the assumptions used in the projections provide a reasonable basis for a forecast or a projection. The accountant must provide a report on any attestation service provided, as described in the various attestation and auditing standards. (See Exhibits 6-4 and 6-5.)

AICPA Online Professional Library Database

The AICPA Online Professional Library database includes a comprehensive compendium of the AICPA literature, consisting of Professional Standards, Accounting Trends and Techniques, Technical Practice Aids, Auditing and Accounting Guides, and Audit Alerts. This database is available by subscription from the AICPA.

To conduct auditing research using the AICPA's online database would consist of the following steps. The opening screen of the online version of the database appears in Exhibit 6-8. This screen lists the various subdatabases available, such as audit risk alerts and PCAOB Standards. Clicking on the AICPA Professional Standards link provides the opening screen to the Professional Standards as depicted in Exhibit 6-9. The table of contents (TOC) appears in Exhibit 6-10. Note the various standards under Professional Standards, from auditing standards and valuation services to quality control and tax service standards.

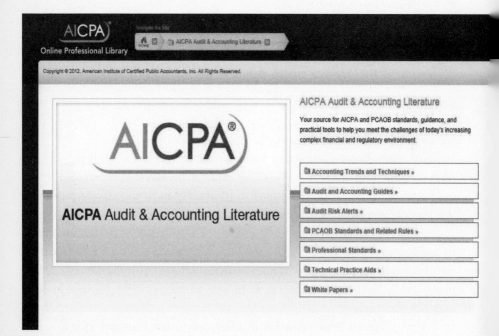

Exhibit 6-8 AICPA Online Publications Screen
SOURCE: Copyright 2012. American Institute of Certified Public Accountants, Inc. All rights reserved.

Exhibit 6-9 AICPA Professional Standards Screen
SOURCE: Copyright 2012. American Institute of Certified Public Accountants, Inc. All rights reserved.

To conduct a specific search using the Professional Standards, enter a keyword search term such as *going concern* in the search window, and the results appear in Exhibit 6-11. Clicking on the second item, AU Section 341, results in the guidance for an auditor's consideration of an entity's ability to continue as a going concern, as depicted in Exhibit 6-12. This Professional Library is a major database in providing guidance for the practitioner by offering various services.

AICPA Code of Professional Conduct

A distinguishing mark of any profession is the establishment and acceptance of a code of professional conduct. Such a code outlines a minimum level of conduct that is mandatory and enforceable on its membership. A code of ethics emphasizes the profession's responsibility to both the public and colleagues. Every CPA in the practice of public accounting has the responsibility to follow the AICPA *Code of Professional Conduct* and its applicability to audit, tax, and consulting services.

The AICPA's Professional Ethics Executive Committee (PEEC), in order to improve the code, has restructured the institute's ethics standards to help members and others to apply and interpret the rules more

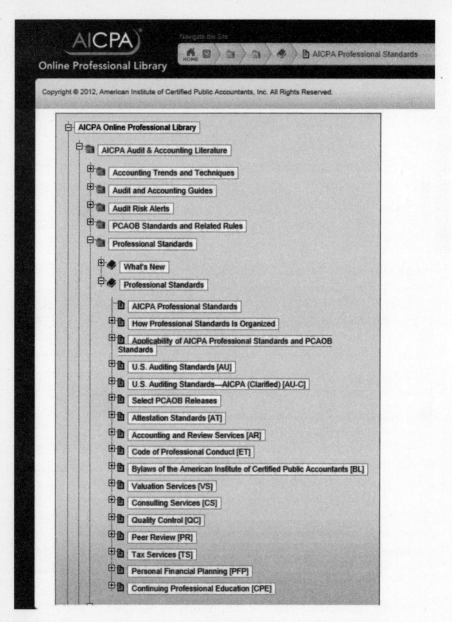

Exhibit 6-10 AICPA Online Library Table of Contents

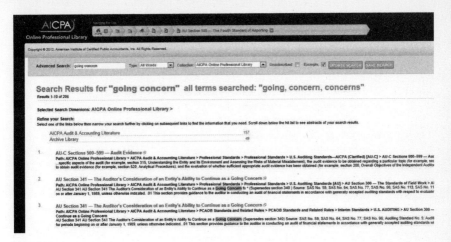

Exhibit 6-11 Search Tab

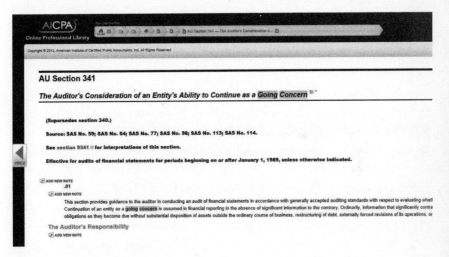

Exhibit 6-12 Search Screen Results

easily. The restructured code is now organized by topic, which also incorporates a conceptual framework for members in the practice of public accounting and those in business. This conceptual framework, referred to as the "threats and safeguards," aids members in the application of the code. The restructured code has several parts, including a Preface that is applicable to all members, a section for members in the

Exhibit 6-13 Hierarchy of the AICPA's Code of Professional Conduct

Level 1	**Principles**—The Principles provide the framework for the development of the Rules.	Official Section of the Code
Level 2	**Rules**—The Rules serve as the enforceable part of the Code that governs the professional services of the AICPA members.	
Level 3	**Interpretations of the Rules of Conduct**—Interpretations are those that have been adopted by the Professional Ethics Division's executive committee to provide guidelines as to the scope and application of the Rules.	Members who depart from interpretation of rulings must justify such departures.
Level 4	**Ethics Rulings**—The Ethics Rulings consist of formal rulings made by the Professional Ethics Division's executive committee. Their Rulings summarize the application of the Rules and Interpretations to particular factual circumstances.	

SOURCE: Modified from *Accounting & Auditing Research: Tools & Strategies*, 7th ed. Reprinted with permission of John Wiley & Sons, Inc.

practice of public accounting, a section for members in business, and a section applicable to all members, such as those who are retired.

The restructured code, available in the AICPA's Online Professional Library, consists of principles, rules, and interpretations. The principles serve as the basic framework for the rules. The rules are mandatory and enforceable. Periodically, the Professional Ethics Division issues interpretations for the purpose of clarifying the code. The interpretations render guidance to the accountant as to the scope and applicability of the rules. The hierarchy of AICPA Principles, Rules, and Interpretations is depicted in Exhibit 6-13.

Departure from the rules may result in disciplinary action, unless the accountant can justify the departure under the circumstances. Disciplinary action may lead to suspension or termination of AICPA membership. Furthermore, a violation of professional conduct may result in revocation of a CPA certificate or license to practice by a state board of accountancy. In many cases, the revocation is also sanctioned by the Securities and Exchange Commission for auditors of public companies.

Although the AICPA's Code of Professional Conduct applies to all members, certain rules are specifically applicable to the independent auditor. One specific rule requires compliance with professional standards and is stated as follows:

> A member who performs auditing, review, compilation, management consulting, tax, or other professional services shall comply with standards promulgated by bodies designated by the AICPA Governing Council.[4]

The following rule generally prohibits the auditor from expressing an opinion that financial statements are in conformity with GAAP if the statements contain any departure from the official pronouncements of the Federal Accounting Standards Advisory Board (FASAB), the Financial Accounting Standards Board (FASB), the Governmental Accounting Standards Board (GASB), and the International Accounting Standards Board (IASB) for international accounting standards. The Accounting Principles Rule is stated as follows:

> A member shall not (1) express an opinion or state affirmatively that the financial statements or other financial data of any entity are presented in conformity with generally accepted accounting principles or (2) state that he or she is not aware of any material modifications that should be made to such statements or data in order for them to be in conformity with generally accepted accounting principles, if such statements contain any departure from an accounting principle promulgated by bodies designated by Council to establish such principles that has a material effect on the statements taken as a whole. If, however, the statements or data contain such a departure and the member can demonstrate that due to unusual circumstances the financial statements would otherwise have been misleading, the member can comply with the rule by describing the departure, its approximate effects, if practicable, and the reasons why compliance with the principle would result in a misleading statement.[5]

As noted in the previous two rules, it is important to emphasize that the CPA must comply with GAAS or PCAOB standards and also have familiarity with GAAP when expressing an audit opinion. Therefore, the practitioner should master the research methodology in order to determine whether the audit is in compliance with GAAS and the entity is following GAAP.

The Accounting Principles Rule was clarified with the issuance of the following interpretation.

> Reference to generally accepted accounting principles in the Accounting Principles Rule means those accounting principles promulgated by the bodies designated by Council. . . . It is difficult to anticipate all circumstances in which accounting principles may be applied. However, there is a strong presumption that adherence to GAAP would, in nearly all instances, result in financial statements that are not misleading . . .
>
> The question of what constitutes unusual circumstances as referred to in the Accounting Principles Rule is a matter of professional judgment involving the ability to support the position that adherence to a promulgated principle would be regarded generally by reasonable persons as producing a misleading financial statement.
>
> Examples of circumstances that may justify departures from GAAP include new legislation or evolution of a new form of business transaction.[6]

Auditing Standards in the Public Sector

Government officials and the general public are concerned about how the public's money was spent and whether government is achieving its goals funded by taxpayer dollars. Thus, to a large degree, the standards and guidelines used in a governmental audit are similar to auditing requirements in the corporate sector. Federal, state, and local governments have historically placed substantial reliance on the auditing requirements of the AICPA's Auditing Standards Division. However, various governmental regulatory bodies have addressed specific governmental audit concerns.

The GAO's Government Auditing Standards, commonly referred to as the "Yellow Book," are applicable to all governmental organizations, programs, activities, and functions. The Government Auditing Standards have the objective of improving the quality of governmental audits at the federal, state, and local levels. These governmental standards were founded on the premise that governmental accountability should go beyond identifying the amount of funds spent, to measure the manner and effectiveness of the expenditures. Therefore, these standards provide for an audit scope to include financial and compliance auditing, as well as auditing for economy, efficiency, and effectiveness of program results. Under federal legislation, federal inspector generals must follow these GAO auditing standards. Also, these standards are audit criteria for federal executive departments and agencies.

Currently, three audit levels affect governments. The first level consists of the generally accepted auditing standards (GAAS) issued by the AICPA. Building on the AICPA standards are the Government Auditing Standards and federal audit requirements. The Government Auditing Standards, considered add-ons to GAAS, are also known as "Generally Accepted Government Auditing Standards" (GAGAS), promulgated under the auspices of the U.S. Government Accountability Office (GAO) by the Government Auditing Standards Advisory Board. The federal requirements are found in the OMB Circular A-133, Audits of States, Local Governments, and Non-Profit Organizations.

The GAO recognizes other sets of professional auditing standards under GAGAS § 1.15. AICPA field work and reporting standards are incorporated by reference for financial statement audits. PCAOB and IAASB auditing standards are used in conjunction with GAGAS for financial statement audits. The Institute of Internal Auditors' standards are used in conjunction with GAGAS for performance audits.

Other major audit guidelines for nonprofit organizations are listed in Exhibit 6-14. The issuance of the Single Audit Act of 1984 (Public Law 98-502), was particularly important because it incorporated the concept of an entity-wide financial and compliance "single audit." This act requires an annual audit of any state or local government unit that receives federal financial assistance. The single audit concept eliminated the need for separate financial and compliance audits conducted by the various federal agencies from whom the entity has received funding.

Exhibit 6-14 Major Guidelines for Public Sector Auditing

GAO	(Government Accountability Office)
	Government Auditing Standards (the "Yellow Book")
OMB	(Office of Management and Budget)
	"Single Audit Act"
AICPA	(American Institute of CPAs)
	Attestation Standards
	Generally Accepted Auditing Standards (GAAS)
	Audit Guides: Audits of Not-for-Profit Organizations
	Audits of Federal Government Contractors
	Audits of State and Local Governments
	Audits of Health Care Entities
	Statements of Position

SOURCE: From *Accounting & Auditing Research: Tools & Strategies*, 7th ed. Reprinted with permission of John Wiley & Sons, Inc.

By congressional directive, the director of the Office of Management and Budget (OMB) has the authority to establish policy, guidelines, and mechanisms to implement single coordinated financial and compliance audits of government grant recipients.

Compilation and Review Services

In response to the needs of nonpublic clients, regulatory agencies, and the investing public, the public accounting profession offers compilation or review services to clients, rather than conducting a more expensive audit examination in accordance with GAAS.* Compilation and review of financial statements are defined as follows:

- **Compilation.** A service presenting, in the form of financial statements, information that is the representation of management without undertaking to express any assurance on the statements.
- **Review.** A service performing inquiry and analytical procedures that provides the accountant with a reasonable basis for expressing limited assurance that there are no material modifications that should be made to the statements in order for them to be in

---

*The distinction between a public versus a nonpublic client is based on whether the entity's securities are traded publicly on a stock exchange or in the over-the-counter market.

conformity with GAAP or, if applicable, with another comprehensive basis of accounting.

Therefore, the basic distinction between these two services is that a review service provides limited assurance about the reliability of unaudited financial data presented by management, whereas a compilation engagement provides no assurance as to the reliability of the data. In a compilation, the CPA prepares financial statements only from information supplied by management. The CPA, in a compilation, need not verify this information furnished by the client and therefore provides no assurance regarding the validity of this information.

The AICPA established guidance for the public accountant for compilation and review services with the issuance of Statements on Standards for Accounting and Review Services (SSARS). To date, the committee has issued 17 statements.

Role of Judgment in Accounting and Auditing

Accountants and auditors exercise professional judgment in considering whether the substance of business transactions differs from its form, in evaluating the adequacy of disclosure, in assessing the probable impact of future events, and in determining materiality limits. This informed judgment on the part of the practitioner is the foundation of the accounting profession. In providing an attest engagement, the result is often the rendering of a considered opinion or principled judgment. In effect, the auditor gathers relevant and reliable information, evaluates and judges its contents, and then formalizes an opinion on the financial information or statements.

A review of current authoritative literature reveals that certain pronouncements require disclosure on the applicable accounting principle for a given business transaction. Other pronouncements provide only general guidelines and in some cases suggest acceptable alternative principles. The process of applying professional judgment in choosing among alternatives is not carried out in isolation but through consultation with other professionals who are knowledgeable in the area. In rendering professional judgment, the accountant/auditor must exercise critical-thinking skills in the development of a solution or an opinion.

The codified Statements on Auditing Standards make the following points on the use of professional judgment in conducting an audit: professional judgment is essential to the proper conduct of an audit. This is because interpretation of relevant ethical requirements and GAAS and the informal decisions required throughout the audit cannot be made without the application of relevant knowledge and experience to the facts and circumstances.

In particular, professional judgment is necessary regarding decisions about the following:

- Materiality and audit risk.
- The nature, timing, and extent of audit procedures.
- Evaluating whether sufficient appropriate audit evidence has been obtained.
- The evaluation of management's judgments.
- The drawing of conclusions.[7]

To render an opinion based on professional judgment, the auditor often considers the opinions of other professionals. In such cases, the practitioner can use several published sources to determine how others have dealt with specific accounting and reporting applications of GAAP. The AICPA publishes *Technical Practice Aids*, which contains the Technical Information Service. This service consists of inquiries and replies that describe an actual problem that was encountered in practice and the interpretation and the recommendations that were provided, along with relevant standards and other authoritative sources.

Economic Consequences

Because time is a scarce commodity, the auditor should weigh the cost/benefit tradeoffs in extending the audit research process. The researcher should address the problem until he or she has eliminated all reasonable doubt relating to the issue, recognizing the hidden costs of making an improper audit decision.

Enforcement of professional audit work occurs at many levels. Quality control reviews are expected within a CPA firm. Peer reviews are conducted by other firms. The PCAOB conducts inspections of

CPA firms. The inspections are generally used for the enhancement of the audit process but also used for PCAOB enforcement sanctions. Audit quality has improved because of PCAOB inspection reports. The SEC can still issue an Accounting and Auditing Enforcement Release on a CPA firm. Litigation results in a review of audit quality. Besides the legal damages from an association with a negligent audit, the auditor can face criminal penalties; SEC, FTC, and other government sanctions; loss of reputation among the auditor's peers; and a significant loss of existing clients in a competitive environment.

If sloppy audit work is revealed to the public through failures of major corporations or investment vehicles, pressure is placed on Congress to change the audit environment, as happened under Sarbanes-Oxley. As congressional and other investigations continue in financial reform, only time will reveal the effects on the audit environment.

Summary

This chapter has presented an overview of assurance services, the auditing standard-setting environment, standards for international audits, compilation and review services, and professional ethics. Familiarity with this information, in particular the types of authoritative pronouncements that exist, will aid the practitioner in the research process.

In researching an accounting or assurance services issue, the practitioner must use professional judgment in the decision-making process. Experience is undoubtedly the primary factor in developing good professional judgment. However, this text presents a research methodology that should aid in the development and application of professional judgment.

Notes

1. AICPA *Professional Standards*, vol. 2, section CS-100.05.
2. AICPA *Professional Standards*, vol. 1, section AT–Introduction.
3. AICPA *Professional Standards*, vol. 1, section AT 100.01.
4. AICPA *Professional Standards*, section ET.
5. AICPA *Professional Standards*, section ET.
6. Ibid.
7. AICPA *Codification of Statements on Auditing Standards* (*Clarified*), sections AU-C A27–A31.

About the Authors

Thomas R. Weirich, PhD, CPA, Jerry & Felicia Campbell Endowed Professor of Accounting, received his BS and MBA degrees from Northern Illinois University, and a doctorate in accountancy from the University of Missouri–Columbia. Dr. Weirich, former chair of the School of Accounting, has served on special assignment as the Academic Accounting Fellow to the Office of the Chief Accountant at the U.S. Securities and Exchange Commission in Washington, D.C. He has completed a Faculty in Residence position with a major accounting firm in their Business Fraud & Investigative Services Division whereby he participated in various fraud and background investigations. He has served as a member of the Technical Working Group for Education in Fraud and Forensic Accounting funded by the U.S. Department of Justice that created the "Model Curriculum in Forensic Accounting." He also served as a consultant to the Public Oversight Board's Panel on Audit Effectiveness. Dr. Weirich was recently reappointed by the governor of the state of Michigan to serve on the Michigan State Board of Accountancy. He currently serves as the chair of its board.

Dr. Weirich has public accounting experience with an international firm as well as with a local firm. He has served on the editorial advisory board to the *Journal of Accountancy* as well as various committees of the AICPA, American Accounting Association, Michigan Association of CPAs, and the National Association of State Boards of Accountancy. He has published over 100 professional journal articles on various issues. Dr. Weirich has been the recipient of the School of Accounting/Beta Alpha Psi's Outstanding Teacher Award, Ameritech/SBC Teaching Award, the College of Business Dean's Teaching Award, the Michigan Association of Governing Boards' Distinguished Faculty Award, and the Michigan Association of CPAs' Distinguished Achievement in Accounting Education Award. He has received the national Beta Alpha Psi "Outstanding Faculty Advisor" Award. He has served as an expert witness for the SEC and in other cases. He has also served as the mayor of Mount Pleasant, Michigan.

Dr. Weirich is the lead coauthor of a popular text titled *Accounting and Auditing Research: Tools and Strategies*, 7th edition, and also coauthor of *Mastering the FASB Codification and eIFRS: A Case Approach*. His primary teaching and research areas include auditing, financial and forensic accounting, and SEC issues.

■　■　■

Natalie Tatiana Churyk, PhD, is the Caterpillar Professor of Accountancy at Northern Illinois University. She teaches in the undergraduate and LMAS programs and also develops and delivers continuing professional education in Northern Illinois University's CPA review program. Dr. Churyk is a CPA and a member of the American Accounting Association, the AICPA, and the Illinois CPA Society. She serves on state and national committees relating to education and student initiatives, including the American Accounting Association's Teaching Learning and Curriculum Section (treasurer and strategic planning committee member) Midwest Region (vice president–academic and program chair). Dr. Churyk is a member of the editorial review boards of the *Journal of Forensic and Investigative Accounting* and the *Journal of Accounting Education*. She is a coauthor of two textbooks, *Accounting and Auditing Research: Tools and Strategies* and *Mastering the FASB's Codification and eIFRS: A*

Case Approach and is a contributor to *Wiley CPA Exam Review, Financial Accounting and Reporting.*

■   ■   ■

Thomas C. Pearson, JD, LLM (tax), is Professor of Accountancy at the University of Hawaii at Manoa (UH). Mr. Pearson has previously served as UH's director of the School of Accountancy. At the graduate level, he regularly teaches accounting and tax research. Mr. Pearson serves on the UH Honors Council and the Oral Communication Board for General Education. Mr. Pearson is a CPA and a member of the American Accounting Association, the AICPA, and the Hawaii Society of CPAs. He is a coauthor of two textbooks, *Accounting and Auditing Research: Tools and Strategies* and *Mastering the FASB's Codification and eIFRS: A Case Approach.* Mr. Pearson has published 40 articles, most of which are on taxation. His article titled "Creating Accountability: Increased Legal Status of Accounting and Auditing Authorities in the Global Capital Markets (U.S. and E.U.)" was published in the *North Carolina Journal of International Law and Commercial Regulation* and received the 2005 George A. Katz Memorial Award in Securities Law at New York University.

Index

a posteriori research, 4
a priori research, 4
AAA. *See* American Accounting
    Association
AAERs. *See* Accounting and Auditing
    Enforcement Releases
AAG. *See* Auditing and Accounting
    Guides
Abbreviations, 31, 157
Academic view, 66
Accounting and Auditing Enforcement
    Releases, 39, 42–43, 45
Accounting and Review Services
    Committee, 221, 223
Accounting, auditing, or tax research,
    18–19
Accounting Interpretations, 63
Accounting Principles Board, 40, 47,
    50, 62–64
Accounting Research Bulletins, 47, 57,
    62–63, 65

Accounting Research Manager, 121,
    127–129, 157
Accounting Series Releases, 42–43, 66
Accounting Standards Executive
    Committee, 49, 63
Accounting Standard Update, 49,
    56–62, 64, 73
Accounting Trends and Techniques,
    26, 49, 154, 230
Acquiescence, 184–185
AcSEC. *See* Accounting Standards
    Executive Committee
Advance pricing agreement, 205
Advanced keyword search, 67,
    78–79
Advanced search, 67, 78–79
Advisory boards, 52–54
AFTR. *SeeAmerican Federal Tax Reporter*
AICPA. *See* American Institute of
    Certified Public Accountants
audit and accounting manual, 154

AICPA (*Continued*)
  Code of Professional Conduct, 32,
    211, 218, 231–235
  Management Consulting Executive
    Committee, 218
  online professional library, 154
  Online Professional Library
    Database, 154, 230
  online publication, 220
  professional standards, 31, 154,
    231–232
  Special Committee on Assurance
    Services, 216
  technical practice aids, 127–128, 154
AIN. *See* Accounting Interpretations
Albrecht, W.S., 14
American Accounting Association, 32,
  38,
American Federal Tax Reporter, 180–182,
  189
American Institute of Certified Public
  Accountants, 38, 40, 47, 49–50,
  57, 63–65, 73, 90, 123–124,
  127–128, 154
AOSSG. *See* Asian-Oceanian Standard-
  Setters Group
APA. *See* Advanced pricing agreement
APB. *See* Auditing Principles Board
Applied research, 4, 7, 30
ARBs. *See* Accounting Research
  Bulletins
ARSC. *See* Accounting and Review
  Services Committee
ASB. *See* Auditing Standards Board
Asian-Oceanian Standard-Setters
  Group, 94, 104
ASRs. *See* Accounting Series Releases
Assurance services, 216
ASU. *See* Accounting Standard Update
Attest
  definition, 219
  engagements and guidelines, 221
  research environment, 220

standards, 223
Attestation services, 219
Attestation standards, 219
AU-C, 225
Audit and Accounting Guides, 63,124,
  128, 154, 230
Auditing authoritative support, 230
Auditing standards, 5, 8, 157, 223
Auditing Standards Board, 221, 223
Audit procedures, 154, 223
Authoritative, 44, 49–50, 54–55, 57,
  61–66, 73, 85, 96, 119

Basic keyword search, 76, 78
Basic view, 66–67
Beresford, Dennis R., 12
Bloomberg, 146–147
Blue Book, 171
Browse, 67–68, 70–71, 73
Business Europe, 104, 105–106
Business Insights: Global, 147–148

CAP. *See* Compliance Assurance
  Program
Capital Markets Advisory Committee,
  93
CCAs. *See* Chief Counsel Advice
CCH. *See* Commerce Clearing House,
  Inc.
Center screen, 74–76, 78–80, 83, 109,
  113, 116
Certified Public Accountants, 50, 53
Certiorari, 182
CESR, 89, 106
CF Disclosure Guidance Topics, 44
Chief Counsel Advice, 177, 179
Citations, 23–25, 31, 72, 81–83, 127,
  157, 170, 172–175, 181, 187–192,
Clarified SASs, 225
CMAC, 93
Code of Professional Conduct. *See*
  AICPA Code of Professional
  Conduct

Codification, 38, 41–59, 61–74, 78–79, 85, 89–90, 108, 111, 114–118

Comment letters, 49, 61

Commerce Clearing House, Inc., 25, 47, 121, 127–129, 157, 165, 167, 169, 180, 187, 189–191,

Compilation and review services, 219, 238–239

  compilation services, definition of, 238

  research tools, 154

  review services, definition of, 238–239

Compliance and Disclosure Interpretations, 44

Compliance Assurance Program, 204

Compliance checks, 210

Compustat, 142, 147

Concepts, 51, 55, 64, 123

Conceptual framework, 55–56, 90, 101–103

Consulting engagement, 218

Consulting standards and services, 217–219, 221, 223

Copy, 73, 81–83, 119

Corporate Affiliations database, 140

Corporate Finance Center, 145

Court of Appeals, 180, 182–185, 189, 191

Court of Federal Claims, 180, 182–186, 189

CPA. See Certified Public Accountants

  PerformanceView, 216

  Prime Plus, 216

  WebTrust, 216

Critical thinking, 2, 7, 9, 13, 19

  definition of, 10–12

Cross-reference, 67–68, 74, 113

Database, 1–2, 5–7, 20, 25–26, 28, 30, 40, 46–47, 61, 65–66, 73, 78, 85, 109, 127–131, 133–147, 149–158, 164–165, 167–171, 174, 176, 180,

185, 187–188, 190, 212, 218, 220, 225, 230–231

Delegation Orders, 177

Directives, 179

Directory of Foreign Firms, 152

Direct search, 115–116

Disclosure, 39, 41, 43–44, 50, 54, 59, 104, 106

Discussion paper, 60–61, 97–98, 112

Division of Corporation Finance, 39, 43–44

Division of Corporation Finance Financial Reporting Manual, 44

Division of Investment Management, 44

Division of Risk, Strategy, and Financial Innovations, 40

Division of Trading and Markets, 40

Documentation worksheet, 23–24

DOs. See Delegation Orders

DPOC. See Due Process Oversight Committee

Due Process, 88, 97–101, 103, 110

Due Process Oversight Committee, 97

Earnings per share, 36

Economic consequences, 14–15, 21–23, 25, 240–241

EDGAR, 38, 46–48

EECS. See Europeans Enforcers Coordination Sessions

EEG. See Emerging Economies Group

Effective communication, 9, 14

EFRAG. SeeEuropean Financial Reporting Advisory Group

eIFRS, 12–13, 89–90, 101, 107–109, 111, 113–119

EITF. See Emerging Issues Task Force

Electronic Reading Room, 179–180

Email, 68, 81–83, 99, 108, 112

Emerging Economies Group, 93

Emerging Issues Task Force, 32, 38, 52, 54–55, 57, 63–66, 68

En Banc, 184

Enforcement, 39–40, 42–43, 45, 95, 104, 106

Enforcement Division, 39–40

EOC, 106

EPS. *See* Earnings per share

ESC. *See* European Securities Committee

ESMA. *See* Europeans Securities and Markets Authority

Estate tax audits, 209

ETF. *See* Exchange-traded funds

EU. *See* European Union

European Financial Reporting Advisory Group, 88, 94, 105

European Securities and Markets Authority, 105, 106

European Securities Committee, 106

European Union, 88–89, 94, 105, 106

Europeans Enforcers Coordination Sessions, 106

Exchange-traded funds, 149

Executive Orders, 177

Exemptive Letters, 44

Exempt Organizations Examination, 209–210

Exposure draft, 60–61, 98, 112

Factiva, 151

FASAB. *See* Federal Accounting Standards Advisory Board

FASAC. *See* Financial Accounting Standards Advisory Council

FASB. *See* Financial Accounting Standards Board

FASB Accounting Standards Codification, 8, 11, 25, 31, 38, 57–58, 61, 64, 65–66

FASB due process, 59–61

FCAG. *See* Financial Crisis Advisory Group

Federal Accounting Standards Advisory Board, 64, 121–123, 157, 235

Federation of European Accountants, 105–106,

FEE. *See* Federation of European Accountants

Field Service Advice, 177–178

Financial Accounting Standards Advisory Council, 52–53, 61

Financial Accounting Standards Board, 6, 11–13, 14, 25, 28, 31–32, 37–41, 43, 45–47, 49–55, 56–70, 83, 85, 88–90, 103, 105, 108, 111, 114–116, 124, 127, 235

Financial Crisis Advisory Group, 93

Financial Reporting Releases, 39, 42–43, 45, 66

Financial Report Surveys, 154

Financial research, 20, 127

Financial Times, 150–151

Form S-1/F-1, 41

Form 8-K/6-K, 42, 44, 46

Form 10-K/20F, 41–42, 46

Form 10-Q, 42

FRRs. *See* Financial Reporting Releases

Funding, 90, 103–104

G20 leaders, 94

GAAP. *See* Generally accepted accounting principles

GAAS. *See* Generally accepted accounting standards

GAGAS. *See* Generally accepted governmental auditing standards

GAO. *See* Government Accountability Office

GARS. *See* Government Accounting Research System

GASB. *See* Governmental Accounting Standards Board

GCMs. *See* General Counsel Memoranda

General Counsel Memoranda, 178–179

Generally accepted accounting
    principles, 16,24, 30, 36, 38,
    40–42, 46, 49–51, 54–55, 57–59,
    61–62, 64–66, 68, 85, 88–90, 102,
    106, 119, 122, 124, 128, 154, 215,
    218, 223, 224, 228–229, 235–239,
    241
  definition, 49
Generally accepted accounting
    standards, 219, 220, 224
Generally accepted government
    auditing standards, 237
GLASS. *See* Group of Latin American
    Standard Setters
Global Preparers Forum, 94
Global Resource Directory, 151
Glossary search, 57, 66–67, 71–72,
    74–75, 96, 112–116
Government Accountability Office,
    225, 237
Government Accounting
    Research System, 121, 123–126,
    157
Governmental Accounting Standards
    Board, 14, 28, 38, 52, 64, 121,
    123–126, 235
Governmental auditing standards,
    225
GPF. *See* Global Preparers Forum
Group of Latin American Standard
    Setters, 94

Hierarchy, 24, 40, 44–45, 61–62, 66,
    90, 101, 106–107, 119, 122, 124,
    140, 154, 181, 183, 191, 212, 229,
    234–235
Higher-order reasoning skills, 11

IAASB. *See* International Auditing and
    Assurance Standards Board
IAPC, 227
IAPSs. *See* international auditing
    practice statements

IAS. *See* International Accounting
    Standards
IASB. *See* International Accounting
    Standards Board
IASB Due Process, 88, 97–98
IASC. *See* International Accounting
    Standards Committee
IFAC. *See* International Federation of
    Accountants
IFRIC. *See* International Financial
    Reporting Interpretations
    Committee
IFRS. *See* International Financial
    Reporting Standards
IFRS Advisory Council, 91–93, 99
IFRS Foundation Trustees, 91–93
IFRS Interpretations Committee,
    91–93, 95–96
Industry codes, 131–133, 136, 140,
    157
Industry research, 131, 133–134
Information letter, 179, 187
Institute of Internal Auditors, 225
Internal Revenue Bulletin, 169, 175
Internal Revenue Manual, 176, 178
International Accounting Standards, 24,
    25, 38, 88–89, 95–96, 104, 107,
    116, 119, 128, 235
International Accounting Standards
    Board, 38, 42, 88–110, 112, 119
International Accounting Standards
    Committee, 88–89, 92, 95, 105
International Auditing and Assurance
    Standards Board, 223, 226–222
International Auditing Practice
    Statements, 227
International complexities, 29
International Federation of
    Accountants, 64, 88, 94,105, 227
International Financial Reporting
    Interpretations Committee, 89,
    95–97, 99, 100–101, 106–107,
    110, 112, 119

International Financial Reporting
  Standards, 24, 25, 29, 42, 58–59,
  87–97, 99, 101–102, 104–110,
  110–113, 115, 117, 118–119,
  128–129, 227
International Organization of Securities
  Commissions, 89, 91–92, 94–95,
  104–106
International Standards on Auditing,
  225, 227
Interpretations Committee, 99,
  100–101, 106
Interpretations Committee Due
  Process, 99–101
Interpretive Letters, 44
Investors Technical Advisory
  Committee, 53
Investor Task Force, 53
IOSCO. *See* International
  Organization of Securities
  Commission
IRB. *See* Internal Revenue Bulletin
IRC. *See* Internal Revenue Code
IRM. *See* Internal Revenue Manual
ISAs. *See* International Standards on
  Auditing
Issue identification, 8
ITAC. *See* Investors Technical
  Advisory Committee
ITF. *See* Investor Task Force

Jacks, Hugh B., 12, 14
Join sections, 68, 70
Judgment, 2–4, 10, 16, 21–22, 65, 110,
  119, 190, 192, 220, 236, 239–240
  professional judgment, 2–4, 21–22,
  65, 190, 192, 220, 236, 239–240
  role of, 238–239
Judicial sources, 180

Keywords, 20, 25–26
Keyword search, 67, 74, 76, 78, 120,
  187–188, 230

Knowledge, 1–3, 5, 10–16, 18,25, 28,
  131, 168, 178, 181, 186, 191, 194,
  196, 199, 223, 239–240
Kompass, 155

Large Business and International, 179
LB&I. *See* Directives, Large Business
  and International
Legal research, 16
Legislative history, 171
Levels of U. S. GAAP, 55, 61–62, 66,
  68, 85
LexisNexis, 40, 121, 138–142,
  144–145, 150, 158, 165, 167
LIFE. *See* Limited Issue Focused
  Examinations
Limited Issue Focused Examinations,
  204
Login, 67–68, 108, 113

Management Consulting Services
  Executive Committee, 221
Master glossary, 66, 71–72, 74–75
Masters of Tax Guide, 164
MD&A, 135
Measurement, 50, 54, 56, 59, 62,
  102–104
Memorandum of Understanding,
  88–90, 204
Mergent Online, 135–139, 158
Monitoring Board, 91–92
Morningstar Investment Research
  Center, 149
MOU. *See* Memorandum of
  Understanding

NAC. *See* Not-For-Profit Advisory
  Committee
NAICS, 131–133, 136
National Standard Setters Group, 95,
  105
Navigation panel, 58, 71, 73–74, 109,
  114–116, 117–119

NetAdvantage 121, 142–144, 158
Nonauthoritative, 47, 62–63, 65–66
Not-for-profit Advisory Committee, 53
Notices, 63, 179
NSS. *See* National Standard Setters
    Group

Objectives, 38, 51, 55–56, 90–91, 102,
    106, 116, 119
OCA. *See* Office of Chief Accountant
Office of Chief Accountant, 39
Office of Ethics Counsel, 39
Office of Management and Budget,
    132, 237

Paste, 73, 81–83, 119
PCAOB. *See* Public Company
    Accounting Oversight Board
PCC. *See* Private Company Council
PCFRC. *See* Private Company
    Financial Reporting Committee
Pension plan audits, 207–208
PIOB. *See* Public Interest Oversight
    Board
PLRs. *See* Private Letter Rulings
Pre-Filing Agreement, 204
Primary support, 64–65, 74
Print, 68, 81–83
Private Company Council, 54
Private Company Financial Reporting
    Committee, 53
Private letter rulings, 175, 179
Problem distillation, 20
Professional practice, 39
Professional judgment. *See* Judgment,
    professional
Professional standards, 1, 26, 28, 29, 37,
    46, 90, 154, 211, 217–218,
    225–226, 231–232, 231–234
Professional view, 66–67
Public Company Accounting Oversight
    Board, 24, 128, 154, 220–221,
    223–226, 230, 236, 237, 240–241

Public Interest Oversight Board, 95,
    105, 227

Registered users, 68, 109
Registration, 39, 41, 6–68
Regulation, 39, 41–47, 64, 66, 89–90,
    95, 104
Regulation AB, 41
Regulation Fair Disclosure, 41
Regulation S-K, 41–45
Regulation S-T, 41
Regulation S-X, 41–45
Regulation of Tax Professionals,
    211–212
Report Builder, 137
Research, 1–9, 11, 13–24,28–29,
    37–39, 41, 43, 47, 53, 64–66,
    70–71, 73, 85, 87, 90, 95, 97–99,
    107, 110, 113, 115, 117–121, 127,
    131, 134–135, 138, 142–143, 145,
    147, 151–152, 154–157, 163–165,
    167–171, 174, 179–181, 183,
    185–188, 190–193, 196–197, 206,
    208, 212–213, 216–218, 220, 225,
    229, 236, 241
definition, 3
navigation guide, 6
process overview, 19–20
process overview, diagram of, 26
professional, 2, 5, 7
strategies, 121, 156
tax, 163–165, 167–171, 174,
    179–180, 183, 185–186, 190–193,
    196, 206, 212–213
Research Institute of America, 25, 47,
    127–128, 130, 157, 165, 167–169,
    174, 180, 189
Researching corporate news, 131, 133,
    149
Revenue procedures, 164, 174–175,
    178–179, 191
Revenue rulings, 164, 167, 174–179,
    191

RIA. *See* Research Institute of America

RIA Checkpoint, 25, 47, 127–128, 157, 168, 169, 174

S&P NetAdvantage. *See*NetAdvantage

SABs. *See* Staff Accounting Bulletins

Sack, R.J., 14

SASs. *See* Statements on Auditing Standards

SBAC, *See* Small Business Advisory Committee

SCAs. *See* Service Center Advice

Schedule 14A, 41

Search, 67, 71, 74, 76, 78–80, 83, 85, 112–120

SEC. *See* Securities and Exchange Commission

SEC Staff Interpretations, 43–44

Secondary support, 64–65

Section links, 81

Securities and Exchange Commission, 6, 7, 15–16, 22, 24–25, 37–47, 49, 60, 64, 66, 69, 73, 85, 88–90, 92, 104–106, 128, 136–137, 202, 207, 228, 241

SEDAR, 135

Service Center Advice, 179

SFAC. *See*Statement of Financial Accounting Concepts

SFASs. *See* Statements of Financial Accounting Standards

SFFAS. *See* Statements of Federal Financial Accounting Standards

SIC. *See* Standards Interpretations Committee

Single Audit Act, 237

Small and Medium-sized Entities, 91, 94

Small Business Advisory Committee, 54

Small Claims Division, 185

SME Implementation Group, 91, 93–94

SMEs. *See* Small and Medium-sized Entities

SOPs. *See* Statements of Positions

SSAE. *See* Statements on Standards for Attestation Engagements

SSCS. *See* Statements on Standards for Consulting Services

SSTSs. *See*Statements on Standards for Tax Services

Staff Accounting Bulletins, 39, 43–44

Staff Legal Bulletins, 44

Staff No-Action Letters, 39, 44–45

Standards Interpretations Committee, 47, 89, 96, 131–132, 136, 138

Statement of Financial Accounting Concepts, 55–56

Statement of Financial Accounting Standards, 57–58, 61

Statement of Positions, 49, 63–65

Statements of Federal Financial Accounting Standards, 122

Statements on Auditing Standards, 223–224

Statements on Quality Control, 224

Statements on Standards for Accountants' Services on Prospective Financial Information, 221

Statements on Standards for Accounting and Review Services, 221

Statements on Standards for Attestation Engagements, 219, 224

Statements on Standards for Consulting Services, 218

Statements on Standards for Tax Services, 211

TAM. *See* Technical Advice Memoranda

Tax Audit Guides, 197, 199, 206

Tax audits, 196–206, 208–210

Tax Court, 180–185

Tax Management Portfolios, 164
Tax research. *See* Research, tax
Tax services, 167, 169, 171–172, 175, 187–188, 211
Tax treaties, 169, 206
Technical Advice Memoranda, 179
Technical bulletins, 28, 54, 63–65, 122–124, 126
Technical Information Service, 240
Technical Practice Aids, 240
Terminology lookup, 112–115
Theoretical research, 3–4
ThomasNet, 135
Thomson One, 149
Topical categories, 71, 72, 74–75, 76–77
Transfer pricing audits, 204–206
Treasury regulations, 164, 167, 171–176, 191, 212

U.S. GAAP. *See*Generally accepted accounting principles
U.S. tax cases, 180–182, 189
USTC. *See*United States Tax Cases

Valuation Resource Group, 54
Value Line Investment Surveys, 133
Value-added services, 215
VRG. *See* Valuation Resource Group

Wall Street Journal, 150–151
Westlaw, 144–146
Wildcard characters, 168–169
Wilson Sporting Goods, 221

XBRL, 46, 58, 73, 113–114

Yellow Book. *See* Governmental Auditing Standards